SCRIPTWRITING FOR HIGH-IMPACT VIDEOS

SCRIPTWRITING FOR HIGH-IMPACT VIDEOS

Imaginative approaches to delivering factual information

JOHN CHARLES MORLEY

iUniverse, Inc.

New York Lincoln Shanghai

SCRIPTWRITING FOR HIGH-IMPACT VIDEOS
Imaginative approaches to delivering factual information

iUniverse books may be ordered through booksellers or by contacting:

iUniverse
2021 Pine Lake Road, Suite 100
Lincoln, NE 68512
www.iuniverse.com
1-800-Authors (1-800-288-4677)

Because of the dynamic nature of the Internet, any Web addresses or links contained in this book may have changed since publication and may no longer be valid.

The views expressed in this work are solely those of the author and do not necessarily reflect the views of the publisher, and the publisher hereby disclaims any responsibility for them.

ISBN: 978-0-595-44938-5 (pbk)
ISBN: 978-0-595-89260-0 (ebk)

Printed in the United States of America

TABLE OF CONTENTS

Chapter 3

CHAPTER 7

CHAPTER 8

CHAPTER 9

CHAPTER 10

Appendix

PREFACE

It's not the glitz on the screen but the impact on the audience that's the measure of an informational program. This book will help writers strengthen that impact by showing them how to make the best use of their time and creativity. It suggests hundreds of ideas that can be used as starting points and insightful touches. It covers all of the analytical and creative decisions that add up to an effective script for a video.

The skills taught in this book are also critical when scripting for film, PowerPoint® presentations, Web sites and other types of interactive media. And specific advice is provided on adapting these skills to those media.

The central focus however is on video and readers are assumed to have a basic understanding of video production and writing skills.

Unique Features

➢ Prepares the reader for an area of employment that is widely perceived as offering more job potential for a writer than the entertainment industry and broadcast journalism combined.

➢ Presents a step-by-step creative process within the context of writing for a living, offering many techniques for presenting and discussing ideas, and for building group consensus.

➢ In plain language, lays out the basics of dramatic structure, advertising concepts and instructional design as they can be applied to informational video.

➢ Includes dozens of suggestions that provide a head start on developing a creative approach.

Overview of Content

Chapter 1 provides a background, history and overview of the realities of the current market.

Chapters 2 through 9 present a step-by-step process for taking a project from initial needs analysis to a completed script. The creative process is at best organic and the creation of video presentations requires the balancing of several interconnected, shifting variables. In this book the process is made as linear as possible and steps are grouped into specific training areas—while still allowing for contingencies of content, application, creative approach and working situation.

Chapter 10 provides advice on finding employment and reviews the major legal, ethical and career decisions faced by a scriptwriter.

The Profession as It's Currently Being Practiced

This book describes the realities of human frailties, time pressure and budgetary limitations rather than a rigid process for idealized situations. It prepares the reader for situations in which clients, content experts and even colleagues may not agree on—or even be aware of—accepted conventions. The ideas and techniques presented are based on over two decades of experience during which no two projects were alike and none were ideal.

The process on which this book is based has been presented and discussed in trade-show and convention seminars, and while teaching informational scriptwriting at California State University, Northridge. It has been refined during hundreds of projects and discussions with working professionals, who are seldom shy about pointing out any weakness.

This is proven advice that works under pressure. It can be applied with confidence by anyone seriously interested in writing for video—whether their concerns center on earning a living, making a difference or some combination thereof.

Case Studies

Following its own advice—to show rather than tell—the text illustrates every major point by applying it to both of two case studies. This approach gives the reader a constant frame of reference as each new step builds on previous steps. The finished scripts for the case studies—a voice-over narration and a dramatization—are included in the Appendix.

In addition to these two case studies, a wealth of examples from dozens of other scripts are used to clarify points throughout the text.

A Tool for Working Writers

This is more than a good how-to textbook; it is also a reference source that can be used often—for ideas to blast past writer's block, for help with selling words and ideas to clients and colleagues, and for insight into a process that keeps making more sense the better it's understood and the more it's practiced.

Terminology

A continuing challenge in this industry is deciding what to call informational video. Contenders include *non-broadcast, corporate video, private television, multimedia* and *non-entertainment television.* All work well in specific situations. All have their limitations. *Informational video* will be used as the umbrella term to include all of the above and the amorphous industry this book addresses.

Every show has a writer, a producer, a client and several other more or less talented accomplices. Any number of these roles may be played by a single individual, but for the purposes of this book these roles are considered separately.

Acknowledgments for the First Edition

Perspective becomes clouded after so many words; escaping that fog was possible only with the help of several reviewers: Dan Mueller, The Lawrence Company; Joseph R. Chuk, Kutztown University; Stan Denski, Inidana University, Indianapolis; Mark Hall, Butte Community College; Michael J. Havice, Marquetter University; Robert Main, California State University, Chico; and David H. Ostroff, University of Florida. Their insight and their dedication to both teaching and the moving-image media have been invaluable in creating an effective tool for learning.

Becky Hayden, publisher, and the production team Elaine Brett; copy editor, Kaelin Chappell, designer; and Sandra Craig, production editor—have been valiant in coaxing an intractable scriptwriter into the conventions of publishing.

Special thanks must also go to Alan Armer, CSUN, for the opportunity to teach and the encouragement to finish this book; Marc Tapper and Glen Otto for the opportunity to lecture at UCLA; Chuck Holmes, Corporate Strategies for being as close to a mentor as I've ever enjoyed; Don Wrege, Eye Songs for incisive comments that were pivotal in shaping the tone and voice of this book; and most of all, thanks to all of my clients, who have provided the opportunities and experiences on which this book is based.

Acknowledgments for the Second Edition

Having a book published can change your life. My gratitude goes out to everyone I have met through this book who has changed my life in so many positive ways.

Massive gratitude must also flow to my wife and life partner, Millie, for her support, suggestions and putting up with me lavishing time on writing projects that I would prefer to be spending with her. And a sincere thank you goes out to my clients and colleagues who have allowed me to practice and refine the ideas in this book.

CHAPTER 1

REALITIES OF THE MARKETPLACE

The Invisible Giant

"Television is a medium because anything well done is rare."
—Fred Allen (1894–1956)

Video displays are common in many stores and public buildings. CDs and DVDs are common marketing and training tools, and an increasing number of Web sites include video elements. Most large businesses, government agencies, non-profits and religious organizations produce video programming to be used either self-standing or incorporated into their Web sites and PowerPoint presentations. Yet when people hear the term *scriptwriter*, they usually think only of the entertainment industry. The reality is that the number of writers working in informational video may well exceed the number working in entertainment and broadcast journalism combined.

One factor contributing to this relative anonymity is that the idea of an *informational video industry* is more of an abstract concept than a specifically defined industry, with its own national organization, annual convention and statistic-generating investment analysts. Communicating with moving images has become so integrated into most human endeavors that it is now simply taken for granted.

Of course there are easily identified industries that make heavy use of informational video, such as training, marketing, public relations and education. But these focus on the purpose, rather than the process, of

1

creating video. The process itself is no more appropriate for defining an industry than activities such as driving a car or using the Internet.

The very fact of this amorphous ubiquity supports a conclusion that informational video, whether it's broadcast, cablecast, used in meetings or classrooms, distributed on CD or DVD, or posted on the Internet, rivals the size of the entertainment industry and is still growing. And more to the point, many writers of informational video scripts enjoy an income that is more consistent, and equal to or better, than their counterparts in journalism and entertainment.

A Quick History

World War II military training films brought the first wide-spread use of film outside of entertainment and news. At the same time, filmstrips were also proving to be an effective informational medium—as long as someone would manually advance the film when a beep was heard on the sound track.

After the war, as the auto industry turned from manufacturing military equipment to putting civilians behind the wheel, it also became the most frequent user of film for training and marketing. The rest of corporate America and government and religious organizations were also finding uses for informational films—when they could find large enough production budgets. Filmstrips were much less expensive and were more widely used.

In the 1950s, Ampex and RCA introduced video tape to the television industry, in the form of 2" quad-head video tape recorders. The 1960s brought smaller-format helical scan video tape recorders, creating a distinctly separate market for this less expensive "industrial" grade of video equipment. The technical quality of this early helical scan equipment was usually too low for the shows produced on it to be broadcast on television but the quality was high enough to offer an alternative to film for informational programs that were never intended for broadcast.

By this time, filmstrips were not only advancing automatically but had evolved into a whole new medium called multi-image. This medium used two or more slide projectors, synchronized with a recorded sound track. For larger corporate events, this could mean dozens of slide projectors, thousands of slides and enough opportunities for error to keep even the most professional of staging crews up all night. Advances in computers and digital production have allowed this truckload of gear and time-intensive setup to be replaced by a laptop computer and a video projector.

As video technology evolved and went digital, the price of equipment plummeted and quality improved. Today most professionally produced informational video is technically of broadcast quality and the differences between broadcast and industrial video equipment have become largely semantic. These leaps forward in technology also mean that the video image—once restricted to about the size of a human head—can now be projected to fill auditorium-sized screens.

In the 1980s, computer technology began merging with video to create interactive video. This initially meant computers connected to laser disc machines, touch screens and/or a variety of other user-interface devices. Improvements in technology have moved all of this functionality into the computer or onto the Internet, and "point and click" now comes as naturally to most of the industrialized world as eat and breathe.

Today, video is not so much a discrete format as an element that can be mixed and matched with the full palette of film-based and digital production media. This entire spectrum, from linear video to video elements on CD, DVD or Web sites are referred to in this book collectively as *the informational video industry.*

Current Opportunities

"The harder you work the luckier you get."
—Gary Player, golfer

Unlike the entertainment and journalism industries, which are largely autonomous in deciding which products they will produce and sell, informational video is a service industry. It's still show business but it's focused on solving the problems of other industries.

It is difficult to categorize the areas within the informational video industry. Specializing in training could lead you into working for business, government or health-care. Specializing in marketing could mean creating shows for industrial equipment, hotels and resorts, or the latest fashions. Working for a specific company may mean writing everything from nuts-and-bolts training to a fund-raising show for United Way.

In practice, writers often move from one industry to another. Though clients often think that it is critical to have experience within their industry, most video professionals understand that a good grasp of writing for video can be applied to any content area. On the other hand, it is not that common to move among business, government, military and religious institutions because significant cultural differences exist among these clientele.

What Scriptwriters Write

Business, government and religious institutions have discovered many bottom-line justifications for getting into show business:

- Annual reports
- Business theater
- Corporate image
- Employee motivation
- Employee relations
- Exhibits
- Fund raising
- Infomercials
- Information kiosks
- New product introduction
- Patient information
- Point-of-purchase (POP) marketing
- Product information
- Public relations
- Recruitment
- Sales meetings
- Seminars/workshops
- Training
- Video magazines
- Visitor information
- Web sites

Multiply this list by the number of different types of business, industry, levels of government, non-profits and religions in the world, then add how-to videos and the Internet and you begin getting an idea of the area covered by informational scriptwriting.

But don't be overwhelmed by the razzle-dazzle. It all boils down to a very simple common denominator: helping someone get a job done. This is a very results-oriented profession. The idea of helping someone is essential to information scriptwriting—not so much out of altruism but because it works. If you can genuinely help clients and employers solve problems, you'll find a stable and rewarding career opening up to you.

A Mix of Disciplines

Informational video contains elements of journalism and Hollywood; advertising and education; corporate conservatism and futurist thinking. In short, those of us who create informational media don't exactly fit in anywhere. Writing informational scripts means never being able to easily explain what you do for a living.

Those who work in entertainment and commercials often call—and perhaps dismiss—the shows we create as *industrials*, a somewhat dated term implying a droning narrator spouting facts and figures over footage of the latest in assembly-line technology. The reality is that the production values of the best corporate shows now rival those of prime-time entertainment, and our messages usually represent a postindustrial world view.

Sophisticated production value is now mandatory in any form of communications. Americans are deluged with demands for their attention. To be remembered, a message must capture their imaginations.

Audiences are now media-literate. Their frame of reference for moving images includes high-end Web sites, movies and prime-time television. As a result, any show that an organization doesn't take seriously enough to present professionally probably won't be taken seriously by the audience either.

We must understand the persuasive techniques of advertising, and practice them on audiences made fickle by television commercials with six-figure budgets.

The advertising goal of heightening the sense of need in viewers is only part of the job. Corporate media must also fill a need for information. The techniques of entertainment and advertising must be blended with the educator's and the journalist's concise delivery of facts.

The bottom line of this mixture of skills is of course controlled by our clients, and large organizations are by nature conservative. So we are often the agents of change in a culture dedicated to the status quo. Many at the top often understand the need for change and innovation but their colleagues and subordinates—our audience—must be eased carefully into anything new.

The opportunities in informational scriptwriting are many, varied and increasing daily. Although this conceptual "informational video industry" is large and established, it is still relatively new and open to anyone who can appreciate the opportunities provided by rapid change, while tolerating the uncertainties that change often brings.

Current Challenges

"If you have a job without aggravations, you don't have a job."
—Malcolm Forbes

Informational video is less competitive than the entertainment industry and has deadlines that are more forgiving than those of a daily news show. But it has its own demanding conditions. Analysis of these conditions is at best subjective. The following descriptions of the industry are based on my own experiences and the consensus of others I have worked with and competed against, and who have freely stated their opinions, whether pragmatically or philosophically inclined.

Techno-Bias

During a tour of a video facility, my host used a sweeping gesture to indicate all of the switches and glowing screens in the control room, as he grandly stated "This is where we create the magic." Though his point was taken, his aim was off the mark. The source of his pride was only a technological conveyance for the magic. The magic is really created in the imaginations of creative individuals. But don't expect many people in the industry to acknowledge this. My host was very typical in his preoccupation with the technology and there is a good reason for this bias.

Video equipment and computer gear is more fun to play with than any electric train that ever graced the base of a Christmas tree. Just about everyone wants to push some buttons and run a camera, so many people in the industry were attracted by the toys. Although everyone *wants* a good script to work from, they often begrudge the effort and budget necessary to create one, preferring to put their time and money into equipment and studio time.

Another source of this techno-bias is that business and government understand investing in equipment. Investing in people—particularly creative types—is considered more risky. Besides, the ego boost an executive receives from conducting a tour of an impressive video facility just can't be matched by introducing a writer and producer occupying conventional office-space.

Good salesmanship is also a contributing factor. Equipment and software manufacturers have sent forth their best to convince business and government that all you'll need to make shows that look just as good as prime time, is the right product. There are no commissioned salespeople promoting creativity and imagination.

The result of this techno-bias has been a preponderance of shows that are magnificent technological edifices teetering on shaky creative foundations.

The people in the informational video industry and the clients it serves are not stupid. They are beginning to realize the pointlessness of supporting impressive facilities that produce amateurish shows. Scriptwriting is now slowly gaining more respect in the land of the techno-obsessed.

It Seems So Easy

Video is good at creating illusion. Its greatest illusion is that all the elements of a show flow effortlessly together, propelled by an obvious logic. After all, it's mostly pictures. How much writing can that take?

So staffing a media production facility has often meant finding people who know the software and can operate the equipment, while writing the script is often assigned by default, to the available person most likely to be able to fake it—without charging too much. It is assumed that anyone who can write a press release or a brochure can also handle a script. Many of the writers pressed into script duty have seen enough bad PowerPoint presentations and dull videos that they think "I wouldn't do any worse than that." And they're right. They turn out shows that are no worse—although no better—than the ones they disparage themselves.

Over the past few years, the informational video industry has done some maturing. Many decision makers have now seen that good shows are possible, and, at least in the larger markets, there are many experienced writers who are professional in their approach to informational scriptwriting.

But there are still many people in the industry who think that any literate person can write a script. Most scriptwriters are used to hearing clients say "I'd write it myself but I don't have the time." Few people appreciate the hours that go into thinking through a show and writing the script.

Don't expect a lot of appreciation for your unique talents. The better you do your job, the easier it looks. Be skeptical of anyone who assures you that writing their script should be an easy job, something "you can knock out in a few hours." Just remind yourself—and perhaps your client—that an accomplished gymnast makes flowing through a complex routine on the parallel bars look easy. Try it yourself and you'll soon learn a new level of appreciation.

Growing Pains

Career paths and in-service training for writers are usually very individualized, when they exist at all. Many informational script writers got their jobs by pursuing an unplanned sequence of opportunities. My own career began with producing and directing shows—essentially giving away scripts to get the jobs. As I discovered that other producers were also having trouble finding good scripts—and were actually willing to pay for them—I slowly eased my way from behind the camera to in front of a word processor.

The procedures for completing a script that are outlined in this text are not a standard followed by the entire industry. There *is* no universal standard. Instead, I am suggesting a process that has been honed by abrasive reality for over two decades and has proven itself workable during a wide range of projects for dozens of different organizations.

The Power of the Moving Image

"We are drowning in information, but starved for knowledge."
—John Naisbitt, *Megatrends*

Information is as plentiful today as sand on a beach and just about as valuable. But as sand can be transformed into silicon chips for computers or glass for crystal chandeliers, a good video can ignite our audience's imagination, turning raw information into powerful knowledge and focused effort.

High-impact video can demonstrate to managers how to lead more effectively, help salespeople understand the subtleties of human interaction and motivate employees to feel more like team members while striving for personal achievement. Therein lies the power of the moving image.

What the Moving Image Does Well

One secret to harnessing the power of the moving image is using it only for what it does well. Basically, it's best at creating emotion, setting the tone and demonstrating the attitude you would like the audience to adopt for themselves. It's good with overviews that show the big picture of how all the facts and details fit together and what it all means in terms of benefits to the audience.

Creates Intuitive Understanding

Examples are usually the most effective way to make a point, whether presenting a technique or teaching a value. Aesop realized this when writing his fables and so has virtually every successful political and religious leader down through history. Abstract ideas become powerful only when you can show your audience how other humans have applied them.

Video does examples very well. Its strength lies in showing, rather than telling.

> Example: In an annual meeting opener, titled "Proud to be the Best," three vignettes show what it takes to remain the best in your field. At a

thoroughbred horse farm, a trainer showed how her group constantly looks for improvement in every detail.

A craftsman showed the care and pride he takes in living up to a reputation his company has been building for generations.

An athlete used a daily practice to show how extra effort by one team member sets ever-higher standards that the entire team strives to maintain.

Vivid images were created that could later evoke an entire set of emotions and attitudes—feelings strong enough to help a person get through a trying day. Fundamental values were given faces and personalities; the audience could identify with them and use them as role models.

The show was an emotional experience. The audience was left understanding something that did not have to be fully translated into words. Through seeing an example, the audience understood a concept intuitively, without having to remember a list of dos and don'ts or memorize a list of rules.

Lists and objective criteria certainly have their place. They help people act on their new understanding. But this level of detail cannot be effectively presented with a video. You can't use video as a quick reference tool, or post it on a bulletin board. Detail is best left to print media and Web pages. But to inspire humans to use those facts and details, humans need a vision to strive for and emotional rewards along the way.

When you need to convey this vision, when you need to appeal to the imagination and create enthusiasm and excitement … that's when to use video.

Brings the Team Together

It happens to even lesser-known television actors: people stopping them in public as if they were old friends. Video has this power. When we see someone talk to us, we become familiar with their personality and we feel we know them.

In most larger organizations, it's usual to reminisce about the "old days," when a division manager, or even the president, knew everyone by name. Nothing is as good as human contact, but when it's no longer possible, the intimacy of video goes a long way toward building that feeling of knowing the personalities behind the names on the organizational chart.

Video lets those at the helm talk directly to each person in the organization as an individual. In addition to conveying information, this personalized contact helps shape the values and culture of an organization. We all need to know our leaders as people, understand their values and motivations, and know what they expect of us as individuals.

To fill these needs with greatest impact, video must be used as an intimate medium. The person on camera must envision a one-to-one communication situation. The popularity and effectiveness of President Reagancan be attributed at least partially to his speaking style on camera. He never tried to raise the rafters. He talked calmly, conversationally, as if addressing a respected friend. It was a refreshing change from most politicians, who seem to spend their time in front of a microphone yelling at us.

For grand occasions, product introductions and anniversaries, broad oratory addressed to the multitudes adds needed flair and excitement. But the vast majority of the time—especially immediately following a flash of grandeur—video has its greatest impact when used to address individuals rather than crowds.

Video can enhance team building at every level of the organization. When the whole organization understands what the individual parts are doing, the "us and them" mentality is broken down.

When you need a stronger sense of camaraderie, when top management wants to share their feelings as well as their words … that's when to use video.

Creates Excitement and Emotional Appeal

A corporate image show opens with the excitement of formula I race cars and street-tough music. The pit crew moves in split seconds, as leading-edge equipment is bent by human will to excel at any cost.

The show was intended to drive home the point that this product brokerage firm is aggressive in promoting its clients' products. The firm had an impressive client list, its numbers were good, their computers were packed with powerful data; but the moving image allowed us to go far beyond a logical presentation of these facts.

We made the audience feel flat-out performance ... experience intense commitment. Once those raw emotions were aroused, we showed how the intensity that's so obvious on the race track is put to work in the marketplace.

By creating this level of emotional experience, video propels the audience toward making an emotional commitment. Once we have their emotions, they're hungry for the logic to support the gut-level decision they've already made.

That's when the sales rep comes on with the charts, graphs and marketing plans. That's when you provide them with printed information listing the facts and figures that could never be remembered from watching a video.

When you want them to know who you are, to understand what you stand for and to be enthusiastic when going over your printed material or Web site ... that's when to use video.

Models Complex Behavior

In the first few seconds of contact between people, dozens of impressions are made, many details speak loudly and an entire arsenal of social skills comes into play. This brief encounter could take hours to analyze and thousands of words could not adequately explain it, but video can show exactly how an expert sizes up a situation and then responds appropriately

On video, this demonstration can be repeated, sped up, or slowed down, encouraging the viewer to envision the overall performance as a vivid frame of reference for analyzing the crucial details.

Visualization of performance has been well documented as an effective technique for training and motivation. Video enhances this effectiveness by helping viewers experience a situation through the eyes of the on-screen talent, giving them the confidence that they have already experienced performing a skill correctly. It's the next best thing to direct experience—without the danger of reinforcing bad habits.

In the areas of sales, management, sports or manual skills, video captures an excellent performance that can be shown to everyone in an organization. Video demonstrations don't suffer the degradation inherent when techniques are passed from person to person. They also allow you several levels of commentary on how techniques are being applied.

> Example: A program on win-win negotiation opens with two people deciding where to eat lunch. The next scene reveals that this video is being used as a discussion-starter in a classroom and we hear the instructor and students talk about how negotiation techniques can be used in deciding on a place for lunch and other everyday situations. The viewer then stops the video to answer workbook questions.
>
> As more negotiation skills are introduced the video examples show issues more complicated than lunch and subtitles point out skills as they are applied. At crucial points we hear the thoughts of the people who are negotiating—to better understand why a particular skill is being applied and to know what impression it is making on the other person.

Video's power to demonstrate all of the levels working together, then comment on the different levels as they are repeated in context, work best when complemented with class discussions, written exercises and printed reference material; but the effectiveness of video in modeling complex behavior can never be equaled by other training methods used alone.

When you're dealing with the complexities of human interaction, when critical skills must be seen to be learned ... that's when to use video.

Harnessing the Power

"An artist needs a brush, a writer needs a pen, a film director needs an army."
—Orson Welles (1915–1985)

And that army of which Orson Welles writes needs a battle plan. Before there can be powerful images on the screen, there must be a vision in the mind of a writer. A good scriptwriter envisions the entire experience that will be created by a show, then, creates a single document—the script—that will be the primary reference source on which everyone on the production team relies while making their contributions.

During production, tasks become increasingly specialized. Everyone must work with the decisions that have already been made. Only the writer starts with a clean slate. With this freedom comes the responsibility to design a creative foundation that takes into consideration every aspect of the medium's potential, while providing everyone on the production team with the guidelines and inspiration they need to help make real the vision that began in the mind of the writer.

Roles of the Writer

As a term to describe this individual who has the initial vision and creates the overall plan, "writer" just isn't adequate; perhaps conceptualizer or visualization consultant would be more accurate. But the last thing this world needs is another semantic crusade; if *writer* is good enough for the help wanted ads, writers is what we are.

What a writer actually does in creating a battle plan for the director's army can be summarized as playing several complementary roles: salesperson, manager, consultant, designer and psychologist.

Salesperson

Two of the most common war-stories in the business are the great idea that the client wouldn't buy and the great script that was turned to drivel by all of the petty changes that were demanded. It's not enough to simply have brilliant ideas. You must also be able to sell and defend them as being brilliant—often to people with little imagination and a great aversion to anything different or risky.

If you meekly hand over a finished script while mumbling, "I hope you like it," you will convey to most people only one thing: that even the writer is not happy with this turkey, so it's probably going to need a lot more work.

Think about it: If you're not enthusiastic about your work why should anyone else be? Unless you're going to work for your mother, don't expect anyone to expend time or imagination attempting to understand your work and recognize its potential. Any rationales and strong points you would like people to understand, you will have to point out yourself—very clearly and with at least the level of enthusi-asm you would like to see in others.

This sales process can often begin when a project is still only a vague idea that some kind of show might fill a current need. But in our off-the-shelf culture, even clients with vague ideas about their needs still want—and deserve—to be able to point to something and say, "yes, that's it." A well-written creative treatment or proposal provides this frame of refer-ence. And it's often the persuasiveness of this document that sells a job.

Many times when working with a production company that won in a bid situation, the client made it clear that we got the job on the strength of our creative approach; our competition often provided only boiler plate generalities about special effects and technical flash.

Sometimes the client did not even like the specific approach we pro-posed. What they *did* like was that it clearly demonstrated our ability to grasp their needs, think the problem through, then provide an involving and concise show to solve their problems.

They needed someone who could think clearly and creatively; some-one who could use the medium. Finding people to operate the equip-ment was a secondary consideration.

This point is further illustrated by a story from *Corporate Video In Focus*[11]: The chief executive of one of *Fortune's* top ten companies called a meeting with his video department to discuss the possibility of a video annual report. His comment on the meeting was: "I met with these peo-ple for forty-five minutes and I certainly didn't understand what they were talking about—and they had no concept of what I was talking about. They were talking about cameras, sets and lights and budgets, and I wanted to discuss concepts. I guess we're not ready for video annual reports."

The "boys with the toys," with their focus on process rather than results, are usually not the most appropriate representatives of our industry. It's the person who understands concepts and results that is best able to show clients how their needs can be met. A good writer is often the first person taken in to see a prospective client. How well that

---

1   John F. Budd, Jr., *Corporate Video In Focus* (Englewood Cliffs, N.J.: Prentice-Hall, 1983), p. 65.

writer can size up the situation and propose a solution often determines whether the project gets approved and who gets to do it.

Manager

The person with overall responsibility for a production is the producer. This is the person who divides up the budget. The person *providing* the money in the budget is typically the client. The client decides what needs to be done and the producer is then in charge of making it happen.

The producer is traditionally the only person with whom the client needs to have a working relationship; most everyone on the production side needs only to have contact with the producer, or with whomever that producer chooses to take on some part of the decision-making responsibility.

The only consistent exception to this is the writer. It's generally recognized as being more effective for the client to talk directly with the writer. Filtering everything through the producer wastes the producer's time and there is a risk that specific facts and the general essence will be lost as the producer attempts to relay information and decisions back and forth.

Producers vary widely in their working style. Some are very hands-on, needing to control every situation and be a part of every decision. Others prefer to delegate responsibility, minimizing their involvement. Some will ask for several rewrites before you present your script to the client; others won't change a word.

Your opportunities for initiative will vary with different producers. It's usually best to ask: "How would you prefer to handle meetings between me and the client?" "How do you want to handle research?" If the producer has specific guidelines, follow them; otherwise, suggest the process you are about to learn.

Meetings between writer and client are usually arranged by the producer, who is usually also present. But in the vast majority of shows I've worked on, *the meeting is turned over to the writer to conduct.* The producer may participate and ask questions, but it's clearly the writer's responsibility to establish rapport with the client and to get all of the necessary answers and information.

Well-managed projects follow a step-by-step process, with client and producer approval at critical points. It requires initiative to work out an acceptable process and to schedule approval points with the producer. If the producer does not make the client completely aware of the process, the writer must take the initiative to clearly establish with the client representatives when their involvement is needed, when approval points are scheduled and what will be approved at those points.

It's common sense. When a plan has been agreed to, there is a better chance that it will be followed. A writer showing up with an attitude of, "Here I am; just tell me what to do," deserves to get jerked around—and usually will be.

Deadlines are an example of an element of a plan that needs writer initiative. For years I would ask clients, "When do you want the script finished?" Of course, most people want most things immediately. So I sacrificed my evenings and weekends meeting artificially tight deadlines.
A much better strategy is to go into a client-meeting with a clear grasp of current work commitments and a firm date by which a script can be comfortably finished. That date is then what you state as the deadline for finishing the treatment or script.

There's no guarantee your date will be accepted but at least it's a starting point from which to negotiate a deadline. It places a value on your time and opens the possibility of negotiating for more budget or other concessions for finishing sooner than the date you first presented.

This text presents a specific process, based on delegation of responsibilities:

> ➤ The client is in charge of setting a goal.
> ➤ The writer is in charge of developing a plan for reaching that goal.
> ➤ The producer is in charge of making the plan work.

The challenge in your role as a manager is to negotiate the elements of the process and to ensure that everyone is aware of and comfortable with these roles. This management effort usually pays off by minimizing frustration, saving your time and yielding a better show.

Consultant

When the cry goes out that "We need a video," it's a writer's responsibility to ask the profound question "why?" A video may be the wrong thing, or not enough of the right thing.

When a project first reaches you, you may find that not much critical thought has gone into it. It may be a case of "me too"—because a competitor or another department has a video that impressed a decision maker in your organization. Maybe it's a Band-Aid approach: "We have a problem; a video might fix it." Or maybe it's just force of habit.

Whatever the case, when there's budget to be spent, it's to your benefit to help ensure that it's invested wisely. A shelf full of unneeded, little-used programs with your name on them is not good for job security—even if the initial mistakes in judgment *were* someone else's.

Before accepting the assumption that a video or PowerPoint presentation is the best solution, first clarify the problem, then consider all the options. Some information is better delivered live. Print media or Web sites are more appropriate for reference information or for presenting details. A series of modules may be more effective than a single long presentation. Ask the obvious questions up front. It may save everyone from having to answer embarrassing questions later on.

This is a responsibility you share with the producer. But many producers—especially if they've come up through the hardware side of the business—are primarily concerned with operating the equipment and have not been trained in the broader questions of how to use the medium. This was the case in the story cited earlier about the CEO considering a video annual report. He became frustrated when no one in the video department could intelligently discuss concepts and objectives, so he killed the project.

It's your responsibility to let both client and producer know that you are concerned about and ready to discuss the broader questions and to make suggestions on how to more effectively use moving-image media.

It's also to your benefit to suggest any extra mileage that can be had from a show. One of the case studies you will be following is a sales training video done as a dramatization in a department store. While the show focuses on sales techniques, the background action and the background itself can help reinforce the proper way to stock shelves and maintain a department.

Since the characters will be having dialogues with customers, this is an opportunity to reinforce product knowledge. In their sales presentations, the characters can point out the features and benefits that are important for salespeople to know, thereby reinforcing product knowledge.

These are secondary opportunities that may be overlooked if you do not point them out. When you do so, your clients may better appreciate the potential of video, and better yet, perceive you as a knowledgeable expert who can help them get more bang for their video buck.

Finishing a script, or even completing the show, does not necessarily conclude your responsibility. Video isn't effective unless it's used to best advantage, so we must make sure that our clients have realistic expectations for what a single presentation can do and then stack the odds in favor of its filling this potential.

It's always a good idea to provide training and instructions for the people using the video materials, particularly with sales presentations. Instructions should include a brief strategy for using audio-visual sales tools and some specific suggestions on probe questions and follow-up. And all of these additional elements are upgrades to the project for which you can negotiate a higher budget.

For seminars that are designed to be presented by the client's own people, an important element of the overall project is to train the trainers. This could range from written introductions to a separate workshop on how to present the seminar, including a complete role-play of the full seminar and several variations.

Scripting itself is also a form of consultation—with the producer and production team. In addition to organizing all the words and ideas, a good script also includes realistic thinking on how to get those ideas on the screen. Writing a *Star Wars* concept for a talking-heads-budget does no one any good, unless you've built it around public domain stock footage to which you just happen to have access.

Designer

Wordsmithing is only the final, and relatively minor, aspect of completing a script. As an architect designs all aspects of a building, you must envision and integrate all aspects of your show.

Rather than simply stringing words together, you are creating a set of instructions for bringing to the screen the full impact of the show you have envisioned.

The visual and sound effects, the music, the tone and the interplay among all of these elements must all first coalesce in your mind, then be transformed into a clear set of instructions for the entire production team.

Your responsibility is more than writing dialogue and narration; it is to create a framework for supporting all aspects of the emotional experience that will produce the greatest impact on your audience.

Psychologist

Informational video is a form of behavior modification. Every project we write is intended to make an audience think or behave differently. We are in essence unlicensed practicing psychologists—analyzing how our audience thinks, understanding their motivations, and then creating an experience that will in some way make them better prepared for the challenges they face.

CHAPTER 2

INITIAL DECISIONS

The Process

"It isn't what you know that counts, it's what you think of in time."
—Anonymous

There's a self-fulfilling prophecy in the informational video industry: that long, crazy hours, last-minute changes and never having enough time to do things right are all unavoidable. This prophecy manifests itself in many projects as five distinct stages: initial excitement and enthusiasm, panic, desperation, search for the guilty, and recognition for the nonparticipants.

Initial Excitement and Enthusiasm

You've got the job. It's the kind of budget you need to work with and the type of project that's going to look great on your demo reel.

Panic

The "script we already have that just needs a little rewrite" turns out to be notes from a lunch meeting scrawled on napkins. The "great footage" we only have to "jazz up a little" has all been pirated off the Internet and can't be used. The life history of a retiring department head now has to be worked in somehow. The budget and deadline are etched in granite.

Desperation

All hope of profit is abandoned. Everyone's so overextended that major responsibilities are being delegated to the new intern. Cots are set up in the office so that no one has to go home to sleep.

Search for the Guilty

An accountant begins reviewing all receipts and bookkeeping. You're asked to compile a day-by-day chronology of all communications with the client, who still refuses to even consider paying overages.

Recognition for the Nonparticipants

As you continue with damage control, the client representative premieres the show to top management, who then invite him to introduce it at the annual convention in Hawaii. The technician who spent all of 10 minutes setting up the playback equipment receives a warm round of applause "for the guys with the technical know-how who make this all possible."

It happens. When the project team is asked why, clients are often blamed. "They don't understand what it takes to write and produce a show." "They interfere." "They keep changing their minds." The reality of the situation is that clients aren't *supposed* to understand the process. That's *our* job.

A Better Way

Professionalism requires taking initiative in leading clients through a process that includes opportunities for constructive involvement and clear approval points. It's our responsibility to explain this process, invite involvement at appropriate points and explain the consequences of changing earlier decisions.

Followed correctly, this process can help keep the whole team on track and pulling together, reducing the frequency and impact of unpleasant surprises while minimizing panic, desperation and searches for the guilty. The practice of giving awards and recognition to non-participants is so entrenched in all bureaucracies that techniques for its minimization have yet to be developed.

Like any effective process, the one you are about to learn can be quickly summarized in a few basic steps.

Summary of a More Effective Process

> **Needs analysis**—The situation is analyzed. The bulk of this research is often conducted during meetings with clients and content experts who respond to research questions.

> **Project proposal**—A brief document is created that states what the problem is, who the audience is and how the audience needs to change for the problem to be solved. The project proposal is approved by the client.

> **Input meeting**—Further research is conducted as needs, objectives and the current situation are discussed among the team assembled to respond to the project proposal.

> **Research and creative treatment**—The situation is further studied and a specific plan of action is written.

> **Creative treatment approval**—There is a meeting of the minds.

> **Scripting**—Creative logistics are arranged and a plan is developed for the production team to implement.

Variations in the Process

Every situation is different. Some writers work for independent production companies. Others work for in-house media production departments. Some work freelance.

Independent production companies are hired by a client and are designed to make a profit above actual costs. In-house departments may charge back for their services. We're all ultimately responsible for staying within some type of budget, whatever our employment situation as scriptwriters.

Your "client" may be a committee—too bad. Or someone other than your current client may have initiated the project. The project proposal may already have been written by the client before you became involved.

In other situations, before you even talk with a client you may be expected to write a project proposal that will then be used in the initial client contact to sell them on doing the project. You may find yourself working with a group that uses a term other than *project proposal* or that doesn't feel this step is necessary by any name.

None of these variations are ideal but they *are typical* of situations you will be asked to deal with. The process you're learning is versatile enough to accommodate any of these variations, as long as you consider it a set of guidelines rather than rigid rules.

There are no industry-wide accepted procedures for pre-production. So don't expect anyone to follow this process exactly or to use the exact same terms. But you can be confident that this process has been proven and refined on hundreds of shows done for a diversity of organizations. It's a good road-map to follow from the beginning. It's also a good fallback plan when direction from your client or your boss are either not clear or not working.

The Case Studies

This book can't teach you to be creative. "Where do ideas come from?" is a timeless conundrum that no one has successfully answered. The best this book can do is follow its own contention that examples work best. Two case studies are included in the Appendix and will be used to illustrate the major steps in the process as they are explained.

Case Study #1

Case Study #1 includes all documents that are discussed. The first three are incorporated in the text:

- ➤ Project Proposal
- ➤ Free-association list
- ➤ Outline

The Appendix includes:

- ➤ Creative Treatment
- ➤ Script

This fictionalized project is for the Elgin Medical Corporation, which needs an employee orientation show. The decision to produce this video is part of a larger operational change: responsibility for new employee orientation is shifting from the individual departments to the personnel department.

In earlier years, this company had been like a large family. The top leaders had personal contact with virtually every employee and regular contact with everyone in a management position. This contact provided ample opportunity to informally pass on their vision for the company—particularly the values and beliefs on which that vision was based.

With growth, sheer numbers made personal contact with every employee impossible. The company's culture began to change, becoming more bureaucratic. Employees did not understand the basis for decisions that were made. The organization was no longer united by a common set of values. Flexibility was being lost. Without a sense of heritage or corporate culture on which to base their decisions and initiative, employees were retreating into the security of rigid rules and attitudes of "not my job" and "don't make waves."

Upper management wants a video that will both encourage initiative and provide a set of values and a sense of heritage on which independent decisions can be based.

Case Study #2

Case Study #2 is illustrated only by its finished script, which is included in the Appendix. It's a dramatization and it is included to show how this approach can provide effective training.

This fictionalized project is for a chain of department stores that needs to improve its customer service. Turnover in retail sales is so high during the first few years of employment that it was not considered cost-effective to give all new salespeople in-depth classroom training. Video is seen as an effective compromise.

The decision was made to produce a series of video modules, accompanied with workbooks and printed reference materials. Employees can watch these modules as self-paced study or in a group. The modules can be conversation starters that stimulate employees to discuss their own experiences and techniques for improving customer service.

The example script is the first module in this series. The rest of the series includes:

- ➢ Defining customer needs.
- ➢ Matching needs with product benefits.
- ➢ Handling objections.
- ➢ Asking for the sale.
- ➢ Turning customers into clients.
- ➢ Handling returns and complaints.

Turn to the Appendix now to read the sample creative treatment and the scripts for both case studies. It will help you to keep the end results in mind as you study the steps in the process that led to the treatment and finished scripts.

Operative Concepts

In informational media, as in life, there are certain basic concepts that seem to hold true, even when everything else dissolves into a confusion of shifting variables. Throughout this text, it will be pointed out when one of these concepts applies. A complete list follows:

Change the audience.

Create an emotional experience.

Focus on results rather than process.

The sharper the focus the greater the impact.

Abstracts on the track, specifics on the screen.

Show it; don't tell it.

Boil down and simplify.

Base humor and drama on training or selling points.

This is an excellent list to copy and keep handy. Refer to it at every critical point in the process to make sure you have considered these concepts in making your decisions.

These are the basics. You can memorize them in a few minutes, then spend the rest of your life realizing their expanding levels of application. Regardless of how sophisticated, imaginative or profound your ideas become, you jeopardize your show any time you overlook the basics.

Video Commandments

Though concepts are handy for philosophizing, it's more practical to have specific guidelines to apply during the heat of creation. The following list of Video Commandments will be referred to throughout the text.

Thou shalt make it quick and snappy. The get to the point commandment.

Thou shalt introduce, demonstrate and reinforce. The Three T's commandment.

Thou shalt knowth thine audience as thy knowth thineself. The research your audience commandment.

Thou shalt respect the intelligence of thine audience. The write for your equals commandment.

Thou shalt express all features and all ideas as benefits unto thine audience. The become an advocate for your audience commandment.

Thou shalt involve the hearts and souls of thine audience. The create an emotional experience commandment.

Thou shalt illustrate how others have embraced thine message and prospered. The tell a people story commandment.

Thou shalt not be pompous and obscure. The get off your high horse commandment.

Thou shalt use thine medium to its fullest. The death to talking brochures commandment.

This is another good list to copy and use for constant reference. When every sentence in your script obeys every commandment, you probably have a good script.

Comfort Factor—Buttoning Down

"Be Prepared"
—Boy Scout motto

Unlike poets and novelists, scriptwriters must be team players and a crucial aspect of team play is to inspire the confidence of your team—or at least to ease any doubts about your ability to play your position. Even if the resulting show is excellent, but you put your client and producer through an ordeal of ego clashes and last-minute heroics, your employability will be diminished.

In short, the process is as important as the product. To help ensure your future, a little comfort factor must be built into every step of the process. This simply means being professional: plan your work and work your plan. Encourage input at the appropriate points. Be prepared to explain your ideas, rather than expecting everyone to instantly recognize the brilliance of anything you commit to paper.

Comfort factor is created by demonstrating to your client and to the rest of your production team that you're buttoned down; you know what to do and how to do it without wasting anybody's time.

Professionalism

Professionalism is the essence of being buttoned down. Central to a profession is having an agreed upon language for discussing and discharging professional responsibilities. We are otherwise reduced to pleading, "just trust me," or threatening "do it my way or you'll be sorry." Part of professionalism is the ability to explain the rationale behind your ideas. Someone expressing skepticism may be satisfied with an explanation rather than a rewrite.

This text presents a working language, including terms such as *premise*, *structure*, *voice* and *subtext*. To win acceptance of your ideas and respect for yourself, you must learn to express yourself and to explain your ideas using this language. Even when working with people who *don't* understand this language, they are more likely to accept you as an authority if you are comfortable expressing yourself using an appropriate and professional vocabulary.

Another aspect of professionalism is that of following a specific procedure. You can win cooperation from your associates and clients by keeping them aware of where they are in the process, what to expect next and how responsibilities need to be delegated.

In practice, this means calling a meeting at every presentation and approval point. State what needs to be accomplished during the meeting, what happens next and who's responsible for making it happen. This keeps the process buttoned down and focused on taking one step at a time. You don't get bogged down in discussing details that aren't yet a factor. Once major decisions are approved, everyone understands that changing them will have consequences for the budget and schedule.

Know Who You're Talking To

You've just spent some of the worst weeks of your life doing rewrite after rewrite for a demanding client. Finally, your client likes it. You relax. The phone rings. It's your client calling to say, "I showed it to my boss and it needs a lot more changes."

Got'cha. You thought you were working with the decision maker when you were actually working with a recommender. It happens. It's frustrating. It will waste your time.

Buttoned down writers know who they're dealing with. It's easy, just ask either or both of these questions"

> ➢ "Who will be making the final decisions on this show?"
> ➢ "Whose approval will we need on the finished show?"

The operative word here is "show." Scripts are sometimes not taken seriously. They're considered an intermediate step that subordinates can handle.

This slight of logic is based on the assumption that the final decision maker will be able to make changes after the final video is shown to them. Sure, it's possible. It's just a lot more expensive and time consuming that way. It's better to have the final decision maker involved earlier on than to have to rewrite the script for a show that had already gone all the way through production.

Be aware of what contingencies await you. Ask whose approval is needed for the finished project—not just the script, creative treatment or project proposal.

It is usually quicker and easier to work directly with the decision maker, but it's not always possible. Working with recommenders is also all right, but requires a different strategy …

Working with Recommenders

When working with recommenders, your objective becomes not so much to influence the recommender as it is to help prepare that recommender to influence the decision maker.

Get yourself on the same side with the recommender. Ask specifically "what can I prepare, what can I do, that will help you get approval on what we've done so far?" View a recommender as a conduit rather than a wall. Ask what the decision makers are looking for; learn the values, attitudes and expectations that shape their decisions.

Form a team, so that the recommender understands your expectations and what you need to do a good job, and further understands that fulfilling your needs for information, direction and at least indirect decision-maker involvement is the most effective means of reaching the recommender's own goals.

Getting the Sign-Off

Even if you're working through a recommender, you need to have the decision maker involved at the critical approval points:

➤ Project Proposal

➤ Creative Treatment

➤ Script

Without the decision maker's buy-in at these critical points you greatly increase the likelihood of those total rewrites and last-minute changes to which the less-professional in this business seem constantly prone.

If there is reluctance to involve the decision maker at any point, you can still move forward as long as someone takes the responsibility of signing off at the approval points. By taking this step, if the project does come apart at the seams, you at least have documentation that the breakdown happened in spite of your efforts—not because of them.

Working with Committees

Your client may often be a committee. This can make it easier to get information on a variety of areas but it makes coming to decisions harder. The best approach is to request that one individual be in charge of getting group consensus, so that you're effectively dealing with only one person. It's now that person's problem to coordinate the group.

This is particularly important during approval of the creative treatment and script. What are you going to do when one group member tells you it's too hard-sell and another tells you it's too soft sell? It's common for committees to ask for contradictory changes. Becoming the group's arbitrator in this situation is a thankless task for which you are not qualified. Only a member of the committee has the authority to impose decisions on the group.

The next best approach is to get the whole group in the same room. You can then more easily point out that some requested changes are contradictory and then become an observer rather than a referee as the free and open marketplace of ideas becomes heated.

Hold off on rewrites until all comments are in. A committee member may ask you to "just get started working in the changes you already have." This may seem like a way to get a head start on the rewrite but it's more like rushing off on a trip without making sure you have everything. You usually have to go back and get something you forgot. You'll waste the time you thought you were saving and your level of stress has just been kicked up a notch.

If you're asked to begin a rewrite before all comments are in, be diplomatic. Explain your reasoning but be firm. Explain that latter comments and changes often contradict earlier ones, so you're more likely to be creating confusion than making progress.

If you're told to do it anyway, this may give you a good opportunity to discuss additional payment or comp time for any extra work that may be created.

Involvement and Interference

The primary difference between involvement and interference is timing. Involvement is helpful information provided in time to prevent problems. Interference is changing work you've already done.

Being buttoned down means getting your timing right. The time for client involvement is during needs analysis and research, when you will need as much help as possible with compiling information and understanding the client's needs and current situation. Other times for client involvement are the approval points for the creative treatment and script. This is when a buttoned-down writer actively encourages questions and revisions.

A more heavy-handed writer may be inclined to discourage involvement, particularly if it concerns questions or revisions to a completed treatment or script. I've found that this approach has the opposite effect: When people realize they were rushed through something without having an opportunity to ask questions and make revisions, they tend to overestimate the impact they could have had at that earlier point. Discouraging involvement at any point often creates resentment; undermining your comfort factor.

By encouraging clients and producers to get involved early in the process, you make them feel they've made their contribution and they are less likely to interfere later. If early on they are told "Now is the time to make any revisions," most people can later more easily accept that they have already had their chance and that revisions made now may legitimately affect the deadline or budget, or even jeopardize the quality of the show.

People accept contingencies much better when they're clearly explained ahead of time; if at the beginning, you make clear those points where involvement is welcome, you stand a better chance of keeping involvement from becoming interference. And besides, when they're put on the spot to revise anything they want right now, most people run out of ideas pretty quickly.

Needs Analysis

"You've got to be very careful if you don't know where you are going because you might not get there."
—Yogi Berra, b. 1925-

The first step in writing a video is to forget about writing a video. Concentrate instead on figuring out where you want to go, which means defining needs and goals. The means of taking this first step vary widely, since most organizations have their own procedures and paperwork. Some are well thought out; some are haphazard. Some organizations haven't a clue.

In the best of all situations the writer would be involved from the very inception of a project, participating in the needs analysis and writing the project proposal. In practice this seldom happens since the writer or video production group are either a separate department or an outside vendor.

A video is often only one component of a program to accomplish a goal such as launching a new product line or training an organization on a software upgrade. This level of needs analysis focuses on broad strategies and a video is only one of many supporting tactics. When this level of needs analysis is properly conducted, the decision to use some form of audiovisual media is made during the needs analysis rather than previously assumed. By the time clients are ready to talk with video specialists, they have usually already defined their needs and audience and are ready to get on with what they've decided to do.

The exception to this situation is when you or your organization is *initiating* the project. It's crucial that you formally study the situation before committing resources. Without a needs analysis you risk creating a show that is irrelevant or factually incorrect, or that duplicates existing material.

Whatever the case, on your initial involvement with a project, you need to get up to speed with a project proposal or needs analysis. If no one mentions this step, it would be a good idea for you to suggest it or volunteer to write one yourself.

The project proposal for a single video is an important step but it is most effective when kept short and simple. It's basically a reality check and an agreement on the identification of a specific problem. It determines that the problem can be solved by the effective application of a good video. It's a tentative initial step to save the time and grief that so often result from charging off with only vague assumptions or verbal directions.

Research

"Get your facts first, then you can distort them as you please"
—Mark Twain (1835–1910)

Assuming that you are initiating a project and therefore have complete responsibility for developing a project proposal, you need to complete some initial research to make the project proposal effective. In-depth research may not be needed until you are writing your creative treatment, but any research done now will be out of the way and will help you know what to ask for later during any additional research.

Research often begins by meeting with the client or content experts.

Getting to Know Your Client and/or Content Expert

We have established that you need to determine whether you are working with a decision maker or a recommender. Once you know who you're dealing with, you need a rapport with your client. Basically, this means that your project proposal, treatment, and resulting script will sound like what the client would have written, if only that client had your skill and expertise.

Even if you are initiating a project, you need someone else's support to finance or at least to distribute it. You need to be sure that what you are creating complements their values and goals of these people. A good approach to discovering someone's values and goals is by asking them questions and listening carefully to the answers.

The Initial Research Meeting

On some jobs there will be a content expert in addition to the client. It's best to get them together for your research meeting in order to resolve any differences that may arise. For example, a client's need to keep a show short may reduce the amount of detail the content expert wants included; a content expert may not have a broad overview or be aware of anticipated revisions in procedures or policy; or what your content expert is used to doing may conflict with what management thinks should be done and the change your show is supposed to help bring about.

If you can't get the two—or more—together you'll have to spend more time conducting multiple meetings and acting as a go-between, looking for contradictory messages and resolving them with the person who has final authority. In short, you'll waste a lot of time. And not just your time; your panel of decisions makers can burn up hours on the phone, exchanging email and passing around multiple drafts of documents revising revisions of revisions, when the issues in question could have been resolved in a relatively short face-to-face meeting.

Like any good business meeting, your research meeting should be opened with a clear statement of what you need to accomplish and what the next step will be. Specifically, the purpose of this meeting is to identify the problem to be solved, define the audience and work out the best means for solving the problem. In short, it's the client's turn to talk.

The "Research Questions" listed in the Appendix provide a good outline for this meeting. Focus on what you need to accomplish. It's still too early to discuss creative approach or what the video will be like.

Any creative flashes that do pop up ... write 'em down. They'll be useful to you later when you're free-associating and looking for creative ideas. It may also be helpful to discuss how other videos excelled or failed to meet needs similar to those of your client.

But the bulk of the input meeting must focus on answering your research questions. There will be ample time to discuss creative approach later in the process, when there is a written creative approach to react to.

These clearly defined process steps are by no means universally accepted wisdom. Many writers and producers feel obliged to brainstorm and rough out a script immediately. There are several problems with this approach.

Time is valuable. Spending it to speculate on solutions to a problem you don't yet understand is usually a waste of time. Even worse, an initial idea may feel really good. You fall in love with it and force the realities to conform to the video you want to do, rather than altering the brilliant flashes to meet stated objectives.

In writing a script, as in most endeavors, it's best to first decide where you're going, before charging down paths that may lead only to confrontation and frustration.

Mixed Agenda Meetings

Another distraction that may soften the focus or your research meeting can occur if the client and producer plan to discuss production details or other factors outside of your immediate concern. No problem. This is what agendas are for.

Be buttoned down. Write an agenda and hand it out at the beginning of the meeting; or better yet, hand it out ahead of time. Agendas are best coordinated with the producer, but it's often hard to fit the meeting itself into busy schedules—much less a discussion on the agenda for that meeting. Volunteer to write the agenda. Most producers and clients will appreciate your initiative, and if they do want involvement in deciding on the agenda, you can give them the option of writing it themselves or working on it with you. A written agenda benefits everyone, focusing and shortening the meeting by helping you plan your work and work your plan.

Begin the agenda with time devoted to answering research questions, so that you get your needs out of the way before bladders and schedules begin exerting pressure on attention spans.

If you don't find out until the meeting that others plan to discuss topics outside of your research questions, take the initiative to sketch out an agenda on the spot. There's a certain power in writing something down. Give copies of your hand-written agenda to everyone—with your research questions at the top of the list. Once everyone sees and agrees with your agenda, it's easier to keep them on track than if they had agreed to an agenda you suggested verbally.

If anyone strays from research-related items during the meeting, simply remind them that they've skipped ahead to the next agenda item and you need to finish the current agenda item before any of the remaining items can be given the attention they deserve.

Research Questions

The list of research questions in the Appendix is a useful tool for conducting interviews. The development of this list began when I noticed that I was asking the same basic set of questions during most research meetings but couldn't always remember all the good ones. This list is the product of many years of compiling and refining my favorite research questions.

The list includes questions for any situation and you would never ask them all during any single interview. The best plan is to modify the general list before any research meeting. Some questions are best reserved to ask after the project proposal is approved, as additional research before moving onto the creative treatment. On the basis of what you already know about the project, remove the questions you don't need and add questions about your specific situation.

Working the Questions

More thought is better. This makes it a good idea to provide your written questions to your interviewee at least a day ahead. You have then at least given them the opportunity to be more thoughtful in their answers.

During your interview, use your questions as a loose guideline, rather than a rigid agenda. Rather than insisting that every question be fully answered in order, make this an improvised performance, using the questions only as an occasional reference, an aid in organizing information under appropriate headings and a prompt for questions you may forget. This increases the spontaneity of the interview and helps you to follow the other person's train of thought.

To understand the need for spontaneity in a research meeting, envision the situation: There you sit with a list of questions geared to your way of thinking. There sits the client, who knows backward and foreword the things you need to find out but who does not share your exact perspective or way of doing things. It is far better to get that client on a roll, gleaning the information you need as it shoots past, than to attempt forcing the client into your way of proceeding. Interruptions, even when intended to keep the meeting on track, often cause people to lose their train of thought and to forget important information.

It's similar to memorizing a song or a poem, or even reciting the alphabet. It's easier to start at the beginning and go straight through. If you interrupt interviewees, forcing them to stop and start their train of thought, you risk them loosing that train of thought.

Experts who explain the same ideas over and again develop patterns. When you interrupt those patterns, you jeopardize the rapport you need to establish and deprive yourself of the full benefit of their knowledge.

To facilitate this relaxed approach to interviews, I number the interview questions and keep a pad of paper handy during the interview. When the response to a question is too long to jot on the same page with the questions, I quickly write the number of the question on the note pad and follow it with the interviewee's continuing response.

I also record interviews, using a recorder that has a counter. Then, along with the number of the question, I jot down the number showing on the counter. Later, when working from my notes, if I need to review a response, I can go straight to it, rather than wasting hours searching for a few words buried among thousands. In this way I typically listen to only a few short sections of any recording. But those few words that I need to hear again are often a real time and frustration saver.

Another benefit of following the order of the questions loosely is that many of these questions approach the same information from different angles. For example, comprehensive answer to a question about the audience's "Previous knowledge of the subject" may bring out all you need to know about "problems the audience has had with this client in the past," "negative preconceptions," and "positive preconceptions." And answers to any one question may lead naturally to a line of questioning that does not include the next question on the list.

In short, this list of research questions is a tool to help you stay buttoned down, but not a crutch to take the full weight of responsibility for deciding what questions to ask and when.

When you keep the research meeting focused loosely on answering these questions, rather than attempting to impress the client with ideas you've had for other shows or improvising a creative approach on the spot, you more effectively demonstrate your expertise. You're conducting your client through a well-thought out process, showing that you know exactly what you need and are wasting no one's time in getting it.

Some of these questions may seem obvious, such as "What is the primary impression you would like your audience to leave with?" "Is there a problem this show should solve?" "Why produce a show now (since you have been getting along without one)?" But these are the very questions that are often overlooked, only to blind-side you in the heat of making a deadline, when some crucial fact appears that lays to waste hours of work. Use these questions well and you'll probably soon be complimented on your insight, or be told "that's a good question we hadn't thought about." That's your comfort factor in action.

The Danger

The only danger with this strategy of encouraging the client to talk spontaneously is that the client may lose sight of what the meeting is about and seize the initiative to run you off the track. No problem.

If the client, or even the producer, gets seriously sidetracked into creative approach or production details, simply remind everyone that they have jumped ahead to the topic of your next meeting. You might add that using everyone's time most effectively is the reason for taking things a step at a time. The producer should appreciate this, since budgeting and scheduling is less dangerous when it can be based on an approved script.

The clinching rationale is that you want the client to have a clearly thought-out written document to consider as a starting point, rather than to be forced to spend time on extemporaneous brain-storming.

Ideas and concerns of any sort can be given a full airing during a research meeting; this is after all, the client's turn to talk. If anyone has an idea for a good opening or the big ending, be polite and listen. Then jot it down as something to consider later. Rather than squelching spontaneity, you're goal is to manage the meeting to avoid turning it into a skull session, where everyone is forced to sit around watching everyone else grope for ideas.

Questions about creative approach are best not asked during a research meeting. Your only purpose at this point is to help your client define the problem, the audience and a possible solution.

Know Your Audience

Turn to the "Research Questions" listed in the Appendix. It will be helpful to refer to these questions as they are discussed in the next few pages.

The most crucial question to answer during a research meeting is "Who is your audience?" The reason for this contention is stated by the operative concept:

Change the audience.

Video is behavior modification and anyone who presumes to change a group's behavior had better first get a firm handle on that group's current behavior. What are their values? What are their needs? What gets them excited? In short, obey the research-your-audience commandment:

Thou shalt know thine audience as thou knowest thyself.

That's why the Research Questions begin with a section on the audience. The entire research process is more effective if everything is considered from the audience's point of view. The realities of the situation are not nearly as important as your audience's perception of those realities.

Your Audience

There are three generalities we can safely state about your audience. Most modern Americans are:

- ➤ Informal
- ➤ Informed
- ➤ In a hurry

Being informal, they are most easily involved in presentations with a conversational tone. Anything officious or pretentious is more likely to induce sleep than alter behavior. This fact leads to the get-off-your-high-horse. commandment:

Thou shalt not be pompous and obscure.

Being informed, audiences will usually know something about your subject already. They don't need a refresher on the history of computers. Most audiences want a clump of very specific knowledge that will plug neatly into what they already know.

Don't insult them by dwelling on the obvious or telling them what they already know. And never talk down to an audience. Even youngsters and the unskilled are more readily involved when they are addressed as equals, this leads to the write-for-your-equals commandment:

Thou shalt respect the intelligence of thine audience.

Being in a hurry, audiences have no patience for unneeded detail or philosophical musings. So make your point, be concise, then finish big. Obey the get-to-the-point commandment:

Thou shalt make it quick and snappy.

In addition to these generalities, the more you understand about your specific audience, the more effective you will be in designing an emotional experience for them. Learn what's going on in their lives; understand their concerns and their goals. For the purpose of writing a project proposal, you need only a general understanding of the audience, but you will need a detailed understanding when writing the creative treatment and script.

While asking your client about the target audience, you may encounter a common malady, the General Audience Syndrome.

The General Audience Syndrome

"One size fits all" sounds like a good idea; but those of us who are tall or portly understand how poorly it usually works in practice. The same is true when you design a video to fit an audience.

It's natural for clients to want to get the most for their money with a program "That we can show to everybody." But, like the one-size-fits-all garment, it is sure to bag on some and bind on others, which leads to the operative concept:

The sharper the focus the greater the impact.

The other way to state this reality, and what you want to avoid is: The broader the message the softer the impact. For example, an orientation show, such as Case Study #1, is basically a general overview of the organization. A resourceful executive may think, "Hey! We can show this to patients and shareholders, too."

The problem is that, in addition to being an overview, an orientation show must also be a personal welcome to the team and an encouragement to personally apply the organization's values to achieving its mission.

These messages are of little interest to patients and shareholders. If you attempt to brush by these ideas you diminish the show's impact on its primary audience. While the issues that are of greatest importance to these "add-on" audience segments may hold little interest for your primary audience, or even be sensitive issues that need to be positioned quite differently for different audiences.

For example, shareholders may be happy to hear how costs are being controlled by aggressive bargaining with labor unions. While employees would hear that and realize, "Hey, that's me they're talking about. And 'aggressive bargaining' means less in my pay check."

While every issue should be treated honestly, it's simply being professional to pare away issues that aren't central to a specific show and to state issues that *are* central in a way that is most appropriate for a specifically defined audience. And the only effective way to do that is to avoid the general audience syndrome.

Life is full of compromises, sometimes a single show must be made to do where several different versions would be more effective. Don't fight realities but be aware of your responsibility to advise your client that the impact of the message is diminished every time that it's made suitable for a broader, less-focused audience.

Determine the Desired Change in the Audience

Here is the real bottom line of your show. Finding out what it is often requires asking specific questions that your client may not yet have considered:

> ➤ How should the audience think or act differently?

> ➤ What is the primary impression you would like your audience to leave with?

Focusing your client on answering these questions can do wonders in cutting through the clutter and getting down to what the project is all about.

The questions on measuring results are included as an encouragement. Most serious practitioners and students of marketing or training are reverent about the sanctity of measuring results. Despite this, virtually all professionals with whom I have discussed this topic have never worked on a program that was followed up with formal research to measure results.

It is amazing that billions of dollars are being spent based on seat-of-the-pants opinions about what works and what doesn't. If we keep asking about measuring results, some day someone may actually do it.

This section includes a profound question: "Is there a problem that this show could solve?" It's so obvious a question that it's often overlooked. By asking your client to specifically consider the program as a problem-solving tool, you may help identify the real issue that must be dealt with.

Understand The Message

Once you understand your audience and how they need to change their thinking or actions, it's time to learn about the information you will use to bring about this change, keeping in mind the become-an-advocate-for-your-audience commandment:

> **Thou shalt express all features and all ideas as benefits unto thine audience.**

To help you in obeying this commandment, it may be a good idea to ask your client to explain the benefits of the main points. While conducting this content discussion with your client, you may run into another common video malady the while-we're-at-it-syndrome.

The While-We're-At-It Syndrome

"As long as we're doing a video anyway," a client may reason, "Let's put in all this other stuff they need to know too." It sounds like a way to get more for your money. But in practice you're more likely to end up with a show that leaves your audience overwhelmed and confused. You can't get around the operative concept:

The sharper the focus, the greater the impact.

Broadening the message softens the impact, often to the point that none of it is delivered particularly well. Consider the Swiss Army knife. With all of those blades it works in a pinch to do all sorts of things but it does none of them very well. A specialized tool is always easier to use and usually does a better job.

Case Study #2, "Success In Selling," teaches a few fundamental techniques for improving customer service. If it were also expected to teach procedures for ringing up a sale and opening charge accounts the show would lack focus. The audience would be overwhelmed with more information than could be absorbed and remembered from a single presentation. They would probably remember nothing at all—besides the confusion and frustration they felt while watching the show.

In practice, this show reinforces some product knowledge and closing procedures but this is included only as credible background action and never takes the focus away from the show's primary purpose.

In situations where a client begins loading on content beyond what's necessary to achieve your fundamental objectives, it's your responsibility to remind them that with every additional fact and detail, you're softening impact rather than increasing value.

Get the Background

Smart people learn from their own mistakes; geniuses learn from the mistakes of others. This section asks how your show's objectives have been accomplished in the past. Ask about any phrases, examples, analogies, or techniques that have worked before. Take them from any source: Speeches, advertisements, news releases, seminars, classroom training materials, magazine articles, annual reports and Web sites may all contain something useful to consider in writing your script.

This section also includes questions on how your show fits into a broader context. By contributing to solving broader problems—rather than focusing only on getting this show out of the way—you may create a more useful show with more depth and levels of interest. You will also position yourself as more involved and knowledgeable, and of long-term value to your client's organization.

The question, "What books/authors have been shaping the client's thinking on this subject?" is included because it's common for someone in executive management to request—or require—all management-level employees to read one of the management theory books that often make it onto a best-seller list.

By reading these books, understanding their concepts and adopting the language they use, you have a head start on tone, direction and language for your script. Your audience is already up the learning curve on a vocabulary of terms and how an author has specifically defined them. It just makes sense to tap into that shared experience of reading the same book and the energy that comes from grasping a new perspective.

How Will the Program be Used?

It's been several millennia since farmers randomly scattered seeds over the ground. But video tapes, through substantially more expensive than seeds, are to this day often cast into the field with nothing more than the hope that someone may figure out what to do with them.

Video is a tool for altering behavior or attitude. Like any tool, it must come not only with a user's guide, but with a comprehensive plan for how it will use—and be used with—other resources. By considering the video as only one component of a program, you can define everything the program must accomplish, assigning to the video only what it does best.

> **Example:** As a sales tool, a video can quickly introduce and demonstrate a product, answering the questions most often asked. It doesn't address every application for the product or ask for the sale, but it sets the scene for a salesperson to address the specific needs of the prospect. The salesperson then asks for the sale.
>
> The video can become a point of reference during the live sales presentation: "The video showed how our SP380 withstands hazardous environments. How do you think that would help you in your spray-painting operation?"

Incorporating a video into a sales presentation is an effective technique for getting extra mileage from a video. But it will only happen if salespeople are trained to do it and will be most effective when a system of follow-up tactics are integrated into the same program with the video—strategies such as direct mail, follow-up calls and sales promotions—all hammering away at the same message, with a clearly coordinated look, feel and theme.

Make sure that your client is aware of the different ways in which the program can be made more effective. This may even be a good opportunity for you to take on the additional responsibility of writing a larger part of the program. It also helps you deal with the While-We're-at-it Syndrome. You can respond to a client who is trying to smother a show in details by advising "it would be more appropriate to include that in the collateral material."

Consider *where* a video will be used. A video used at a trade show, in a lobby, or in a retail store, must grab and hold attention at whatever point a person starts watching. In a controlled environment, such as a classroom or seminar, you can assume it will be watched from beginning to end. Large groups respond differently from individuals. A crowd may stand up and cheer a motivational show that might seem corny and manipulative to a solitary viewer.

Subtleties in sound and intricate graphics that are truly astounding on a high-quality playback system, can be muddled or lost when played back on inexpensive, poorly maintained equipment, on a hand-held digital device or in a small window on a Web page.

Timing is also crucial. A group that's spent all day in training needs review and reinforcement; any new information thrown at them probably won't be absorbed. You may expect a group to come in early for a video about the new equipment that will make their lives easier, but a video about a cut in health benefits had better be shown on company time. A patient about to undergo surgery wants a lot more detail about the procedure than an investor who is considering buying stock in a company that makes medical supplies.

Who Will be Administering the Program?

Like any tool, video must take into account the people using it—so talk with these people. You may discover that one type of audience won't pay attention to a show unless they know they'll be tested, while another group may resent being tested so much that they discount the video's message.

If the people administering the video have poor presentation skills, they may need a detailed facilitator's guide—or even need training in how to lead a group. If they're polished speakers they may resent this intrusion.

Presentation counts, not just during the show but before and long after. A video's effectiveness can be enhanced by making a big deal about it. For example, as part of initial research, having your potential audience answer a short questionnaire creates a feeling of ownership and curiosity to see what it will be like.

A teaser campaign let's the audience know something special is on the way. Posters, announcements, and articles in a newsletter and the organization's intranet can all build expectation.

If your show is being sent or given directly to the person who is to view it, packaging is crucial. It must look important and include some form of collateral material the viewer can keep and refer to.

If your show is posted on a Web site, make sure that the framing, or download, page builds anticipation for your work. Entice your prospective audience with concise statements of what they will learn and/or how they will benefit, if only they watch your video and embrace its message.

Any collateral material that can't simply be posted to the same Web site should also be easy to download or link to from this page.

If your show is part of a presentation—a sales pitch, seminar or live event—part of its design must include material on how to introduce it, how it complements and sets-up other elements in the presentation, or discussion questions that use the show as a point of reference.

After the fact, follow-up in newsletters, emails, online forums, posts to Web sites, or on-going training. All of these tactics can leverage a video-based program's effectiveness. Every time an audience sees a reference to what it remembers from one of your shows, the initial knowledge is reinforced and becomes an existing context within which new information is easier to understand and mentally file away into an expanding framework of well-structured knowledge.

It can all work together so that the whole is greater than the sum of its parts, but only if you're smart about crafting those parts so that they all build on each other.

These additional program elements may be outside your area of responsibility as a scriptwriter but it's important that you're aware of them so that you design a show that leverages all aspects of the environment in which it is used.

Production Details

Details. Learn them now, before they sneak up and bite you. It could be very embarrassing to write a twenty minute show when the client has only a ten minute slot available. It could also mean hours of work down the tube.

Learn the resources that will be available. Where can the production crew shoot? Where can't they shoot? What existing footage, graphics, photography or other program elements are available to you? The following list summarizes what you as a scriptwriter should do.

Research Meeting Overview

> Determine who the decision makers are and follow the best strategy for working with the people with whom you have direct contact.

> Clearly state the objective of the meeting.

➤ Clearly state the next step: to return with a written creative treatment, at which point anything can still be changed.

➤ Encourage the client or content experts to state the problem and objectives, and current situation in their own terms, taking notes on the paper containing the Research Questions (a legal pad is also helpful for taking notes that can't be quickly organized onto the question sheet).

➤ Refer to the list of Research Questions so that ask for information that has not been volunteered.

➤ Use the Research Questions as probes, encouraging the person answering to continue at their own pace.

Additional Research

Taking a tour of your client's facility, or doing field research, is always a good idea. Even writers who are staff employees and are familiar with corporate headquarters need to get out in the field or on to the factory or shop floor to personally experience the tone and feel that needs to go into the show.

The most consistent criticism I received on a video dramatization done for insurance claims representatives was, "The guy in the video looked like he had only one thing to do, I have to balance three or four things all the time." After spending more time in a branch claims office and paying more attention, I was able to write into the next script more background action, a steady flow of realistic interruptions and frequent references to several other priorities that our character had to manage simultaneously. The audience liked that show better.

Taking photos during your tour is also a good idea. This is a visual medium. Photography forces you to look for the visuals. And by studying them back at your desk, you may see important points in the pictures you missed while on-site. These pictures can also double as location research for the producer. Other items that may help you in your research include:

➤ Annual report.

➤ Web site.

> ➢ Videos and scripts of previous, similar efforts, or those of a competitor.
> ➢ The Client's advertising.
> ➢ Press releases.
> ➢ Newspaper and magazine stories.
> ➢ Company newsletter.

Determining the Budget

"Money never meant anything to us. It was just sort of how we kept score."
—Nelson Bunker Hunt, who made his fortune in Texas oil, then lost it in silver speculation

No project is real until it has a budget for production. Checking for budget helps you separate the buyers from the idle curious and can save you from devoting many uncompensated hours on someone else's free education. So before committing your time and effort to a project, first make this simple two-part reality check:

> ➢ Is there a need?
> ➢ Is there a budget?

How Big a House?

Shows range in price, just like houses. A little cabin prices out differently from a gracious mansion, so no one would ask an architect to design a house without first specifying a budget range, size, and level of amenities.

Video budgets are similar. You must know both needs and budget before you can realistically design a means of bringing them together. Only by knowing the budget can strategies and creative approach be intelligently selected. Many hours and dollars are wasted by people who think video is like a sack of potatoes: if the whole sack is too much, they'll just take half. It doesn't work that way. A video is a critical balance of many elements, all of which must be at a comparable level of quality.

To substantially cut a show's budget requires scaling back all of its elements consistently. This takes time, which can legitimately be charged back to the budget, making it even tighter.

Top value comes with reaching agreement on a firm budget range before making any other decisions about your show. You will waste your own time if you guess at a budget range or design a video without budget constraints.

Understanding the Budget

Knowing the dollar amount of your budget is not as critical as understanding the number and level of elements with which you have to work.

The basic questions you need answered to understand the budget's impact on your script includes how much is allocated for:

➢ Number of locations?

➢ Days of photography?

➢ Number of professional talent?

➢ Level and size of production crew?

➢ Original or library music?

➢ Level and amount of graphics and animation?

➢ Stock footage that can be incorporated?

➢ Level of audio sweetening?

➢ Level and amount of post production and special effects?

Answering these budget-related questions is a necessary step toward intelligently designing any video. If you have questions about any of them, sit down with your producer—or whomever is managing the budget—and button down how much you can afford of every element of production.

Different Media for Different Needs

"Consistency requires you to be as ignorant today as you were a year ago."
—Bernard Berenson (1865–1959)

Video can be mixed and matched with a number of different distribution methods. And the process you are now learning can also be used to improve PowerPoint presentations, Web sites, self-paced learning, and other interactive media that do not necessarily incorporate a moving image.

A traditional use of video is a stand-alone presentation, now typically distributed on disk-based media. This is a good choice if your message would have the greatest impact seen beginning to end. In other cases your video may be more effective broken up into modules that could be interspersed throughout a live presentation or framed within different pages of a Web site.

To choose the most effective way to deliver a message, it's a good idea to consider the strengths and weaknesses of all options. Then select the one that best serves the needs of your client and audience. Often, these decisions are made without the writer's involvement, but if you're writing for moving-image media, it's important to understand the issues involved.

The two highest-level issues are acquisition format and distribution format. The issue of distribution format includes the environment in which your video is seen.

Acquisition Format

Acquisition format is simply the type of camera used. For our purposes, we need consider only the two highest-level options: motion or still image.

Motion Video

It's often just assumed that video means motion, and motion video is often the obvious best choice. Interviews typically need to be captured on motion video, along with documentation of most things that move, dramatizations, modeling of correct behavior, and the real-time world as we generally perceive it.

Still Images

Although the term video may *imply* motion, good videos can be crafted from still images. This is not a black-or-white issue. One of the strengths of video is its ability to combine still and motion images.

Sometimes still images are all that is available. This is common when addressing an historical subject, or an event that was documented only with still images. In other situations, still images may actually be the better choice.

Cost is one issue. A single photographer may be able to document an event as effectively as a video crew. And depending on the level of documentation needed, still images may actually be a better choice. We tend to remember events as single moments that captured the essence of the situation. And still photographers are by their nature more attuned to seeking out those telling moments. A candids module, which is described later, is usually better when composed from still images rather than motion footage.

Still photography also offers some quality advantages. Being less obtrusive, a photographer can often get better candid shots than a video crew. In situations requiring lighting, a still camera can work with strobes, which can light a larger area than can be lit with an equivalent amount of video lighting.

Starting with still images you can then add motion. Examples of this are documentaries created by Ken Burns on the Civil War, baseball and jazz. To the still images that comprised the bulk of his source material, he added camera moves, panning or tilting across the images, zooming or combining them as inserts over computer or video-generated backgrounds.

Video effects such as page-turns, flying images in and out of the frame and creating three-dimensional shapes with different images on the different surfaces open up opportunities for transitional, continuity and instructional devices. But this advice comes with a critical warning:

> **Overuse of camera moves and video effects is distracting and the mark of an amateur.**

Limit your camera moves and visual effects to a very few that are clearly motivated by the overall design and pacing of your show. Consistency, simplicity, and discretion should guide all decisions on visual and sound effects.

Distribution Format or Environment

To design an effective show you must understand how it will be used and then design for that environment. This can be straight forward. A video on the history of an organization can be a self-standing presentation. Your client may want to use it for a kiosk in the lobby at headquarters, for recruitment at colleges and job fairs, and as part of employee orientation.

On the other hand, that same basic content can be used in a number of more sophisticated ways. Audience interaction may be desired, either on a Web site or as interaction during a live event. A survey may be needed to measure audience reaction, or a test needed to judge comprehension and retention. Different versions may be needed for different audiences. In any case, to design the best show, you need to know how it will be used.

Linear Video

Linear video is the most traditional use of the moving image. Your audience sees it from beginning to end. There is no interaction with the audience. Although it can be coordinated with, or supported by, brochures, study guides, tests or other collateral, those items exist separate from the video itself and the facilitator or audience must make some effort to obtain and use that collateral material.

Typical uses of linear video include programming for broadcast or cable television, a show distributed disk-based media that can be taken home to watch or can be shown in a meeting or classroom, a video-format computer file that can be downloaded from a Web site or viewed online, or a show to be used in a kiosk or tradeshow booth.

Linear video is good for providing an overview or introduction, similar to the employee introduction in Case Study #1. It's good for setting a tone that is then paid off by a live presentation or other types of digital media. For example, a video that introduces a planned community can be distributed on a disk that also provides information on available floor plans for houses, pricing levels and the schedule for when different phases of the community will be finished.

Linear video is good for taking an audience to destinations that are difficult or impossible to reach, such as foreign countries, inside the human heart or to the bottom of the ocean. It's also good for showing things that are difficult to stage, such as crash tests or heavy equipment in action.

Linear video is poor at presenting a lot of factual detail, or information that is likely to change frequently. It's not well suited for use as reference material, because it's hard to get back to that specific image or fact you need.

Table 1: Strengths and weaknesses of linear video.

Strengths	Weaknesses
Full control, ensuring that every audience has the same experience.	Audience can't self-select pace, order of presentation or specific segments of content.
Good for creating an emotional experience, setting a tone or motivating.	No random access ability to quickly find specific images or segments.
Good for affecting overall opinions or attitudes, or reinforcing a singe idea.	Audiences can't remember a large number of facts and details from only seeing a video.
Can incorporate other media such as diagrams and charts.	Poor at presenting visuals that are complex or highly detailed.
Relatively inexpensive, standardized and widely available playback options.	No embedded means to track audience reaction.
Easy playback, requiring no computer literacy.	No embedded means to test audience comprehension or to offer additional information.

Web Sites

Online digital media (Web sites) promise the best of both worlds. Linear video elements can be posted right along with the collateral and reference material needed to introduce, support, and reinforce them. Surveys and testing can be incorporated so that audience interaction is required before the next motion video element is made available.

Audiences may proceed at their own pace, be allowed to select the type and amount of content they see, and bookmark Web pages for future reference. This makes Web sites not so much an alternative to linear video, as a distribution environment that both leverages the effectiveness of linear video and compensates for its shortcomings.

The downside is that the more control given to the audience the less assurance there is that they have the experience you intend for them. Whether or not this is a problem depends on the goals and objectives of your video project.

Table 2: Strengths and weaknesses of video used within a Web site.

STRENGTHS	WEAKNESSES
Introductory, support and reference material can be provided on same webpage with the video element.	Little control over how much collateral information the audience reads and uses.
Audiences can pick and choose content of greatest interest and order of presentation.	No assurance that audiences have the same experience with the Web site or are exposed to an appropriate level of content.
Good for random access. Specific segments can be posted as discrete video elements that can be easily found and played independent of other video elements.	Video elements can be played out of sequence and out of context.

Strengths	Weaknesses
Text, data and other reference information can be made available on the same Web site.	Access to the Internet is required.
Playback is possible over any Internet browser with appropriate add-ins.	Audience members must have the appropriate, software, hardware, Internet connection and level of computer literacy.
Content can be continually updated.	Quality control can be no better than quality control for the Web site.

Offline Digital Media

Web sites deliver many advantages for distributing and framing video content. But you can't always assume reliable access to the Internet. Would you want sales reps to be unable to give presentations in a customer's office if Internet access was not easily available? What's the best way to show video at a tradeshow where an Internet feed to your booth is prohibitively expensive? Once you've gone to the expense of incorporating leading edge graphics into a video, would you want it to be unwatchable by anyone without the latest browser and the newest add-ins?

There's also a greater perceived value to a disk. Many people are more likely to keep and watch something on a disk than if you simply provide a Web site address and ask them to go online to find your video and watch it. And most disks can be played back on inexpensive players, rather than a computer.

Disk-based media, such as CDs and DVDs, shield you from the vagaries of distributing video over the Internet. You don't have to worry about audience members having an adequate browser, properly configured, with plenty of bandwidth. As with Web sites, disk-based media are not so much an alternative to linear video but a distribution environment that both leverages the effectiveness of linear video and compensates for its shortcomings.

Quick disk content can be created by making a copy of an existing Web site on a disk. Disks also open a wider world of playback options that aren't Web-compatible. You can also enjoy the best of several worlds by putting your more permanent and bandwidth-intensive media on disk, which can then connect to a Web site that provides content that is more dynamic, including prices, schedules, availability of rental items or inventory levels.

Table 3: Strengths and weaknesses of video distributed on disk-based media.

STRENGTHS	WEAKNESSES
Access to the Internet is not required.	A physical object (the disk) must be provided to everyone in the audience.
Can be played on inexpensive, easy-to-operate players.	Once released, can't be updated.
A disk can also contain collateral material and an installer that places files on a computer's hard drive.	For playback on a computer, audience members need equipment that meets system requirements.
Can be included with print collateral and other support material to create a complete package with high perceived value.	Duplication costs drive up expense, complicate logistics and require additional time.
Can use technologies that are not Web-compatible.	Leading edge technologies may not play back on some equipment.
Distribution is easier to control.	Distribution becomes more complicated, expensive, and time consuming.

Live Presentations (PowerPoint)

Love it or hate it, Microsoft PowerPoint is currently the most common tool for providing visual support for many different types of presentations. Rather than recommending this Microsoft product over other options, this book uses the term *PowerPoint* simply because it has become a generic term that is more widely used and recognized than any equivalent generic term, such as *speaker support,* or *visual support.*

Although PowerPoint-type presentations can include video elements and even be configured to run as self-standing presentations, it is being included in this section to represent the live-presentation option to pre-recorded video. As such, PowerPoint has replaced 35mm slides and overhead transparencies as the standard means of incorporating visual support into live presentations.

Although PowerPoint-type speaker support can be less expensive to produce than motion video, for presentations that need to be given many times, the cost of a live presenter can make the over-all cost of this option much more expensive than pre-recorded video. It should be considered primarily for presentations that are given only a few times, that require a live presenter in any case (such as classroom training or sales presentations) or that must be tailored to an individual audience every time it is given.

Because PowerPoint is so easy to use, it is frequently misused. The concept of "death by PowerPoint" strikes a responsive chord throughout most large organizations. Many authors and consultants have risen to the challenge of saving audiences from bad PowerPoint. Perhaps chief among them is Edward Tufte[2], Professor Emeritus at Yale University, who goes so far as to suggest that the "cognitive style of PowerPoint" was a factor in the engineering decision that contributed to the Columbia Space Shuttle exploding shortly after launch.

The bottom line however is not so much that the software is to blame as the human beings who make poor use of it. Too often, "planning" a live presentation begins with creating a new PowerPoint file. This short-circuits the most critical steps of the creative process. Every step in the process

---

2   Edward D. Tufte, The Cognitive Style of PowerPoint (Cheshire, CT: Graphics Press LLC, 2003)

presented in this book can improve a PowerPoint presentation. Any step left out, or brushed over, weakens the effectiveness of the presentation.

Any presentation, even without visual support, is strengthened by a thorough analysis of audience needs, careful positioning of the message and skillful structuring of content. And there are no buttons on the PowerPoint user interface to do any of that.

Another shortcoming of typical PowerPoint presentations is a lack of adequate collateral material. Again, it's an issue of ease. It's so easy to simply print out a copy of your slides, audiences usually request them, and presenters too often feel that nothing more is needed.

The reality is that thoughtfully designed collateral material is essential to any presentation, whether this is a brochure, a white paper, study guide or a Web site that provides these types of elements. As Tufte makes clear, PowerPoint slides have *low resolution*. A single, well-designed page of text and images can convey more information than dozens of PowerPoint slides. Also, by their very nature, PowerPoint slides are designed to be seen while the presenter is being heard. So without the presenter there to explain them, PowerPoint slides are too often more baffling than illuminating.

Table 4: Strengths and weaknesses of live presentations.

STRENGTHS	WEAKNESSES
Can be individually tailored to every audience.	Requires the expense of a trained presenter.
Cost of creating visual support can be kept low.	Cost of presentation is high (due to cost of presenter).
Relatively easy to produce.	Because the production tools are so easy to use, they are frequently misused.
Can include pre-recorded mini-modules.	Ease of adding visual embellishment and special effects encourages their amateurish overuse.

STRENGTHS	WEAKNESSES
Can be updated and revised right up to the last moments before the presentation is given.	Ease of last-minute revisions is used as an excuse for poor preparation.
Live presentations are perceived as more important and the presenter can interact with the audience.	The presentation can be ruined by a poor presenter or one who is not familiar and current with the content.

Film

Although largely replaced by digital media, film still exists in the rarified atmosphere of high budgets and special applications.

Film has a softer look. It can appear more elegant, or more removed from the immediacy of current problems. Film is a good look for evoking the past, or for showing the present or future as we would like it to be. Film is the look we associate with movies and high-budget commercials.

However, what many people think of as the "film look" often has more to do with lighting and production value than with grain patterns in film emulsion. Film budgets are often higher budgets. Film makers are more often craftspeople rather than technicians. And most important, film makers usually spend more time lighting and art directing their shots. This same attention to lighting and art direction can also bring to video some of what is admired in the "film look."

Business Theater

Live performances—singing, dancing, stage skits—have a tremendous impact. Mixing them with live speeches, projection video or film blends the best of all worlds into an experience that will not be easily forgotten.

The downside is expense and logistics. A cast and production crew must be assembled, fed and transported for every performance. Business theater is best reserved for special events, annual meetings, awards banquets, product introductions, program kick-offs and world fairs.

Planning the Project

It is a bad plan that admits of no modification.
—Publilius Syrus (first century B.C.)

Though information will seldom be ladled out to you in its proper order and your ideas and insights may come in a jumble, it's still necessary to understand the formal organization of how decisions build on each other.

There are six important tasks at the planning stage.

Summary of Planning Tasks

- ➤ **Purpose and goal** are the fundamental decisions on which all others are based.
- ➤ **Audience** must then be identified—the people who will accomplish the stated goal by changing their thinking and/or behavior.
- ➤ **Behavioral objectives** specify what those changes must be, taking into consideration the situation and attitudes of the audience.
- ➤ **Content** is based on audience and objectives. It must be at their level of understanding, building on what they already know; adequate to achieve the objectives and unburdened with anything extra.
- ➤ **Creative approach** flows from the content, presenting the content as a benefit to the audience in a way that best involves their imagination.
- ➤ **Scripting** is the final step—converting the creative approach into plans the production team can work with.

Writing a Project Proposal

A blank page is God's way of showing you how hard it is to be God.
—variously attributed

With initial research completed, it's time to summarize the situation. Short is better. This is an initial document to get everyone moving in the same direction. The next step, the creative treatment, will include a more complete statement of objectives, strategies, and execution. The project proposal needs to concisely answer four basic questions:

➢ What is the problem?

➢ Who is the audience?

➢ What change in the audience will help solve the problem?

➢ What basic strategy will help bring about this change?

Focus on the problem—a specific problem. Rather than stating that sales are falling off, look further to define the underlying problem, which may be that salespeople don't have adequate product knowledge or that dealers don't understand how to use promotions effectively. Rather than stating that the tiles in the heat shield on the space shuttle are falling off, define the underlying problem: that technicians are not properly selecting among the different options for attaching those tiles.

The problem must be specifically defined before producing a show can be justified. Once stated, determine whether that problem—or at least part of the problem—can be solved if a specific group acts or thinks differently. This conforms with the operative concept:

Change the audience.

Video is a behavior modification tool, so your desired solution must be defined in terms of the behavior or attitudes you want modified, for example, the target audience will:

➢ More closely observe safety procedures.

➢ Identify the top three benefits of using the new product.

➢ Take more initiative in suggesting quality improvement ideas.

Once the solution is clearly stated, it's much easier to select strategies and create tools to make it happen. But be sure that your project proposal states real solutions, not just empty jargon.

The too-often heard, "to make aware" or "provide an overview" is vague rhetoric that only sounds like a solution. Think about those phrases. There's no substance, they imply scattering information over your audience without changing their behavior or thinking—much less motivating them to action. With such a vague goal, the only result will be to waste time and resources.

What are some substantive solutions that a show can help accomplish? Take a look at the project proposal for Case Study #1, written for a fictitious for-profit hospital corporation called EMC.

Project Proposal for EMC Employee Orientation

The Problem:

Recently hired employees lack the big picture of how they fit within EMC. There's confusion as to how and why the overall organization is structured. Top executives are barely known to them as names, much less as personalities. The heritage and values on which this company was founded are being lost and are no longer providing the focus and basis for decision-making that they once did.

Supervisors are usually too busy to provide a comprehensive orientation and often are not clear on this information themselves.

The Audience:

The audience will be employees recently hired by EMC hospitals and affiliated companies. Most of them are recent college graduates in their 20s and 30s. Though primarily in health-related fields, some are in administration and support services. They are assumed to have little previous knowledge of EMC.

The Solution:

New employees must better understand the history and heritage of EMC. They must better understand the values that have shaped our growth and be able to apply those values when making their own decisions. They need to be more aware of top executives and begin to perceive them as accessible leaders who are concerned about every member of the team.

Strategies:

Provide the personnel department with video and print materials that will expand its formal orientation procedures to include information on the organization's history, corporate culture, and company values.

You now have specific needs to fill. Rather than broadcasting some information that an audience may do with as it pleases, this expression of a specific solution helps you focus on creating a behavior modification tool that will help your audience:

➤ Better understand the history and heritage of EMC.

➤ Better understand the values that have shaped that history.

➤ Apply those values when making decisions.

➤ Begin to perceive the top executives as accessible leaders who care about every member on the team.

You are now ready to act on a basic operative concept:

Focus on results rather than process.

Focus on changing your specific audience in this specific situation, rather than assembling all of the usual elements that fit some abstract idea of what an orientation show should contain.

Project Proposal Approval

Though brief, the EMC project proposal clearly lays out the basic factors on which you need consensus. *This is a major approval point.* All subsequent decisions will be based on the project proposal. Once you are further into the process, changes to the project proposal may create big problems that are expensive to fix, or even kill the project completely. Be sure that everyone who must approve the finished show understands and has approved the project proposal.

Collateral Material

"Trust in Allah, but tie your camel"
—Arabian proverb

Video is good at stirring the emotions but if you want your audience to remember any details, you'd better write them down.

For the employee orientation addressed by the preceding project proposal, a printed employee handbook would probably be the best solution for informing new employees about paid holidays, shift changes, and performance reviews. But that's not the key problem. The key problem is that new-hires do not understand the company's heritage, values, and corporate culture. To best convey these things, which are subjective and emotional, a moving-image medium is usually more effective.

In practice, a combination of the two is usually best, with printed collateral material as a reference and reminder of the video's message and a way to convey all of the factual details that would not be remembered from a video.

Another example of a useful combination of media is that of introducing a new product line. A brochure or Web site are good media for conveying facts and specifications but a video is much more effective for showing how the new features and benefits will change the life of a customer, sales rep, dealer or employee.

Video can set the tone and provide an overview or demonstration. Printed collateral material or a Web site can then fill in the details and provide reference material. Everyone then has easy access to the reference material needed. Once the video motivated the audience to seek out and use the reference, it is no longer needed, but the reference material needs to be available for the long-term.

Video modules can also add pacing and introduce discussion points for live events and training. Video helps to fill the gap between live training and no training at all, and is often tied to online or printed training materials.

> **Example:** For a self-paced program on negotiation, short video vignettes dramatize a negotiation situation. The video shows a group discussion of the techniques just demonstrated, then tells students to answer a series of exercise questions in a workbook.
>
> On re-starting the video, students see a discussion of the questions they have just answered—providing immediate feedback. A new vignette, building on the previous one, continues the cycle.
>
> After completing the program, a supervisor conducts a discussion with the student—based on a list of prepared questions—and answers any remaining questions that students may have.
>
> The completed workbook can also be used as a reference tool in the field.

Breaking the program up into clumps of information conforms to the way we think and learn best: a point is introduced, reinforced, practiced, and then summed up before going on to the next clump of information.

The more interactive a video, the better. Involving students with written exercises, then providing follow-up reinforcement, is more effective than simply bombarding them with information.

To best ensure that these elements are most effectively coordinated, they must all be planned early on. Often, different people will write the video, online, and print components of a program, so your project proposal will be intentionally restricted to the video. But even in these situations it's always best to fully understand the total environment in which the show you script will be used. Coordinate with other elements of the program, take full advantage of any concepts or terminology used elsewhere and avoid inconsistencies with other material your audience may be using.

CHAPTER 3

STARTING IN THE MIDDLE

Research for a Creative Treatment

The skill of writing is to create a context in which other people can think.
—Edwin Schlossberg, Designer, 1945–

High-impact shows are built on a foundation of good data and careful needs analysis. How much research and needs analysis you do yourself will vary. Remember that a scriptwriter is usually not brought onto a project until after the needs analysis and development—however informal—have been completed and the client is at least intuitively clear about what the problem is, the audience, the solution and the basic type of presentation needed. So in terms of analysis and research, you are forced to start in the middle.

In this situation, all the research suggested earlier as preparation for writing the project proposal must still be done—or be provided to you by the client. A good way to do this is to modify the list of "Research Questions" and follow the guidelines suggested in Chapter 2, then arrange the meeting during which your questions can be answered.

The creative treatment is an in-depth summary of a presentation that will solve the client's problem. Your major content, structural, and creative decisions will be made during this step of the process. This means that all of your research needs to be completed before writing the creative treatment. Once it is approved, little or no additional research should be needed to begin writing the script.

The amount of research must fit the project. The more you know the better but there is a point of diminishing returns. A ten-minute show doesn't need as much research as a thesis, or even as much research as a comprehensive term paper. The vast majority of shows I've scripted have been researched during a single meeting with the client and/or content expert, plus a day or two of reviewing the materials provided.

A scriptwriter must be an expert on form rather than content—presenting the majesty of the forest rather than categorizing every tree. Unlike investigative journalists, we work on the assumption that the people we are interviewing are telling us what we need to know. Probing for inconsistencies and contradictions is a critical part of the job, but it's to help focus and refine our client's message, rather than to challenge its validity.

Budget is also a factor. Research contributes to quality by bringing out the insights, historical background and that exact detail that may exemplify a major point. So a high-budget show warrants research consistent with the quality and attention to detail that is going into the other production values. Conducting extensive research for a low-budget show makes about as much sense as searching for the finest hand-finished mahogany to build a shipping crate and may squander resources equally.

There's no exact formula; the right amount of research is what your show needs and what your budget can afford. It's the same process that must be followed when designing any product or service within a budget: Set your constraints, do your absolute best within those constraints, then move on.

You will be making creative decisions while writing the Creative Treatment and you will need the answers to questions that may not have been an issue during needs analysis, for example, in Case Study #2 there is an opportunity to reinforce knowledge about stocking the shelves, closing procedures or product knowledge. So you might ask such questions as:

> ➤ "What are the three most important things to do when closing a department for the night?"
> ➤ "What are the three most important details to attend to when maintaining shelves and merchandize displays?"
> ➤ "What is an example of the product knowledge you would most like a salesperson to mention when presenting merchandize to a customer?"

Answers to these questions give you good ideas for cutaways and close-ups, realistic background action and credible topics for conversations. It also helps your client get extra value from the show by reinforcing knowledge that's outside of, but complementary to, the show's stated purpose.

This is the time to learn everything you need to know about the audience. For example, if you are planning a corporate video, it may be helpful to know that they are very loyal to a certain top executive; or very hostile. This information will help you decide whether the video should include an interview and with whom it should be conducted.

Probe for any emotional baggage with which any part of your message may be burdened. After deciding to use "Productivity Improvement" theme for a program, I discovered that what were known as "productivity teams" had recently decided that a lot of people were no longer needed—creating a strong association between "productivity" and losing your job. We took the hint, changed "productivity" to "performance" and proceeded pretty much as planned.

Shows are never seen in a vacuum. Current concerns and hot topics skew the way an audience perceives your message. A video that was obviously expensive to produce—that would be very appropriate during a successful year—would cause resentment if shown shortly after a pay-freeze. If a softball tournament or a major league play-off has everyone's attention, a creative approach based on a sports theme may be a good idea.

A good reason for putting this much effort into learning about your audience is to prepare yourself to be an advocate for that audience while you pursue additional questions and research. During your research interview, probe for any contradictions or weakness in your client's message. Ask the tough questions that the audience would like to ask for themselves and that may jeopardize credibility if not honestly addressed in your presentation.

Another good reason for considering the audience before you choose the message is that it helps you better understand their concerns, goals, and where they are headed, so that as you discuss the message with your client, you begin positioning that message as a means of meeting the needs of your audience.

Additional research can flow from any of the Research Questions that were not fully explored during needs analysis, or from the suggestions in the section on "Additional Research" in Chapter 2.

The Reality Backlash

Accepted wisdom is that audiences are media literate and will fully accept informational programming only when it has the same look as television. Many writers and producers take this to mean they must imitate the look and tone of prime time TV, right down to the physically perfect actors and slick production values.

In reality, our audiences are sophisticated enough to understand that actors aren't experts at anything other than entertaining us. That's fine if your only purpose is diversion, but if you're presuming to tell people how to do their job or live their life, they may not want to hear it from professional actors portraying idealized situations.

I ran straight into this reality backlash while working with a client at Nissan. My passing suggestion that a dramatization is often a good approach to showing how problems can be solved brought a stinging rebuke about how insulted their salespeople are by anything other than straight facts from the real experts.

The lesson here is summarized by the research-your-audience commandment:

Thou shalt know thine audience as thou knowest thyself

No creative approach is inherently good or bad—it just has to be appropriate to your audience. That's why the section of Research Questions section on audience includes the question "Who would your audience find most credible delivering this information?" Notice also that the Background section includes questions on how the client feels about using actors and interviews.

For the client at Nissan, dramatizations were obviously a bad idea for that audience in that situation. But that doesn't mean that dramatizations will never work.

Case Study #2 is a sales training that uses dramatization. The reality backlash not withstanding, this is still an appropriate creative approach for this type of show for this particular audience—newly hired employees who are assumed to be less cynical than car salespeople and more likely to trust training done by their own company. Car salespeople, on the other hand, don't work for the car company; they work for dealerships, so they have less reason to trust anything coming from a source that's once removed from their direct employer.

The content in Case Study #2 also lends itself to dramatization. Sales techniques are best taught through example—sales is partially acting and largely attitude. Dramatization is a good choice; use professional talent to model the behavior you want the audience to learn.

Another option is to use real salespeople to model their skills. But with amateurs, a director doesn't have the control necessary for a tightly scripted show. The only effective way to use amateurs is to have them do what they normally do the way they normally do it, then work with what you get. Asking them to read a script virtually ensures a wooden performance and many retakes.

Real salespeople who may be able to model good selling skills would probably not work for the conversations between the two main characters that provide the continuity and commentary for the show in Case Study #2.

Another problem with using real people is that, although they may be good at what they do, they may not necessarily do it exactly the way management would now like new employees to learn. You're then backed into asking non-professional talent to break old habits and learn new tricks, while under the pressure of being in front of a camera. It's usually easier to just have professional talent read the approved words exactly as management wants it done.

Using dramatizations does not preclude incorporating real people into the show—improving credibility and tempering reality backlash. Interviews with real salespeople could be intercut with the dramatizations. Segments of real salespeople going through role-plays could be intercut with dramatizations to demonstrate variations on specific sales techniques.

This gives you the best of both worlds: the control and professionalism of using actors in the dramatizations and the credibility of actual experts who critique the behavior and techniques being demonstrated. The big tip here is to ensure that your experts offer meaningful criticism, rather than simply function as cheerleaders, enthusiastically endorsing every detail as "just the way to do it."

This gets tricky. Your audience is most likely to remember and emulate what they see in the dramatizations. So it's self-defeating for the dramatizations to model anything other than exactly what you want your audience to do. And it's naïve to think that you can get around this by having an expert suggest a better alternative to the dramatization. There is little chance that the audience will discount what they've seen with their own eyes and emulate instead what thy have only heard described.

The technique for making this all work is to ensure that the constructive criticism from your experts focuses on setups, cautions and payoffs. This means that once your experts endorse the dramatization there is usually a "but" or an "and then." For example: "That's good, but to make it work you need to do your homework and make sure that you already ..." Or a caution, such as, "That's good, but if your customer then tells you, 'That's not important to me.' you need to be able to ..." And a payoff can follow the pattern of, "That's good because later on in the process you can ..."

This level of discussion builds credibility because the on-screen experts aren't simply accepting the company line as being perfect. They agree it is correct but feel compelled to add their own tips and insights.

The challenge is getting this level of discussion out of your experts while still following the advice to not script non-professionals or tell them what to say. The way to do it is to ask the right questions or to provide in your script directions to provide to your experts. For example:

> ➤ Discuss what you think of the technique demonstrated in terms of what you need to know or do before hand to make it work.

> ➤ What type of unexpected responses could you get if your tried this and how would you handle them?

> ➤ Discuss a time when you've used this technique and how it made things easier later on.

The order of your dramatization and discussion can work either way. Group discussion segments could show salespeople discussing their opinions. Every major conclusion they reach could then become a setup for a dramatization. Or the dramatizations could be intercut with segments in which the real salespeople comment on the sales technique just demonstrated, specifically commenting on the credibility of the dramatization the audience has just seen.

There are no absolutes. Do whatever is appropriate for your audience. If research shows there may be a reality backlash, do whatever it takes to temper it. But don't completely write off an entire category of creative approach just because some audiences in some situations do not react well to it.

Acknowledging "The People"

Current management theory is that we should heap new respect on human resources (that means people). Writing as a human, these are admirable intentions but we know where good intentions often lead. In this case, they have led to a new set of tired clichés that belie our refreshing intentions.

Business meetings everywhere now feature a genre of shows that either center on "our people" or have at least a segment full of smiling faces, generally introduced with a phrase such as: "People are our most important asset," "People make the real difference," "You make the difference," "The difference is you."

These increasingly familiar phrases are beginning to sound as empty and heavy-handed as the "And here's a picture of our company president with a little crippled child," school of audience manipulation.

One way to transcend this patronizing tone is to *Just Do It*. It's not necessary to bring the show to a halt and solemnly announce "But the real difference is our people." Instead, go straight for the jugular. State the benefit. It may be better service and quality for the customer, or a more fulfilling work life for the employees themselves. For example:

Product shot of most recent milestone product.	We've set the standard ...
Montage of people at work.	and these are the people who are moving it higher.
Group in lab with working model of a control panel.	With attention to detail, like a work group assembled to design more ergonomic controls.

Group in conference room intensely working on architectural plans of their work area.	With cost reduction, achieved by employees helping redesign their work areas to minimize materials handling.
Assembly line stops, as small group assembles to inspect a part.	And with a commitment to quality, giving every employee the authority to stop the assembly line—preventing defects from slipping past.

When the dialogue, interview or narration begins referring to benefits derived from dedication, professionalism, and innovation, the audience will quickly figure out that you're not talking about the new office furniture—especially if the screen is filled with *imagery* of people *being* dedicated, professional, and innovative.

A good strategy for improving your section on people is to ensure that it supports your theme and central idea. In the above excerpt, the show's overall theme was "Advancing The Lead." The central idea was that leadership means pushing the boundaries to a level that no one else can attain. The section on people is given the substance it needs by demonstrating how individual and collective effort help achieve this goal and the hollowness of token rhetoric is avoided.

Another strategy is to avoid generic fluff phrases. Instead, convey the specific values driving these people on to accomplishment. Avoid adjectives—just show how these values are actually being applied, using examples that show people investing extra effort, attention to detail, commitment, and involvement.

This requires that you identify the underlying values during research. This is often difficult; deeply held personal and organizational values are often not easily verbalized. Most people are uncomfortable explaining and justifying their beliefs—which is why clichés are so often used instead.

However, many organizations have formal statements of mission or philosophy. During research, use them as a starting point; ask for specific examples of the people or situations that demonstrate the underlying values. If this formal statement doesn't exist, offer to help create one.

Don't settle for rhetoric. Keep probing until you really understand these values and how they have shaped the organization's culture. If you don't, there is no way you can transcend empty cheerleading when attempting to convey them to your audience. The people who are making this country work deserve more thoughtful recognition than a generic rendition of the latest human resources clichés.

Turning Facts into Ideas

"To treat your facts with imagination is one thing, but to imagine your facts is another."
—John Burroughs (1837–1921)

Now is the time to immerse yourself in the research you've gathered. Don't even think about the show you're writing yet. Instead, concentrate on being an advocate for your audience and imagine the impact the material you're absorbing will have on them.

The process that works best for me is to begin organizing by culling through all notes and materials, making a "Free Association" list of anything that seems of note, including:

> ➢ Key concepts and ideas.
> ➢ Key words and phrases.
> ➢ Personal impressions.
> ➢ Quotes.
> ➢ Main points to be covered.
> ➢ Audience needs.
> ➢ Major benefits to the audience.
> ➢ Values and attitudes that have shaped the client's current situation.
> ➢ Similarities to more basic or universal situations.

Don't worry about the order and organization of this list. Your purpose now is to sift through your material and wrap your mind around the problem at hand. It may help you to make copies of the material you've gathered so that you can cut and paste it together. it may help you to highlight key phrases, or to organize material into separate folders.

Follow any personal work habits that help you absorb and organize your material. Rather than one list, you may be more comfortable organizing the entries into several lists. Do whatever works best for you.

But don't skip writing a list. That simple act of writing something down—or entering it into your computer—helps fix it in your mind. Your list becomes a distillation of everything you think is most important, filtered through your own thought process. It will be an invaluable reference source later in the creative process as you are groping for ideas.

The free-association list for Case Study #1, an orientation program for new employees of a for-profit hospital company, included items such as:

➤ Hires from within, grooms people for higher positions.

➤ Management style is action oriented, management by objectives (MBO).

➤ Values: innovation and problem solving.

➤ Rapid growth, during period of rapid and dramatic change in the healthcare industry.

➤ Good management means creating an environment where the standard is excellence.

➤ "Excellence in healthcare."

➤ Values: quality, caring, economic strength.

➤ Avoid term "vertical," use "integrated healthcare."

➤ Very literal, logical, and practical.

➤ Take initiative to find problems and fix them.

➤ Early days were like a big family, with close personal relationships.

If you are presenting new ideas that may not be readily accepted, check your list or your research for an earlier era in the organization's history that illustrates how these "new ideas" are really proven concepts that have worked in the past. The organization may have a heritage of "pioneering new markets," or "going against conventional wisdom." By showing how these strategies have worked in the past they can be made less threatening today. For example, an automotive company that helped move disc brakes from daring innovation to an accepted standard could state that heritage as the success they will duplicate by pushing the technology of braking systems even further.

If your list contains any "similarities to more basic or universal situations" you can begin developing analogies and metaphors—like the "big family" in the example list. Can your message be made more involving or more easily understood by expanding on an analogy or metaphor? Can the concepts of management you're trying to teach be better demonstrated by showing how a coach improves the performance of an athletic team? Can the quality in your product be compared to the craftsmanship of an earlier era? Does the situation your sales force faces in a new market have anything in common with the frontier of the Old West?

The range of possible analogies is endless, if one seems appropriate, check to see whether it holds up as a device for delivering all your main points. If so, you may have a head start on a creative approach. If not, forget it. Don't distort the content to make it fit a creative flash.

Don't push for the creative ideas just yet, but don't ignore any that crop up. The important thing now is to look for patterns in how this information fits together, always analyzing from the context of how all of this can benefit your audience.

You are not yet specifically focusing on the show you are about to write, but you are beginning to make the transition from analytical to creative thinking—the most gratifying as well as the most difficult part of designing a script.

The Creative Paradox

A quick quiz: Creativity and structure are:

    A. Opposites

    B. Mutually exclusive

    C. Necessary for each other's existence

Many people would choose options A. or B., reasoning that creativity means transcending structure. If you chose C., you may already understand the broad distinction between creativity and chaos.

Consider the most wildly imaginative shows you've ever seen. Examine them closely and you'll find a specific logic or reality holding them together. It may be a reality unlike anything you've experienced, but it still has a specific structure.

In *Star Wars*, Wookies and Jedi Warriors each conform to a specific code of behavior. In the *Wizard of Oz*, houses could fly only when propelled by tornadoes. By remaining true to their own sets of immutable rules, these movies create credible realities for our imaginations to inhabit. Shows riddled with inconsistencies, in which super-natural powers are bound by no apparent logic seem hokey and self-indulgent.

Creative Structuring

True creativity means first being imaginative in creating a structure, then using that structure to focus your creative direction.

This creates a need for two levels of structure: a structured process and a structure for all content to support a unifying idea. An appropriately structured process frees you to focus full creative energy on the task at hand, so that you don't constantly slip through a morass of interdependent variables, knowing that any decision is likely to come undone at any time—taking with it hours of hard work.

Structuring the process means first nailing down decisions on all of the structural elements: the show's format, premise, theme, continuity, image system, and central idea. Once you're straight on those fundamental decisions, they provide focus and direction for the next level of free association—as you brainstorm on the stunning visuals, the clever transitions and the inspiring dialogue.

Structuring your show's content means deciding on a specific purpose of unifying idea for the show. Write it down. Attach it to your keyboard, then when anything does not pass the test of directly that purpose, toss it back into the idea bin. Remember, to make a point with power and intelligence, it's best to first know what that point is; then stick to it.

Focusing on specific needs gives your work perspective and substance. You're still free to explore in any direction, but once a discovery is made, you have a standard by which to judge, "Is this important enough to include?" and "Where does it go?"

The Creative Mystique

Many people are fascinated by the creative process. This fascination often manifests itself in two key ideas:

> ➢ The best ideas come at the most unusual times.
> ➢ The best shows come as a flash of inspiration, after which everything else flows effortlessly into place.

There's something comforting about these two misconceptions. They put everything into the hands of divine providence. They free you to work on your backhand swing and enjoy literary lunches until that flash of inspiration hits. It sounds like an intriguing life-style. It's also nonsense.

Thomas Edison is quoted as saying, "Genius is one percent inspiration and ninety-nine percent perspiration." He's right. I get most of my best ideas between 8:00 a.m. and 6:00 p.m., sitting in front of my computer. All of the successful writers whose work habits I am familiar with spend many hours of most days at their desks working. Occasional inspirations may strike while on the freeway or in the shower, but relying on that to happen is no way to make a living.

The ideas that do come are small and raw. They must be chiseled and pieced together before a script begins to emerge. Don't expect it all to come in a flash.

Star Wars is cowboys in outer space. *Hamlet* is about a guy who can't make up his mind. Reduced to their basic ideas, they don't sound very powerful, but their creators built on those simple ideas with more ideas and lots of hard work, finally creating true classics.

Nothing can ensure that creative ideas will come to you. However, following the process that you've now begun will provide several techniques for making you more receptive to ideas. It provides examples of ideas that have worked before. Some of them may work for you. Some of them won't. The important thing is to apply your seat to the chair and keep churning through the ideas, piecing them together in different combinations, and revising and editing until it all feels right.

Ideas don't always come in a logical order. The steps suggested here for writing a creative treatment do not have to be taken in any particular order. They *do*, however, need to be arranged in a specific order to be discussed, and the order in which they are presented here makes as much sense as any.

Writing Behavioral Objectives

A crucial aspect of getting organized is to expand on the solution defined during your needs analysis. Do this by identifying specific behavioral objectives. The operative word here is *behavioral*. The objectives must address the change your show will bring about in the way the audience thinks or acts.

"Explain product benefits" is not a behavioral objective. It doesn't address a change in audience thinking or behavior. It may be typical of the goal or purpose of many informational shows but it does not get down to the change in audience behavior enabling them to achieve that goal. Behavioral objectives look more like this:

After experiencing this video, the audience will be able to:

➤ Identify the three most important features of the XP-47.

➤ Compare those features with similar features on the XP-47's two closest competitors.

➤ Explain the rationale behind the current positioning statement.

These behavioral objectives specifically address a change that will take place in the audience: they will gain the knowledge that enables them to identify features, compare features, and explain rationale.

In the strictest sense, behavioral objectives must be observable and measurable. A test for these example objectives would simply ask:

➤ What are the three most important features of the XP-47?

➤ What are the XP-47's two closest competitors?

➤ How do the three most important features on the XP-47 compare with similar features on its two closest competitors?

➤ What is the rationale behind the positioning statement for the XP-47?

If everyone who sees the show attempts to write answers to these questions, the results could be analyzed to provide an idea of how effective the show was in meeting its objectives.

Many marketing and motivational shows have goals that are much more subjective. Instructional designers describe them as attempting to change affective behavior—changing attitudes rather than providing the facts or skills. The purpose of these types of marketing and motivational shows is to set a tone, to establish positioning, or in the case of Case Study #1, to convey a set of values. A sampling of objectives from different shows might include:

- ➢ Appreciate Executive Office Towers as the premiere business address on Main Street.
- ➢ Feel confident that their efforts will be recognized and appreciated.
- ➢ Better understand the continuity of humankind's previous steps into the unknown and our current need for manned space exploration.
- ➢ Perceive VentureQuest as fully competitive with its larger and more experienced competitors.
- ➢ Recognize that a new level of leadership has taken firm control and has the organization headed in a positive direction.

These can be considered "terminal objectives," in that they address the change that the audience is to experience rather than the specific steps enabling them to make this change. They do not meet the strictest criteria for behavioral objectives.

To be considered a true behavioral objective, the behavior must be observable. Typically, behavioral objectives contain action verbs such as *list, identify, state, perform*. This is a valuable distinction for training and educational programs, but for marketing and motivational shows, the changes we are attempting to bring about in the audience are largely in the way that audience perceives things, which is difficult, if not impossible, to observe. The best we can do is to write objectives that address the changes in the audience's attitudes and understanding.

The types of behavioral objectives you write for your shows will depend on the type of video you are creating. Training videos requires observable, measurable, enabling objectives. Marketing and motivational shows require more subjective terminal objectives.

The one absolute is that you must understand the difference between a show's goal and the behavioral objectives necessary for achieving that goal. Only then will you be able to write behavioral objectives that keep everyone focused on creating an effective show.

A good device for helping you write behavioral objectives is to begin the list with the phrase:

After experiencing this video, our audience will be able to:

This forces you to write in terms of how the audience will react, rather than simply rehashing the show's goal, purpose or content.

The number of objectives you need varies in different shows. Between three and seven is a manageable number and looks pretty good on the page.

Your list of objectives will be included in the creative treatment you will present to your client. Writing it now helps you to focus on the next step in the process, which is to analyze the list(s) you've made and to decide what it all means.

Finding the Central Idea

Simplify and boil down. Understand what it means. Then focus on driving home what you've learned from the facts and details.

Contrary to what you may assume about living in what has been called the "Information Age," bare facts and figures often do more to smother than invigorate. It's the distillation of information into knowledge that helps us to understand the forest without bumping into the trees.

Writers often dissipate their resources on amassing a mound of detail, like deranged junkmen hoarding old auto parts. But just as a pile of parts will never become a functioning vehicle, a show that simply catalogs information will never move your audience to understanding or action.

As you study your research, search for that spark that makes everything else fall into place. A vision must emerge that unites all the facts into a concise summary of what it all means, such as:

➢ Motivated people make the difference.

➢ Getting involved makes your life more fulfilling.

➢ Great service brings customers back.

These concise statements express a "central idea" that can be the core of an entire presentation. When you analyze your research, your task is to boil down and simplify complex data until you have a central idea that can be intuitively grasped.

It's like the trunk of a tree. Every limb can be a clump of new information, growing logically out from the trunk. And every limb can branch out into more related ideas. Your audience can go as far out on a limb as their understanding of your show's content allows. If a viewer gets confused, the central idea is always right there in the middle, holding everything up; it's the one constant that every other idea is tied to. This is why audiences can watch a well-written show several times, finding deeper meaning in every viewing.

In Case Study #1 the central idea became "Take the initiative to find problems and solve them." That's what the company's founder did when he started the company. That's the ability the company is looking for and trying to develop in new employees.

Case Study #2 is a training show on retail sales techniques. Its central idea is "Develop an attitude of customer service." From this central idea you can branch off to introduce different sales techniques, explaining them all in terms of how they help enhance customer service.

What Are You Selling?

Another way of determining a central idea is to ask "What are we selling?" Even for technical and training shows, you're selling ideas, you're selling attitudes, you're selling specific ways of doing things.

When you merely put the information out there without an attempt to sell it, you are making two assumptions:

> ➤ That your audience will figure out for themselves why it's important and what to do about it.

> ➤ That your client is providing a public service in presenting unbiased information.

In short, you're assuming that your audience has time to spare and your client has budget to burn. Get real. This business is about results. If you can't promise in a single phrase the results your audience can expect to get from embracing your message, there's little chance they'll pay much attention. We've all been programmed to pay the most attention when the bottom line Is clearly stated up front.

If your show is training its audience on how to operate a drill press, sell the idea that every procedure contributes to some central goal, such as making the job easier or safer, improving productivity or enhancing quality. If your show presents an entire organization, sell the idea that it's committed to a clear mission, such as quality workmanship, preserving the environment, or making customers feel secure and confident.

Case Study #1 is selling the idea of finding success through turning problems into opportunities. Case Study #2 is selling the idea of finding success by keeping your customers satisfied. People like to succeed. They're more likely to pay attention if you promise them help in finding that success.

Finding the Emotion

To best convey your central idea, heed this operative concept:

Create an emotional experience.

Robert Frost once wrote, "No tears in the writer, no tears in the reader." He was probably not considering informational video at the time, but the concept still applies. As you analyze your research, thinking from the perspective of your audience, what single emotion do you feel most strongly? Pride in past accomplishments? Strength to face the future? Security from working with the best? The excitement of facing a new challenge?

Write it down. Tape it up next to your keyboard to remind you to use that emotion in heightening every point you need to make. It can be one word or a simple phrase. The important thing is to write it down, then envision how the material you have to present can be demonstrated in a situation that would make your audience feel that emotion.

In Case Study #1, the emotion is courage to view change as opportunity rather than a threat. In Case Study #2, the emotion is enthusiasm for developing yourself and for earning respect as a professional.

You are delving into the realm of psychology when you develop the emotional appeal of your show. Your intuitive grasp of what people like—and what they *are* like—may be all you need in some situations. A more solid grounding in human motivation can be gained from studying psychology, including Maslow's Hierarchy of Needs and Ernest Dichter's writing on motivation. Their books are listed in the suggested reading portion of the Appendix.

Once *you* feel the emotions you want your audience to feel and have focused on a central idea, it's time to arrange your material so it can be forged into a show create an emotional experience.

Making a Content Outline

List every fact and idea that must be included, but be a ruthless editor. Remember that video is most effective at changing attitudes. It's pointless to load a video up with specific facts and details. Keep in mind the operative concept:

The sharper the focus the greater the impact.

Decide which facts and ideas are essential. Organize them into a logical list. This is not necessarily an outline of your script; it's a checklist to ensure that nothing's left out.

This content outline may even be a good tool to present to your client as part of the creative treatment. It will help ensure that everyone agrees on exactly what will be included in the presentation.

Here's the outline for Case Study #1:

1. Spanner buys Doctor's Diagnostics

    1.1. Facing bankruptcy

    1.2. Name change to Elgin

    1.3. Made profitable in 2 years

    1.4. Grows to $500 million company

2. Current state of the industry

    2.1. Healthcare too expensive

    2.2. Run by doctors who don't know business management

3. Greater economy through:

   3.1.Reducing mistakes and duplication

   3.2.Sharing expensive medical equipment among several hospitals

   3.3.Motivated, well trained staff

      3.3.1.   Challenging career paths

      3.3.2.   Compensation package tops in the industry

4. Core values

   4.1.Care and concern for people

      4.1.1.   Patients

      4.1.2.   Employees

      4.1.3.   Doctors

   4.2.Commitment to quality and excellence

   4.3.Growth and economic strength

5. Qualities desired in an employee

   5.1.Willing to take initiative—

      5.1.1.   In finding ways to improve the company

      5.1.2.   In finding out what's going on and what's expected

   5.2.Able to adapt and remain productive

   5.3.Self-starters

6. Heritage and culture

   6.1.Family-type of organization—always been that way

   6.2.Under constant growth and change

   6.3.Action orientation

   6.4.Things aren't always spelled out

   6.5.Each hospital and subsidiary operated as profit center

7. Business strategies

   7.1.Economy of scale

      7.1.1.   Centralized labs

      7.1.2.   Can hire better people

      7.1.3.   Higher quality service for smaller hospitals

7.2. Cost containment through professional business management

7.3. Building for the future

7.4. Preventing problems is more economical than fixing them

7.5. Partnerships with business

    7.5.1.   Preferred Provider Systems

    7.5.2.   HMO

7.6. Lean management structure

    7.6.1.   Hospitals are autonomous

    7.6.2.   Operational independence for departments

8.   Growth through buying hospitals

8.1. Bought own best customer when it was facing financial problems

8.2. Early pioneer in investor-owned hospitals

8.3. Service companies

    8.3.1.   EMC Data Processing

    8.3.2.   MedCord medical records

8.4. Uneven growth, layoffs necessary

Creating a Language List

Another aspect of immersing yourself in your subject matter is the development of a language list. Get a feel for the style and the culture that best embodies your message, then list the words and phrases that exemplify that style. Here is a language list for a project for an up-scale hotel:

> ➤ An arpeggio of sunlight.
> ➤ Warm counterpoint.
> ➤ A spacious theme.
> ➤ A baseline of polished marble.
> ➤ A flourish of brass.
> ➤ The day goes legato.

Even without being used in complete sentences, the words themselves deliver a strong tone and feel. They create an expectation of what your audience can experience for themselves by embracing your show's message.

Now read through this list of nouveau-hip automotive Language:

➢ Totally tricked out.

➢ Crank it up—blow it out.

➢ Blast past awesome.

➢ Blasting out a beachhead.

➢ Making a mountain assault.

It cranks your emotions right around to an entirely different feel and set of expectations.

By consciously searching for words with strong imagery during your research, you can develop a vocabulary that will add force and focus to your video.

The language list for Case Study #1 includes:

➢ Delivering quality healthcare.

➢ Excellence in healthcare.

➢ Sound business management.

➢ Growth and strength.

➢ Reducing mistakes and duplication.

➢ Top performance.

➢ Concern and respect.

➢ Building for the future.

The language list for Case Study #2 includes:

➢ Helping.

➢ Good attitude.

➢ Friendly respect.

➢ Welcoming.

➢ Building rapport.

> ➤ Extending yourself.
> ➤ Taking responsibility.
> ➤ Satisfying the customer.
> ➤ Enhancing professionalism.

Begin compiling your language list as soon as you begin your research. It's easier to develop it now, while you're free associating and bombarding yourself with new stimuli. In later steps, when you're actually writing, you're most likely to grab what's already there, using the language most comfortable for you. if you develop your language while you write a treatment or script you are doing two things at once and that usually means you are doing neither of them to the best of your ability.

Learning From Other Disciplines

"He who resolves never to ransack any mind but his own will be soon reduced, from mere barrenness, to the poorest imitation: he will be obliged to imitate himself."
—Sir Joshua Reynolds (1723—1792) To the students of the Royal Academy of Arts

Open almost any video trade magazine. Search the Internet for information or training on producing video. What you're most likely to find is a profusion of technical information and hints on how to take a script to the screen. What will most likely be missing is any comprehensive consideration of how to write a script.

The reality of our industry is that it's obsessed with the technology—and it shows. A great many informational videos are quite sophisticated in their use of technology, while amateurish in their use of the medium. While learning to operate the equipment, our industry has chosen to virtually ignore the fundamentals of several other disciplines that could improve informational shows.

To enhance your own value on the job market, it would be a good idea to study several related disciplines: advertising, training, and entertainment.

Advertising

TV ads are a constant source of ideas for using visuals and sound to communicate quickly. Study them. For a heavy dose of the best ads, look for a compilation of Clio winners (the ad industry's version of the Oscars, http://www.clioawards.com). See it every year you can; it's a good source of both ideas and inspiration.

When watching ads, study how they develop characters and tell stories—all within 30 seconds. Notice how they often stress life-style and image over specific product features. Recognize the symbols and imagery they use. Learn from their tremendous economy, with many levels of communication interacting to make every second count. Study the clarity and focus, as one central idea is driven home over and again on every level.

Benefits are the bottom line in most ads—as they should also be the bottom line in most of your shows. Rather than objectively showcasing features and advantages, ads make very clear what's in it for the audience. In print ads, the fundamental test of a headline is, "Does it clearly promise a benefit." Ask yourself this same question about the theme and every segment of the shows you write.

Positioning is another advertising concept that scriptwriters must understand. At its most basic, positioning refers to the niche in which a product or service competes. A Buick is *positioned* above a Chevrolet and below a Cadillac. It may further be positioned as most dependable in its class. It may also be positioned to a specific market segment, such as upper-middle-class families who have made the commitment to buy American.

A writer may create a positioning statement such as "Most dependable American car in its class." That sounds impressive, even though on closer study you can see that it excludes competition with imported cars, or even other American cars outside of its class, whatever that means. Its performance and handling could be dismal. Its styling could be an embarrassment. The car could be a real dog, but by carefully considering the needs and values of moderately affluent buyers, committed to buying American and primarily concerned with dependability, the writer created a positioning statement that emphasizes the facts that are most important to the ad's target audience.

Positioning also dictates the characters and story portrayed in the ad. In this case it may be mom picking up a gaggle of kids from the riding stable. The imagery may not appeal to hip young singles, macho dudes or poor folks, but since those groups aren't likely to buy the car anyway, it's worthwhile narrowing the appeal to increase the impact among those who *are* likely to buy. Ads gain impact as they are targeted to narrower and better-defined audiences, just as your shows gain impact when you position their message to a very specific audience.

For example, a department store chain was having trouble recruiting male college graduates—most men not having much interest in the perceived glamour that is so effective in attracting qualified female graduates. So the company wanted a college recruitment show that specifically positioned it as having career potential for men.

To achieve this positioning, the hard business aspects were stressed, pointing out that the opportunities in finance, management and information technology are at least as rewarding as in any other types of business. The glamour of fashion was downplayed.

Through this repositioning, a career in retail fashion was presented in terms of the specific benefits that male graduates were seeking. It was a very factual representation of the career opportunities, but the facts presented were selected to be those of greatest interest to a specific audience.

Any of your clients who work in advertising or marketing will probably be familiar with the concept of positioning. During your research, ask specifically about the positioning of their product or service, and of their organization, and you will open up an area of critical discussion, while positioning yourself as being knowledgeable about marketing.

In summary:

> ➢ Express your message in terms of benefits to your audience.
> ➢ Develop your positioning.
> ➢ Target your message.

Training

One of the most basic and valuable concepts in training is what can be referred to as the Three T's:

➤ Tell 'em what you're going to tell 'em.

➤ Tell 'em.

➤ Then tell 'em what you just told 'em.

This axiom can be applied to virtually any show and is the basis for the Three T's commandment:

Thou shalt introduce, demonstrate and reinforce.

This is not to be mistaken as an argument for redundancy; That would be Tell 'em; Tell 'em; Tell 'em—and boring. Instead, the Three T's present the same information from different perspectives:

➤ Introduce the information.

➤ Demonstrate or apply the information.

➤ Reinforce the information.

This is more effective than mere repetition, because it gives your audience the chance to consider information from several different perspectives: In the abstract, how it's applied and how it fits into the big picture. Learning is kept interesting, while it accommodates the different styles of learning.

On the scale of human learners there are two poles: analytical learners, who learn best when facts are presented one-by-one in a logical sequence; and intuitive learners, who learn best by seeing everything in context then remembering the patterns.

A well-designed show accommodates both of these learning types, by presenting major points in both a logical sequential approach and in a broad overview revealing common patterns.

Another training fundamental is that of using examples. This is the "monkey see, monkey do" approach to training. Examples make things real. Most people have an easier time understanding and remembering a single clear example than they do any amount of abstract explanation.

Analogies are another effective teaching device, because they use a familiar frame of reference as an example of how something less familiar works.

The principles that explain how water flows through plumbing are more visual and intuitively obvious then the principles of electricity, so water flowing through plumbing can be an effective analogy for explaining how electricity flows through a circuit.

Finally, one of the most inescapable concepts of training is that the mind can not absorb more than the seat will endure, leading to the get-to-the-point-commandment:

Thou shalt make it quick and snappy

In summary:

> ➢ Introduce.
> ➢ Apply.
> ➢ Reinforce.
> ➢ Write for both analytical and intuitive learners.
> ➢ Examples work best.
> ➢ The mind will not absorb more than the seat can endure.

Entertainment

There is a popular contention that informational shows must be entertaining. This is nonsense, or a least a misstatement of a principle that *is* valid. The valid principle is that informational shows must be involving. Audiences are more likely to learn from and be persuaded by a show that involves them on a personal and emotional level.

Where entertainment comes in is that many of the fundamentals used by entertainment to involve an audience will also add impact to informational shows.

This difference between entertainment and involvement is more than a semantic fine point; it is the difference between an effective show and a bunch of fluff. In an effort to entertain, many informational shows try to imitate the look and tone of entertainment—attempting to bribe the audience with something fun, then slipping in the stuff *that's good for 'em.*

Most people resent being manipulated with such lack of finesse. It also becomes painfully obvious when the fun stops and the boring stuff begins. It's here that the audience usually looses interest, disappointed that the fun's over and insulted by this cheap attempt to trick them into paying attention.

Rather than imitating entertainment, a high impact show applies the fundamentals that make entertainment so involving. Many of these fundamentals have been used to involve audiences since even before the Ancient Greeks created their classic dramas. And they are still more effective in adding impact than anything you can add in post production.

The most basic fundamental is to tell a story. A story adds to the impact of teaching through example by creating characters with whom the audience can identify and sympathize. Most people will become more involved with a story about people than with any compilation of facts about a thing or idea.

The best stories are about a hero dealing with conflict. And the most critical point to understand about that conflict is that the only way to build the stature of the hero is to increase the intensity of the conflict. Without Darth Vader, Luke Skywalker would be just another angst-filled farm kid wondering about life. And without a strong conflict to motivate the training or teaching material in your dramatizations, the audience will have little reason to believe that learning it will help them overcome anything of importance in their lives.

Telling stories can also take full advantage of a visual medium. Many studies have proven that we learn and understand better by seeing than hearing. This fact is also well known to Hollywood. Study a good movie. You will notice that virtually all dialogue comments on the action. No time is wasted in bringing the audience up to speed or providing a lot of background. Instead, you're propelled immediately into the action, while the dialogue focuses on what you need to know at that specific moment to understand the relevance of the action. Hollywood movies as well as good informational shows follow the operative concept:

Show it; don't tell it

Another fundamental is to create curiosity, making an audience hungry to know the facts and background before they are revealed. Few movies begin with biographies of the major characters. Instead, intriguing glimpses into the past are parceled out as commentary on the action, at just the points where the audience is made to wonder "What's going on here," or "why is this character behaving this way?"

In the same way, a corporate image or orientation show doesn't have to start with a history. It may be more involving to first intrigue your audience with that organization's current influence or the position to which the founder has risen; then there is a hunger to know how it all began.

Other fundamentals of entertainment that are often ignored by informational shows, include character development, back story, subtext, and pacing. These are covered in Chapter 7, "The Power of Drama."
In summary:

➢ People care most about other people.

➢ Dialogue is commentary on the action.

➢ Heroes are no stronger than the conflict they face.

➢ Make the audience hungry to know.

Mixing and Matching Disciplines

In practice, the fundamentals of every discipline can the mixed in the creation of any single show. Most training can be enhanced with some sales appeal; most sales shows need to impart some factual knowledge. And any show can benefit from the intelligent application of dramatic techniques.

The world at large is brimming with ideas and inspiration. Formal study and casual observation of the fine arts, commercial art, drama, film, training, current events, advertising, psychology, and religion can enhance your life and improve your writing.

CHAPTER 4

PACKAGING IDEAS: THE CREATIVE TREATMENT

The Purpose of the Creative Treatment

"Writing is easy. All you do is stare at a blank sheet of paper until drops of blood form on your forehead."
—Gene Fowler (1890–1960)

A script is like a blueprint, while a creative treatment is like the architect's initial renderings. The creative treatment conveys the essence of what will follow so that everyone can agree on the general approach, tone, and content before you fill in the details.

Why Bother?

It's tempting to go straight to script. It seems like it would save a step and thereby save time. In reality, this "extra step" usually saves time and if you skip this approval point, you risk increasing your work many times over.

To Reduce Risk

The risk in going straight to script lies in being blind-sided by that one bit of information you never asked for. Regardless of how well you've done your research, there are still some things you don't know.

You may put a lot of effort into a finished script, only to discover it's too much like what was done a previous year, or too much like something everybody hated the last time it was tried, or too much like what the competition is doing, or is based on a premise your client simply won't accept.

In other situations you may simply read the signals wrong and base your script on a misinterpretation of what you've been told, or on bad advice someone else may have given you. On a job for Delta Air Lines, I was told they needed a public relations-type piece to introduce a new fleet of jets to the press and to their corporate customers. The producer gave me a copy of their brochure, telling me that the client loved it and wanted a video just like the brochure—same tone, same style—and that I should even use a lot of the same language. The producer had been working with this client for years. I had worked with both of them before and we all thought we understood each other. Time was tight. I went straight to script.

The client hated it. It was hard sell—just like the brochure. It was features and benefits—just like the brochure. There was no poetry or imagination—just like the brochure. Now time was *really* tight; but none the less I had to make the time to start all over again, sit in an extra meeting and deal with some nervous people looking for a scapegoat.

Once a project gets off course and your team has reason for concern, it's hard to reestablish the comfort level. Everything takes longer. Everything is scrutinized more closely. It's not much fun.

To Save Time

In addition to reducing risk, writing a creative treatment usually saves time in the long run. It's less intimidating to work through an intermediate step than to face a blank computer screen knowing that you have to make all of your decisions at once.

When you write the creative treatment, you can loosen up, work in broad strokes. The concepts and ideas come easier when you're free from the pressure of writing the exact words and scenes to bring those ideas to life.

Then, in the creative treatment approval meeting, you still have room to make adjustments. By asking your client to consider only the general ideas and approach, you avoid nit-picking about he specific wording.

When you go straight to script, every detail must be worked through. You must spend many more hours thinking out every word. If that script is then completely rejected—perhaps for reasons outside your control—you've lost a larger investment in time and emotional commitment. In an all-or-nothing gamble, you've lost it all.

An artist will sketch before working in oils and a sculptor works in clay before casting the bronze; a scriptwriter likewise needs the freedom of working out a creative treatment before being absorbed by the details of writing a script.

To Improve Quality

The clinching argument for writing a creative treatment is that it simply results in a better show. You can concentrate on tone and approach, and on paring down the content to the absolute essentials. When scripting, you have another chance to think things through. You have a feel for where any creative flashes can be worked in and you can quickly recognize the ideas that won't work. You've had some time to live with your vision as a complete, functioning whole, so scripting becomes a second chance to improve an already familiar creation.

The Treatment Format

Though different organizations have their own preferences for formats and section headings, the format followed by the treatment for Case Study #1, reproduced in the Appendix is widely accepted. It is divided into four sections:

- ➢ Background
- ➢ Objectives
- ➢ Strategies
- ➢ Creative approach

Background

The background is an analytical statement of the current situation. It is intended to confirm that what you heard in the research meeting closely approximates what the client and content experts meant to say when they said what they did say.

The background concisely summarizes who the audience is, why the show is being done now, any limitations that may exist and the context within which the show will be used.

Objectives

The objectives section is also analytical. It's the list of behavioral objectives you developed earlier, introduced by a general statement of goal or purpose, such as:

> The proposed presentation will not close a sale. Instead, it will lay a foundation of emotional as well as rational understanding. It will set a tone, helping a business person recognize Executive Office Towers as his own image of the next step his company must take, while creating for the sales representative an informed and motivated prospect.

Your list of behavioral objectives is then introduced by a phrase such as:

More specifically, after experiencing this video, our audience will:

Strategies

The strategies section begins your creative leap of imagination; however, it is still done as a list. It's a creative specifications sheet, stating what will be done, in terms of structural elements, devices, and techniques you will use.

It answers all of the basic questions concerning "What will the show be like?" These questions may include:

➢ What's the format?

➢ What and who are seen on camera?

➢ What provides the continuity?

> ➤ What devices are used to position the organization, product, service or idea?

> ➤ Is a symbol established to represent the central idea, theme, company or product?

> ➤ Is there a conflict between good and evil?

> ➤ Is the "voice" or point of view particularly relevant or unique?

> ➤ How are music, sound effects and graphics incorporated?

Creative Approach

The creative approach completes your leap of imagination. It's a word picture. It must evoke the tone and mood to be set by the video. While weaving this magic it must also make clear what approach will be used for the opening, the closing, the flow, the transitions, the content covered, the number of locations or sets, and the graphics, as well as who and what will be seen or heard.

Read the creative approach in the Appendix. Though not very specific about the words to be heard and visuals to be seen, it leaves no doubt about the tone of the presentation and how it will be structured.

Also notice its form: a present-tense narrative description. It literally takes the reader step-by-step through the show, describing what will be heard and seen. It avoids any explanation or justification: Rather than stating, "High impact music and visuals make the audience feel the excitement of racing a sailboat," a good treatment simply describes what's on the screen, giving a distinct taste and a tease of the impression they will create:

> "A fresh wind fills the sails; there's a new hand at the helm. A racing sloop fills the screen ... sails trimmed for victory. She's a flat-out competitor: sleek lines, well rigged with the latest electronics. The crew is experienced, with minds sharp against the unexpected that every new challenge brings."

The creative approach presents ideas and concepts. It's the most important step in bringing a show to life—moving from facts and objectives to a vision for creating an emotional experience for the audience.

The creative approach must spark the imagination of both the client and the producer—as well as provide you with a certain warm glow of accomplishment. It's the most important section of the creative treatment, which may serve several purposes: It acts as a selling tool, it describes the show itself and it is the point at which you establish the video's "voice."

As A Selling Tool

A treatment may be written either before or after a job is sold. When it is written before you have the job, it's quite literally a selling tool, a description to your prospect of what your team has to offer. In either situation, your creative treatment is a tool for selling your ideas.

As a selling tool, your treatment must ooze comfort factor, reassuring cautious clients—who may have bureaucratic tendencies—that you understand their business, understand their problem and will be thoroughly professional in executing a solution to their problem. They would probably also like a glimpse of dazzling imagination.

A creative treatment becomes the single tangible object representing what your entire team is attempting to sell to a client. As such, a "strong creative" is often what sells a job; at other times it's a low budget. There are no absolutes, other than the fact that a strong creative will improve your chances; whether it will improve your chances *enough* is always an open question.

As a selling tool, a treatment is often more effective than a finished script. A script is longer and includes a lot of detail that may be confusing. Details can get in the way of your client's grasping a quick understanding of the show's essence; and details that—if you get them wrong—may destroy comfort factor: when clients see that you've mangled the facts they know about, it's natural for them to fear that you will also play fast and loose in the areas of expertise they don't know about.

A further problem with scripts is that many clients aren't familiar with the format. They may not be able to understand how it all fits together; and may not have the imagination needed to meld visual and audio descriptions into a coherent whole.

A treatment is written in standard narrative paragraph format, with which all literate persons are already comfortable. If is written well, it's a quick read, giving just the highlights—conveying a better feel for the show's essence and your intentions than a finished script could.

A creative treatment is both specification sheet and creative writing sample. An astute client may reason that the quality of writing in the treatment represents the quality of writing that will go into the script. So it had better be good.

If your treatment doesn't paint a compelling word-picture of what will come through the screen, you'll have a hard time convincing the client that your writing will improve substantially by the time you write the script. Your treatment must capture the same tone and magic that you intend for your finished show.

As Creative Writing

Your greatest leap of imagination is made while you write the treatment. Here is where you make the most fundamental creative decisions and where you sketch out your vision, deciding on structure, tone, and approach.

A script developed from a well-written treatment will contain few surprises. The big decisions are made during the treatment; scripting is finishing off the details.

This is the hard part, as you confront a completely blank computer screen. Everything is a variable. The first decisions are yours. One of the most crucial of those decisions is what voice you will use.

Developing Your Voice

At a writer's seminar, I asked a successful screenwriter how she determined what voice to use. She said she couldn't explain it, but that she was clear on the fact that developing the appropriate voice is what separates good writers from hacks.

"Voice," as the term is used by the literati, is basically the personality of a book, film or video—its attitude and tone. Are you pontificating to the masses, or are you having an intimate chat with a friend? Are you formal or casual? An old curmudgeon or the voice of the avant-garde? Philosophizing or focusing on quick hard results?

A Woody Allen film is different from a James Bond movie. Many of those differences flow naturally from a difference in voice.

Voice reveals a certain worldview, a set of beliefs and convictions. It evokes a specific time and place. Voice means taking a stand, and taking a stand means you will probably be questioned—if not attacked—by someone. This helps explain why informational programs too often assume a passive, third-person voice, conveying no hint of opinion or attitude.

"Voice of God" is the term often used to describe this default choice of voice that many people lapse into when they fail to consciously develop their own Voice. And when mortals presume to speak for God, it comes off as a bit pretentious. Assuming the voice of an all-knowing, all-seeing, ultimate authority is not only a crushing burden for a writer, it's also a bore for the audience. Like a person, a video devoid of personality is seldom very interesting or convincing.

In short, how you say it often has more impact than what you say, and voice is the term describing how you are saying it. No single voice is right for every video. The same audience that needs a cheerleader to present last year's sales figures may respond best to a hard-boiled skeptic introducing new management techniques. The important thing is to transcend the bland and the lifeless. Envision the personality that your audience will find most convincing, then design your video to speak in the voice of that personality.

The voice for Case Study #1, the employee orientation video, is the voice of management. Since this show is designed to present the company's values and heritable, and to be the official welcome from upper management, this voice is appropriate. It's a pledge-of-allegiance voice, unashamedly stating what the company stands for and what its leaders expect from everyone on the team.

The voice for Case Study #2, the sales training show, is the voice of an employee who is slightly more experienced than the audience is assumed to be. It's someone who has been there, passing on helpful words of advice. There's a level of skepticism in this voice—a skepticism similar to what many new employees may be feeling when they're told to improve their attitude. This provides a tone to the show with which the audience can identify. Rather than saying "do this because it's company policy," this voice is saying, "here's how you can make your time here more rewarding on every level—the fact that it's also what's good for the company is just a pleasant coincidence."

The time to develop your voice is when you are writing the treatment. The purpose of the treatment is to give a taste of the show's style and tone. The only way to convey in the treatment the tone that will be created by the finished show is to write them both in the same voice.

An effective exercise to help find your voice for a specific script is to literally envision yourself speaking one-on-one with a member of your audience. What situation would make an individual in your audience most receptive to your ideas? Lecturing from a lectern as you wag your finger at the faceless masses? Perched on bar stools having a heart-to-heart with a new employee? Giving a walking tour of the facilities to an old school buddy? Giving last-minute advice to an associate before charging in to an important meeting? By deciding on the situation and fixing it in your mind, the tone and mood of your video become grounded in a specific reality, taking on an appropriate tone and urgency and you become less likely to lapse into the voice of a pretentious didact preaching to the faceless multitudes.

Often, a single phrase will capture the tone of a voice:

➢ "Make my day."

➢ "The prelude to a sumptuous evening."

➢ "Hard-drivin', flat-out excitement."

Once you have that phrase, use it as a touchstone for the rest of the script. Check every sentence to make sure it's speaking in the same voice.

Different Styles for Different Situations

"Stay committed to your decisions, but stay flexible in your approach."
—Tom Robbins, U.S. Novelist, b. 1935

An earlier section addressed factors to consider when deciding on acquisition and distribution formats for your video. These are sometimes the writer's decision, usually not. In any case you should now already know how your audience will be experiencing your video, whether it's on a Web site, in a classroom, on a DVD or some other means of distribution. Now you must decide how to write for that situation in order to use video to its fullest advantage. If you are accustomed to writing for print media, you will need to adapt your style to write effectively for the screen. Keep these principles in mind:

> *Most sentences must be short and simple.* An audience lost in a confusion of restrictive clauses never has a chance to go back to the beginning of a sentence to untangle its meaning. They have to get it the first time, every time.

> *It's primarily a visual medium.* Things are better shown than explained. The only reason words are needed at all is to tell the audience the significance of the visual.

> *Close-ups are the most powerful images.* Still photographers look for that one image that says it all. Good videographers look for close-ups that allow the story to unfold one delicious detail at a time. Establishing shots are only interesting until the audience is oriented to the action—a few seconds—then they want to see the details. Giving a third of your screen time to close-ups is not too much and may be too little.

> *There are many more elements at your disposal.* It's actually more like writing music than writing for print. Just as a listener simultaneously hears the base, drums, and lead; your audience is simultaneously reacting to the people on screen, their inflection, expressions, and body language; the set or location, and any graphic or design elements; the music and sound effects; and the words. All these different layers must be arranged to work together.

It's a more emotional medium, you actually *can* have violins playing in the background.

It's a more intuitive medium. You can simply show how something is done, rather than having to break it down into words and individual pictures.

It's more linear. Except for interactive video, audiences can't skip sections, glance over at another picture, or speed-read. Your audience has to see everything in the exact order and at the exact pace you decide. And time on the screen goes much more slowly than time on the page.

In some small ways, it is more forgiving. Few people will ever see your spelling errors, unless they are in on-screen graphics.

Now that you've broken out of the print mode of thinking, consider how video can be used to fullest advantage in a number of different situations.

Linear Video

Linear video is the default standard for informational media. It's seen end-to-end, without interruption. Any planned interaction with the audience is structured as either an introduction to the video or as activity that follows the viewing. Virtually all of the procedures and techniques in this book are appropriate to helping you craft a linear video script.

Despite the growing popularity of wide screen and projection television, most audiences will see most of your videos on a screen that's close to the size of a human head, or even smaller. Take this as a hint. Video is a personal medium. The most effective voice to use when writing for video is a personal voice, talking one-to-one, rather than shouting out to the throngs. This makes the often maligned "talking head" one of the most effective shots to use. The obvious secret here is that the head that's talking needs something compelling to say. Follow all of the procedures in this book and focus on crafting a personal message that lets the people in your video talk to your audience as individuals.

Interactive Video

Whether presented as a Web site or distributed on disk-based media, interactive video gives you the opportunity to more tightly integrate your video with its collateral material. This often means breaking up the video into modules so that feedback, or interactivity, is prompted between every module.

This is a natural for training. After a video module presents one or more training points, have your audience respond to a multiple-choice question. A correct response sends them on to the next video module. An incorrect response creates a teachable moment that can be used to explain why this is not the best choice. This in turn can be another video module or a static page that explains why the answer is incorrect. It also provides links to take the learner back to where the correct answer can be found.

Interactive video framed within static pages is also a natural for reference material. A carpenter or mechanic can quickly search for information on a procedure. If all they need are some specifications or a diagram, it's right there as a static image. But if they need a demonstration of how a procedure is completed, they can just click to run a video module that shows how it's done.

Applied to marketing communications, one video module provides an introduction to the company. The viewer then self-selects which product line is of interest. A new video module provides an introduction and overview of that product line. At it's conclusion the viewer is offered information on the specific products in the product line, each of which includes its own video module. The video modules on specific products all end with a clickable button that can put the viewer in touch with a sales representative, of otherwise facilitates the viewer making a purchase.

The big challenge for writing this level of interactivity is that all of the video modules must fit together in a number of different configurations. The end of any given module must make equal sense when the audience chooses any of several other modules to follow it. This requires careful flow charting and designing all modules with a consistent open and close.

Like episodes in a TV series, each of your video modules must be consistent with the whole and also make sense self-standing. This means that the entire process laid out in this book still applies. As you proceed to learn about the seven strategies for improving any treatment and the elements of structure, think about how they can be applied to both your entire presentation and to the individual modules.

Incorporating Still Images

An earlier section established that your visual source material may include, or even be limited to, still images. If this is your situation, now is the time to start thinking about writing for still images.

Still images are often more challenging to write for than motion video; since you don't have the options of on-camera spokespersons, dialogue, talking heads or visuals that simply follow the action. And the danger with still images is that they are even more likely than motion video to be fashioned into a talking brochure. Avoid this danger by paying closer attention than ever to these operative concepts:

Show it; don't tell it

Abstracts on the track, specifics on the screen

Think first of the sequence of visuals that will make your point, then write only the words that are absolutely necessary to fill in what the visuals leave out.

Use simple transitions such as:

"Here at the ..."

"This is where ..."

"Notice that the ..."

These all help direct attention to the visual, making the track a complementary element rather than an attempt to explain everything verbally.

Effective Still-Image Techniques

Interview excerpts can be effective in still images. Just keep in mind that attempting a talking head with still images creates a talking cadaver—not a pretty sight. To have a full-frame head staring out of the frame, frozen in mid-sentence as you hear the person's words flow by can look surreal or discomforting. None the less, people try to get away with it. There are alternatives.

As the person's candid comments are heard, show a series of candid shots of that person: at work, at play, doing anything that's appropriate to what is being said. Limit the shots to wide shots, talking with other people and close-ups that do not include the mouth, anything other than a composition that suggests a talking cadaver. Of course it's also quite appropriate to show images of what the person is talking about.

Sound effects become even more important when working with still images. Street sounds or office noise can bring still images to life in the minds of your audience. Since these sounds have to be deliberately added to the sound track, be sure to add sound effect cues to your script to remind the production team to incorporate sound effects at all appropriate points.

Dramatizations are also possible with still images. The story is told in voice-over, preferably by one of the characters or a voice that takes on some level of characterization. The visuals show the events as they unfold, or the people, places, or artifacts that surround the story.

A stylistic approach to the photography enhances the dramatic effect. Encourage the designer and photographer to develop a distinct "look" that takes photography beyond a literal documentation. Study the work of fine-art photographers to find a mood that fits your material.

How Often do Still Images Need to Change?

The answer is an emphatic, "It depends." For highly technical or "numbers" shows, an important chart or a detail shot of a mechanism could support up to 20 seconds of audio, while a montage may require images to remain on screen for only a second or two.

As a rule of thumb, ten seconds is about as long as you'll want to leave an image up and six seconds is a more pleasing maximum. Varying the length of time the images are on the screen is critical to creating a more involving pace for your show. For every image that lingers on the screen for six seconds, several other images must move more quickly. An overall average of 5 seconds per image is good for a typical segment of still images.

As a writer, you control the pace of image changes by specifying the amount of narration to be heard over each image. This is easily done in a two-column format by placing the visual next to the narration it goes with. You don't have to literally specify on the script a number of seconds for each image. In the following example notice how the arrangement of the narration and visual description makes it obvious how long each image stays on the screen:

27. Housewife sweeping up her kitchen.	NARRATOR: For regular cleaning …
28. Workman kneeling with a broom and dustpan to clean up a spilled bag of concrete.	for spills and emergencies …
29. Teenager sweeping a hallway.	To tidy up inside …
30. Person sweeping a porch.	or to fight back the dirt outside …
31. Close-up on the broom.	brooms are an effective cleaning tool found almost everywhere people live, work or play.
32. Montage shows evolution of brooms through the years.	Over the years, brooms have been a domestic necessity; changing little in their basic design, but constantly evolving in their construction and the materials used to make them.

In this example, images 27–30 would remain on the screen about three seconds. Image 31 would ease the pace and stay on screen for five or six seconds. Then the montage at 32 would change images several times during the 10 to 12 seconds of narration.

For still images that are integrated with motion video, you need a visual device to signal the audience to expect a change in the style of the visual and to reassure them that you're not just trying to get away with throwing in still images because you don't have suitable motion footage. For example, you could call for images to be enclosed in a frame or floated over a video background to tip off your viewer that these images are supposed to look different.

For long segments of still images, you may want this visual treatment to be only a transition. For example, motion video could cut or resolve to an image that suggests a photo album framing up a still image. You may want to let several still images go by within this frame to establish that the images are *supposed* to be stills. At this point, the framing element becomes a bit tiring, so you zoom in just enough to make the still image full frame. The audience now intuitively understands to expect more still images. At the end of this segment of still images, just pull out a bit on the last image, to reintroduce the "photo album" frame, and your audience intuitively understands to expect the style of the visual to change back to motion video with the next cut or transition.

The process you are learning applies equally to writing a sequential presentation of images, whether or not they happen to be moving. Just be sure to think first of what is—or will be—available to go on the screen, than craft your presentation to take fullest advantage of that visual.

Live Presentations (PowerPoint)

As established earlier, visual support for a live presentation typically means PowerPoint. But even through your "sound track" is not prerecorded it's still a visual medium and every step in the process you are now learning helps improve PowerPoint presentations. You can start that improvement by breaking out of the bullet point rut. Heed the operative concept to …

Show it; don't tell it.

Consider every point of the presentation in terms of how you can show it in pictures. Sure it takes longer but it will enhance both your presentations and your reputation as a writer.

Break out of the box. And the *box* at issue is the fancy framing element that has become standard on every PowerPoint slide. There's nothing wrong with having a nice frame on some slides, but why *every* slide? By showing images full frame you can wake up an audience. And you've reclaimed some of the lost screen real estate that causes PowerPoint slides to be criticized for being low-resolution.

Live presentations can also be enhanced by what can be called mini-modules, short pre-recorded videos that introduce speakers or segments, or deliver a cluster of information that is not likely to change, such as a company history or product overview.

In practice, a mini-module may open the meeting, establishing the meeting's tone and setting up an introduction for the first speaker or segment of the presentation. The speaker would then use PowerPoint slides to present information such as this year's sales figures. Other mini-modules would then provide transitions into other segments, such as current sales strategies and quotas for next quarter. A final mini-module would close the meeting with a bang.

In short, live presentations—with or without mini-modules—are no different from pre-recorded video, to the extent that the best ones are the result of thorough research, imaginative design and adequate collateral. And there are no items on the PowerPoint menu bar that will do that for you.

Business Theater

Although it typically incorporates conventional videos and live presentations, business theater is primarily live theater. Forget the intimate appeal of video. The action must be broad and the words must be spoken to everyone in the crowd.

In business theater it is crucial to develop a strong theme that lends itself to a stage set and room decor: Hawaiian beach party, ocean cruise, sports, the wild west or anything else that can be big, bold, and fun while complementing your message. Take-offs on Broadway musicals and hit movies are popular.

Business theater usually means combining a number of elements into a well-coordinated event, from a banquet meeting to a week-long convention. These elements may include any of the following:

Registration and Reception—actors in themed costumes talk with guests, hand out gifts and provide live entertainment. Impromptu skits may build anticipation for the main events and help set the scene. For a

Western-themed weekend, Black Bart and his boys on horseback "held-up" the shuttle buses coming from the airport, warning the guests that "Black Bart runs things in these here parts," and "there might be trouble, so don't be spoutin' off no *dangerous* ideas about good service and customer satisfaction."

Official Welcome—The entire group assembles for an opening video module, perhaps with singing, dancing and a live stage skit. The master of ceremonies takes control of the event, setting the tone and letting everyone know what to expect.

Keynote address—An opening speech is presented, usually with speaker support.

Additional Presentations—Speeches, video modules, and stage skits present the information to be covered. Live stage segments introduce or interact with the modules. Song-and-dance numbers have graphics on the projection screen that are choreographed right along with the dancers.

In a product introduction meeting for a medical equipment company, a James Bond character communicated with his superior via the large projection screen, then had to retrieve stolen trade secrets from the villain whose laboratory was set up on stage. Bond was captured, but cleverly played the product introduction module to find the clues he needed to escape, retrieve the trade secrets, and whisk the pretty lab assistant back to the meeting in progress to see the new product line revealed live on stage.

This is typical of the way all of the different elements interact. The master of ceremonies and actors may interact with the video modules or members of the audience; products may be introduced on screen, then appear on stage and then be taken out into the audience.

Competitions and Games—TV game-show type activities are used to involve the audience and reinforce the information being presented.

Breakout Sessions—The meeting breaks into smaller groups for seminars and workshops, any of which may include their own video modules or speaker support. Topics many include product knowledge, training, hands-on testing of equipment or products, or marketing strategies and sales quotas individualized for specific groups.

Awards Banquet—the event culminates in a formal dinner. It may include "This is Your Life," or recognition video modules, awards for the year's top employees, stage skits, and speeches.

Entertainment—Entertainment themed to the overall event closes the evening.

Though business theater is larger in scope than a singe show, when designing the overall event or writing any of its individual elements, you still follow the same basic process of researching, structuring, and writing. You need a theme, a central idea, and a logical continuity to hold it all together.

CHAPTER 5

SEVEN STRATEGIES FOR IMPROVING ANY TREATMENT

"Don't learn the tricks of the trade—learn the trade."
—Jacob M. Braude

Regardless of how your show is structured, regardless of its format, there are seven strategies that will improve it. These strategies go to the heart of your work—not just how video works but how people think and learn and how your shows can help empower audiences with knowledge and understanding.

These even strategies are the basics. By constantly returning to them, you will create more powerful shows.

Create an Emotional Experience

"Nothing great was ever achieved without enthusiasm."
—Ralph Waldo Emerson (1803–1882)

There is a common self-fulfilling prophesy in our business: Many practitioners believe that non-entertainment shows are dull and they vindicate their opinion by creating dull shows.

Dry data is dull; and no amount of pretentious music or flashy effects will change that. But information can be put in a fresh perspective: Who does it empower? Whose vision brought it into being? Whose life will it enhance? Who can now be challenged to new heights of achievement?

By probing these questions, your script can pierce the shield of indifference we all use to avoid a daily glut of trivial information. Below that filter lie emotions that can be reached by showing our audience that it's all right to dream ... to strive ... to be vulnerable ... to get back up and try even harder.

Even technical subjects can be made interesting—by demonstrating how lives are affected. For a show introducing a new fleet of jets to the flying public, the standard approach would be a deluge of facts on state-of-the-art technology and luxurious comfort. Instead, we used the ageless dream of flight as a theme and analogy, showing how the engineers soared to new heights of creativity in their design, how the production line soared beyond previous boundaries of scale, how pilots felt a new level of power and control.

The hard information was in no way sacrificed—it was given emotional power by being seen through the eyes of those who created the plane and those who now stand in awe of this new marvel of the air. The show evoked the emotional appeal of being free enough to dream and bold enough to make your dreams real.

Emotional excitement is found anywhere you look for it. A product introduction show for jets might be inherently more exciting than a show on accounting procedures, but within any subject area, you can find the excitement of discovery, the fulfillment of helping another person, or the joy of personal growth. Tapping into these emotions is essential to creating a high-impact show.

Video is a nonintellectual medium. Appeals to reasoned analysis are at best secondary reinforcement. Think about dreams ... about power ... about crashing through barriers to new levels of self-worth. Show your audience the excitement of the world from a fresh perspective.

2. Tell a People Story

"If you want an audience, start a fight."
—Gaelic proverb

Most successful movies are about a hero battling an enemy. The setting may be war, Wall Street or another galaxy, but the story is about people. By focusing on a story about individuals, an interesting thing happens: Not only is the audience more involved, the film's statement about the setting or situation is made more powerfully.

The old surf-movies with Gidget and her friends were trite love stories—surfing providing only a background and a weak sub-plot. But they were more effective in introducing surfing to main-stream America than any of the more accurate surfing documentaries—because most movie-goers care more about love than surfing.

This open secret, known to all successful screenwriters, can also be applied to informational videos. For example, rather than a show on management techniques, show how an employee and her supervisor resolve a problem. Rather than parading features and benefits, show how a product or service changed an individual's life. While showing how it's done, show an individual who is personally benefited while contributing to the benefit of others.

Though a dramatization is an obvious format for people stories, any format can be enhanced through demonstrating how your message affects people. Interviews are more effective if the questions center on personal experience or add insight to someone else's experiences, rather than confining themselves to opinion or abstract facts.

Even in a straight voice-over, with no specific reference to the personalities on the screen, a picture story can show specific individuals in a story that applies the ideas or techniques being discussed.

> **Example:** For a sales piece on a national court-reporting network, we opened with a lawyer fielding several problems over the phone. During the show, the narrator explained all of the network's benefits, while the visual demonstrated how those benefits solved all of the lawyer's problems introduced in the opening. Sparse use of sound bites from

telephone conversations increased the sense of urgency, introduced a touch of reality and filled in the details we couldn't demonstrate visually.

Although it was technically a voice-over narration show, it became much more powerful and involving than a lifeless parade of benefits, because it allowed one person's story to unfold through visuals.

Segments of a show can be separate stories. Vignettes can alternate with commentary on what was just dramatized, or establish the problem that your product or service can solve. The critical thing is to give your audience someone with whom they can identify. One specific example, that is emotionally involving, has more power than any amount of reasoned analysis.

Make It Positive

"Nothing succeeds like the appearance of success."
—Christopher Lascl

When riding a mountain bicycle through a treacherous section of trail with a steep drop immediately to the side, an experienced rider focuses on the line the bike must take to make it through the rocks, ruts, and obstructions. The rider's mental focus must be complete and intense— willing the bike along the only line that will take it through the section. Even an instant's thought given to the dozens of things that could go wrong—or the consequences—is enough to break the rider's concentration, or shake the confidence, sending the rider tumbling down the mountain-side.

Focusing on what you want to happen makes it happen. Your audience tends to go where their minds have been aimed. Programming those minds with mistakes and fears weakens your message of how to do things right. If you dwell on negative consequences you can frighten your audience into believing that the less they do the safer they will be.

This has become an accepted tenet in training. Most training professionals feel that the best approach in most situations is to model only correct procedures and behavior. Why clutter the minds of your audience with things you do not want them to do?

Audience recall is never perfect and after seeing your show it's possible that an audience member may remember only the vivid image of something being done incorrectly, rather than the admonition, "don't do it this way." The fine points are often forgotten, so all that's retained is "This is what I saw in the video," and on that association, they assume it's right. By planting a negative image that was imperfectly remembered, your show has actually made matters worse.

In some situations it *is* helpful to point out common problems, but identifying the problem can usually be done quickly and verbally. You might show only the consequences without modeling incorrect behavior, then cut straight to modeling the behavior that will prevent those problems.

In some situations, particularly in sales and management training, it may be helpful to debunk common misconceptions by showing the negative consequences of what many people think is the proper thing to do. Humor can be helpful here. By showing how ridiculous the character who acts this way really is, your audience may then notice themselves doing the same thing and recognize that they are being just as ridiculous as the character in the video that they were laughing at.

The deciding factor is that the audience is already practicing the behavior and not necessarily aware that they are guilty of it, or that it's hurting their performance. By showing only a parody of this behavior, your show is not introducing them to any bad habits they don't already practice.

For marketing shows, positives are also more effective. Avoiding problems mostly maintains the status quo—hardly exciting. Your audience wants to know how their lives can be made better.

A dire warning about head injuries will probably do more to alienate athletes than excite them. But if they can hear top players talking about how much more confident they feel—and aggressive they play—when wearing protective gear … that's what every competitor wants to hear. Make the equipment an icon of the sport. Glamorize it. Make it a prop to be cool with.

Rather than dwelling on the messy, inefficient office, show people enjoying the extra time they've earned by using your product or adopting your techniques to clean up that mess.

Another marketing problem associated with showing negatives is that negative images are often so powerful that your message becomes associated with them, regardless of what you may then attempt to do to position yourself as the alternative to that image.

When I wrote a product intro for a men's cologne targeted to more sensitive-type guys, I opened with a put down of macho meatheads and pin-stripped clones. The imagery was so strong it overshadowed the message that this new scent offers a refreshing alternative. I lost the job.

Safety and human services shows are particularly prone to wallowing in the negative. The broken bodies in the gutter and heart-wrenching poor little crippled children are familiar to most of us.

What do these images do to the audience? They make them uncomfortable. They want it to stop. One way an audience can try to make it stop is to heed the show's message and attempt to change the world, knowing full well that the best of their efforts will only lessen the problem, never really stopping it. The other way to make it stop is to simply turn off mentally—ignore the show. It's quick. It's easy. It isolates them from the problem completely. Which do you think most audience members choose?

Scolding and dwelling on the horrors may help swell the self-righteousness of the already-converted but will only remind others of why they would just as soon not think about it.

Sure, you have to make an audience aware of the problem and its consequences. But how much argument does it take to convince people that poverty, senseless slaughter on the highways, or crippling diseases are bad? How many people in your audience actually advocate death and suffering? Is your goal to beat them over the head, or to motivate them to start solving the problem?

A problem-solving approach would be to show the gratification, sense of belonging and power to change things that are enjoyed by those who are doing something about a problem. Invite your audience to share in this joy and accomplishment, meeting people they will be proud to know. Show them how people who enjoy life are able to prevent drunk driving or deal with other social problems. Show the action you want them to take; show them the rewards.

Negatives don't motivate. You'll never hear cheerleaders chant "Don't loose the ball," or "We're not losers." They shout out what they want to happen, which is exactly what a high-impact video does. Give your audience a goal. Show them how to do it. Give them an image of themselves—confident and successful, to envision. It's easier and more motivating to copy success than to repress failure.

Work Within the Culture

"Laws are sand, customs are rock. Laws can be evaded and punishment escaped, but an openly transgressed custom brings sure punishment."
—Mark Twain (1835–1910)

We all react to the familiar. In-jokes are the best jokes. They make us feel part of a special group. An audience comes alive when you show that you understand their special way of doing things. They open up ... become more accepting.

This can be done with details as obvious as style of dress, or as subtle as body language. Casting, set design, music selection, and language are all crucial to establishing the right tone and feel. It's emotional and highly subjective. When it's right, the audience finds it much easier to believe the video's message. If the tone is off—even when the audience is not consciously aware of it—credibility is lost.

Do your organization's employees speak with perfect diction? Probably not, so it might be better to write dialogue that sounds like real people. Is cost-control an important element of your organization's culture? If so, your sets might need to be more on the minimalist side.

Most cultures and nationalities can be identified by their music. Corporate culture is similar. Your show must have a sound that makes sense from the perspective of both the show's specific message and the client's over-all culture.

Most cultures have not only a dialect and a jargon but a specific tone to their language. Your organization client's may consider itself totally hip and nouveau to the max, or it may prefer the quiet power of understated excellence. Your selection of phrases, tone of voice, degree of formality, and attitude of those heard speaking, often deliver more of your message than the specific words that are used.

Reinforcing Culture

A video can not only tap into your organization's culture, it can also help shape that culture. This may be a subtle secondary objective, but video is much too powerful a tool, and much too well adapted to reinforcing values, to overlook this function when writing a video.

On some level, every show affects a company's culture—whether it's intentional or not. It's essential to be aware of the culture within which you are working and to consciously design your shows to reinforce the positive values of that culture.

If innovation is central to your organization's heritage, your skills-training videos can all carry a secondary message encouraging experimentation and the sharing of new ideas. If being the oldest in your business is central to your client's identity, your videos can use imagery that invokes the craftsmanship of an earlier era.

Shaping corporate culture is a responsibility, giving video a power that is seldom discussed or even recognized. Just as advertising and entertainment media both mirror and shape mass culture, corporate media shape the way employees, customers, and suppliers feel about life in the workplace—where we all spend at least half of our waking hours.

By realistically building on an organization's culture, a video can help endow the audience with a powerful winning attitude. But the operative word here is "realistically." A sales team charging into the fray full of groundless enthusiasm for a lousy product will feel betrayed as well as defeated when the dust finally settles.

Videos must reinforce an organization's assets rather than disguising a lack of them. Pure hype and hyperbole, along with those who indulge in it, do not fare well in the open marketplace.

Myth Making

Although a company's culture is understood by most employees on a gut level, video programming is a way to give it coherent form. The style of those videos become the cultural mode of expression. The tone, the attitude, and any references used all become touchstones by which the entire audience will use to compare their personal goals and values with those of their company.

It's a lot like myth and legend. Just as countries and cultures renew themselves through retelling the old stories, successful organizations must constantly reconfirm a specific set of values, a mission, a reason for coming to work every day that goes beyond a regular paycheck.

Like all myths, corporate myths are based on real people and situations: the founders and the heroes who best embody the company's values, and the humble beginnings or the great innovations that have since shaped the company. By turning these into recognized icons and incorporating them into your video, you help establish a common language.

Invoking a founder's name can become short-hand for all the values he or she embodied. The first successful product can symbolize your closeness to the customer. The organization's first facilities can be developed into an icon representing resourcefulness and perseverance; the archetype of this being the garage from which sprang the tremendous success of Hewlett-Packard.

In Case Study #1, the employee orientation, the show opens with how the company's founder began the company by salvaging a bankrupt medical lab. This opening both illustrates the values on which all employees are now expected to base their actions and helps to establish a company hero who embodies those values. This takes the company values beyond abstracts and slogans to show how a role model has applied them to the real world, and provides a specific act of achievement for employees to strive to equal or beat.

One company that gains strength from its heroes and legends is 3M, where they tell a story about an employee who spent so much time and effort trying to find a use for rejected sandpaper minerals that he was fired. He kept coming to work anyway and his efforts finally led to development of the profitable Roofing Granules Division. He was rehired and by retirement was vice-president of that division.[3]

---

3   Thomas J. Peters and Robert H. Waterman, Jr., *In Search of Excellence*, (New York: Harper & Row, 1982), p.229.

At Apple Computer, Steve Jobs, in his signature black turtleneck, has made himself a symbol of ultra-hip design and "insanely great technology," in an industry otherwise known for being bland and nerdy.

These are the stories that clearly show others what must be done to rise within an organization. They drive home that message with more power than any amount of cheerleading or abstract psychology.

Even in our broader culture, invoking certain names can instantly ground a presentation in a clearly defined set of values. Golfer Tiger Woods epitomizes the pinnacle of success earned with talent and a lifetime of hard work, along with reminding an audience that nice guys—of any race—can and do finish first. Martin Luther King Jr. and John Kennedy are examples we turn to for assurance that it is possible to find public figures with the vision and courage to lead rather than exploit.

Historical events, such as the Freedom Marches, and success stories such as Amazon.com are examples that our collective consciousness continually returns to as proof that our system can and does work. These are touchstones that a skilled writer can use to create instant consensus within an audience before moving on to the points that build on that foundation.

The goal of developing symbols, heroes and milestone events within an organization can't be fully realized with a single show. It must be accomplished through considering and incorporating the organization's heritage into every production. The best show to start with is the one you're working on now.

5. Convey Ideas, Not Words

"An invasion of armies can be resisted, but not an idea whose time has come."
—Victor Hugo (1802–1885)

Baffling them with words is no substitute for dazzling them with ideas. Don't pontificate on intuitiveness when you can hammer home gut-level understanding. A common misconception is that writing a script means stringing words together. In reality, good scripts are composed of ideas.

Before you can say it well, you must fully understand what you are trying to say. During research on a show on corporate culture for an aerospace company, the content experts talked about what other companies were doing, what the management gurus were preaching and about aspects of their corporate culture that had to change. When asked exactly what that change should be, they cycled back into talking about what everybody else was doing.

By explaining that we needed to know what the goal was before we could achieve it, an additional consulting job was created. The project fell back a step while we worked out what specific values and attitudes to reinforce. When we reached agreement on our message, we could then move forward to packaging that message.

Too often, this regrouping never occurs. A writer may attempt to pass along what clients say they want by working specific wording into the script—without fully understanding what it means. This is partially defensive, since the script can be defended by claiming "but this is exactly what the CEO said." Substituting repetition for understanding not only spreads confusion and paranoia, it makes dull shows. Emotion is not aroused; imagination does not take flight by rote repetition.

On a more practical level, the ideas in the message must all be woven into the fabric of the show. This can't be done if the ideas are only mouthed and not understood. Expressing ideas from different perspectives requires that you first understand them.

If autocratic management insists its words be delivered verbatim, showcase them as an insert of that executive talking to the camera. It's your only hope of delivering the understanding and conviction that originally inspired the words.

Once the ideas in the message are understood, *original* ideas are necessary. Imagination must go into the creation of a video before it can spark the imagination of the audience.

Unfortunately, ideas powerful enough to spark imagination are never conceived intact and complete. Ideas must be developed. To say that your product performs like a high-powered race car isn't very exciting. Your audience must be made to feel the power and taste the excitement.

Moving some words around will not do it. The concept must be understood, then re-thought, over and over again until you finally realize how to make it pop off the screen with laser-like clarity. Lifeless words are seldom remembered, while imaginative ideas dwell long in the memory of those they inspire.

6. Show, Don't Tell

"Never explain. Your friends do not need it and your enemies will not believe you anyway."
—Elbert Hubbard (1856–1915)

Examples work best, whether you're showing a tennis swing or a management technique. If your purpose is to position a place or product as elegantly upscale, logic is your weakest appeal. Your video must create an experience that's similar in mood and tone to experiencing the place or product itself.

For a downtown hotel, a musical metaphor was appropriate. A business guest's stay was divided into symphonic-like movements: the morning is bright and vibrant ... the evening goes legato. While showing the details of interior design, we talked of "a baseline of polished marble; a flourish of brass."

We never tried to explain *why* it was elegant; we simply demonstrated the client's understanding of the details that go into a fine hotel, in a style and tone that complemented the message.

Explaining verbally is seldom the most effective or interesting approach, but since it requires little imagination, that's all that too-many shows do. Think how much more effective it is to provide a new context, create a fresh perspective, or show how other people deal with similar situations.

Rather than explaining quality, show examples of an obsessive commitment to quality. Rather than explaining that customers react warmly to personal attention, show their smiles, interview them, or dramatize customer satisfaction as it happens. Rather than explaining how a drill-press works, build something—show how various techniques contribute to a finished product, and ultimately, to satisfying customers.

Beware of abstracts and philosophizing; don't get bogged down in the why's and how's. Simply isolate an important benefit and show it. If that benefit is something that is not an action—like a good diet helping to prevent heart disease—show the results of that benefit: active, happy people enjoying life.

Words of explanation will seldom be remembered, while a vivid image or a clear example can be burned into the memory forever.

7. Use Humor

"I don't make jokes. I just watch the government and report the facts."
—Will Rogers (1879–1935)

While out-right comedy is best handled by a writer who's serious about being funny, imagination and humor can enhance the impact of any video. The pomposity of many informational videos is inexcusable. The voice-of-god narrator stiffly declaring, "We're the Best in the Business," and "We do it for You." Is not only dull and dated but one of the least effective ways to get your message across.

When is the last time you saw a ram-rod stiff announcer on a TV commercial using his deepest authoritative voice? That approach has not been used since the 1960s. Why? Because it doesn't work.

Commercials today use warmth, wit and human interest. Pay attention—they spend lots of money researching this stuff; and some of their techniques may help improve your next script.

> **Example**: A corporate image film for an up-scale luggage manufacturer states, "We're clearly out of step," while demonstrating this fact by showing an airport crowd scene from the knees down. As the scene develops, a crowd of people in scruffy footwear stands back for a pair of elegantly clad feminine legs to make an entrance and then become surrounded by a matched set of beautiful luggage. The video then proceeds to demonstrate that, in a world of mass production and allowable tolerances, being out of step means crafting a quality product.

Not exactly a laugh riot, but turning a phrase with questionable connotations into a positive statement is a refreshing change from the pretentious, more-elegant-than-thou approach that is usually expected.

The secret is to think. Don't just show something—show it in a way that's imaginative. Humor enlivens language in dialogue or narration. It demonstrates an intelligence and personality that's more interesting to experience and more likely to be remembered.

Figures of speech can be twisted: memory like a dead elephant. Before they made him, they broke the mold. The average person thinks he isn't … these lines not only make their point strongly, they also make the audience want more.

Colorful figures of speech, dialect, and jargon—if used with discretion and intelligence—can add life to a video. Not everyone in your video has to sound like a newscaster. In fact, no one in your video should sound like a newscaster. By being playful with language, videos take on warmth and humanity.

> **Example:** In a patient information video, the patient, on entering a radiology lab, is asked, "How are you?" by the technician. She responds: "Other than nervous, anxious, and apprehensive, just fine." To which the technician responds, "You can relax then. Nothing in this room cuts, pokes or punctures."

Hardly hilarious, but certainly more entertaining than the cardboard cutouts populating many informational videos. This exchange doesn't take significantly more time than clichéd dialogue; and in addition to adding entertainment value, it adds depth to the patient's character by showing that she was frightened but being a good sport about it, and holds out a hope to our audience that in addition to cold equipment, they may find a warm human being in a radiology lab.

When you need to make an impact, it's far better to be humorous than lofty. Profound statements are usually filed and forgotten, while we always enjoy remembering and sharing anything that made us smile.

CHAPTER 6

STRUCTURE AND FORMAT

"But most important of all is the structure of the incidents."
—Aristotle (384—322 B.C.), writing on drama

Structure is the most crucial and least understood aspect of designing a show. It's like planning for a large party; if it's done well, no one notices; but if done poorly, everything falls apart. At its most basic, structure is the order in which the facts are presented, and the techniques through which a point of view is imparted to the audience.

Think about the life of a murderer. If we start with a chronological life history, then analyze the facts about why the victim was murdered and why the crime was committed, we've turned human drama into dull details.

Imagine instead jumping right into an emotional moment, opening on the murder itself. Then suffer with a detective digging for clues, not knowing until the final scene who did it. That's a murder mystery! It's entertaining. It's involving. It's the same set of facts, but the structure has turned dry data into intriguing drama.

> **Example:** For a corporate image video on a real estate title information service, we opened on Lindberg flying the Atlantic, then cut to fighter planes, to develop a theme of "Speed and Dependability." Once the excitement was established, we introduced the company: TRW. Its diverse history now has an image of adventure and a common thread. Air planes and information retrieval must both be fast and reliable.

> Cutting to a real estate agent, we show the time pressure, the exten-
> sive liability and the potential problems that could disrupt lives years
> into the future. Speed and dependability are reinforced over and again,
> driving home a memorable theme, bringing excitement to the product's
> main benefits and giving the show a high impact focus.

The show is about a big company moving numbers around but by structuring those facts, the excitement of performance under pressure brings
life to their presentation and imparts an understanding of why they are
important.

Structuring requires the greatest leap of creative imagination in the
video process. It's main goal is to first make the audience hungry to know
why, and only then giving them the facts that satisfy their hunger. Make
them wonder. Intrigue them with improbable combinations. Throw new
perspective on every-day things.

Did you realize that the public water supply could pull waste-water
directly from the sewer if you fill a wash basin so that the surface of the
water reaches the end of the faucet? Does that fact have any more impact
on you than being told that double-check valve backflow assemblies are
important safety precautions? It's the same fact, but the presentation is
structured differently.

Structure for your show must be developed while writing the creative
approach. A clear structure prompts your creativity by focusing your
imagination on specific questions. Rather than having to envision the
complete show all at once, you can take smaller bites and consider the
elements of structure one at a time.

There are several elements of structure, all of which must be considered more or less simultaneously. The most fundamental structural
decision to make is to choose the format of your show.

Format Templates

"Originality is the art of concealing your sources."
—Variously attributed

Format is a show's physical framework. It answers the question, What
type of show is it? Documentary? Interview? Dramatization?

Because it's one of the most fundamental decisions in developing a creative approach, it's often a major stumbling block. To make the format decision easier, this section is organized by format type, with a list of ideas for each. When you need an idea for a show's format, read through this section to find one that can be adapted to your needs.

Voice-overs

The cheapest, easiest, most often used and frequently abused format is to simply have a narrator talk while the pictures go by. There is nothing inherently wrong with voice-over formats, except that they are often unimaginative.

The worst misuse of a voice-over is what's called a "brochure with a light to read by." This is created by a writer explaining everything in words, then going back and adding pictures as an afterthought. Not only is this backwards, it bores the audience with verbal explanation. Your message could be carried with more power by telling your story visually, then using words to fill in any gaps.

There are several variations on the voice-over format: the voice of God, the character narrator and the tag-team.

The Voice of God

In an authoritative voice, the narrator speaks his (it's almost always *his*) words as though they were chiseled in granite. This is clearly the voice of management speaking and it implies a paternalistic and superior attitude.

Although it is the most typical style of informational video voice-over, its effectiveness can be judged by the fact that TV commercials seldom use this approach. The TV advertising industry has good research budgets and tests the effectiveness of different formats, so this is no accident.

You can enjoy the benefits of this research by simply analyzing the commercials you see in prime time. You'll notice that few commercials use the voice of God approach; if they use voice-over at all, they use a voice with a specific personality.

Character Narrator

The obvious benefit of a character narrator is that the personality that's projected can convey a specific attitude and world view that exemplifies your message. "Real people" voices also enhance the intimacy of video, making the message seem more warm and personal.

The voice-over presenting carpentry tools can sound like a carpenter. A discussion of product features and benefits can come directly from a customer who uses that product. Or a hardware company that began supplying miners can have its history given by "the old prospector."

A personality, or a more natural voice, sounds less like the voice of management and implies a third-party endorsement. An imaginative choice of voice can add a new depth of interest to a show.

A car thief can discuss auto security systems. A mailman can discuss the changes he's seen in a neighborhood. A salesperson can tell other salespeople about the benefits of attending a training seminar. The spirit of an early pioneer can return from the beyond to give guests an introduction to a park and garden.

To be even more imaginative, non-humans can narrate a show. The product itself can speak. A parrot may have some interesting views on color coordination within a line of clothing. An intake valve can discuss the benefits of fuel injection. We're all familiar with the privileged position of being a "fly on the wall," why not let that insect finally share some of the sights it has beheld?

Tag-team

Multiple narrators help break up a video, enhancing its pacing. Using a balance of male and female voices works best, since they are easier to tell apart.

Different voices can express different views on benefits or issues. A show on travel packages was done as a couple telling friends about their vacation. She consistently talked about the freedom and adventure of it all. He talked about the good deals and special rates. The audience had the fun of getting to know this couple, anticipating how they would respond to each other's comments and enjoying the satisfaction of having their insight confirmed.

In addition to being more fun, this approach eliminates the more contrived transitions from one perspective to another that are necessary with a single voice. It's another example of how a more imaginative creative approach can deliver more information in less time.

Combinations with Other Formats

A handy thing about voice-over is that it's an effective glue for holding together segments of a show done in other formats, providing continuity or an additional level of commentary. A voice-over approach can easily be enhanced by interspersing it with video bites of interview excerpts, vignettes or some other type of footage—documentary being a typical example.

Case Study #1, the employee orientation, is an example of this. The voice-over is interspersed with excerpts of interviews with company executives.

A voice-over summary could add an additional level of reinforcement in the script for Case Study #2, "Success In Selling." It could list all of the major techniques for demonstrating an "attitude of customer service," either showing a list of those points on the screen, or using flashbacks to the scenes that demonstrate those techniques.

A variation on voice-over is to have the narrator appear on camera as a spokesperson.

On-Camera Spokesperson

Like a host leading a tour, an on-camera spokesperson conducts a video, anticipating our interests and pointing out details that may satisfy them. This format shares many strengths and problems with the voice-over format.

Host

The cliché is a spokesperson who is a bland humanoid. This obvious surrogate of management exudes pomposity and projects about as much warmth as a mannequin with a voice-chip implant. The solution is to create a personality for your host. Have your spokesperson loosen up, show some enthusiasm, and interact with the environment.

*Connections*was a PBS series written by James Burke, who also appears as the on-camera host. His intense enthusiasm and lack of self-consciousness brought the joy of discovery to this blend of history and physical science.

*Connections*is a good example of how an informational program can be made more involving by a script and a host who project energy and enthusiasm—effective production values that cost nothing extra. Three specific techniques were used to demonstrate this enthusiasm:

➤ The host involves the audience by frequently asking "what would happen?" Encouraging them to "imagine this." He leads the audience into assumptions, only to shatter them with a hidden nugget of new information. The audience is kept on guard, guessing what comes next, discovering for themselves how the clues and connections introduced earlier all come together.

➤ Connections are constantly being made between things not normally associated, or between the familiar and the unusual. In a show adapting this approach to convey information on safeguarding the water supply, a scene began with a little girl washing her dog, then a chain of possibilities ends with fleas flowing out of her neighbor's kitchen faucet. This aroused the audience's curiosity about "How could that possibly happen?" So they were much more interested in the information that followed.

➤ The visual direction is playful, with the host injecting himself into the frame in unconventional ways: popping up from the bottom of the frame; kneeling down to get closer to a low-angle camera, or initially blending in with a group, then revealing himself when he turns to address the camera. He frequently uses props or costumes appropriate to the on-camera environment and interacts with his environment by operating controls and moving things back into place.

The impact of an on-camera spokesperson is enhanced by any technique that helps project a personality and point of view. Providing props for the host to handle or other motivations to involve the host with the set or location all help to improve on a host who may otherwise seem like a talking cardboard cutout.

Management or Celebrity Spokesperson

An effective option in creating a personality is using a personality already known by your audience. A celebrity adds a certain amount of glamour and implies an endorsement. The danger lies in using a celebrity whose image does not complement—or even contradicts—your video's message. Select a spokesperson who could plausibly have some knowledge—or a least an interest—in your show's message.

A member of management will have instant credibility as a content expert in many areas and certainly can't be topped for "state of the company" type programs. For greatest impact, the tone for this type of approach must be conversational and personal. Having the executive behind a counter or a workbench or out in the field is often a good idea. This location implies that the executive is in touch with reality out on the front lines; it can convey more credibility than shooting the same scene in a plush office.

The obvious warning here is that any member of management considered for an on-camera spokesperson role must have good camera presence.

Demonstration

An on-camera spokesperson is perfect for demonstrating a procedure or showing off a product. The basic approach is to have the spokesperson talk straight to the camera.

Human interest and a story-line can be added by giving the demonstrator someone on camera to talk to. A precocious teenager can be taken into work on the weekend to show mom how to use her new computer, a neighbor can show off some new power tools, or a newly promoted employee can go visit someone with the same position at another location to see how that person has things set up.

Although these approaches could also be considered dramatizations, most of the show is spent with the camera taking the point of view of the character for whom a demonstration is being performed, so the effective result is a nuts-and-bolts demonstration with the increased audience appeal of a people story.

Massive use of close-ups is a secret to good demonstrations. For manual skills, the hands should often fill the frame. For communication skills, facial expressions—or just the eyes—can effectively punctuate every point.

Breaking the Fourth Wall

This term describes the situation in which a participant in on-camera action turns to address the audience directly, becoming an on-camera spokesperson. The name comes from the fact that a typical studio set has three physical walls as background for the action and one imaginary wall separating the action from the camera. Talking to or even recognizing the existence of the camera "breaks" this imaginary fourth wall.

> **Example**: In an orientation show for a hospital, we showed a new employee's supervisor giving him some advice or encouragement; then, as the employee walked out of frame, the supervisor turned to talk with the audience about why she had told the employee what she did and slip in a occasional hint on what was about to befall this new employee. The audience would then see the employee deal with a new work situation.
>
> To begin following scenes, the supervisor would walk out of the background to talk to the audience and set up the coming action; then, as the new employee walked into the frame, the supervisor would go back into character. At no time did the employee break the fourth wall, or acknowledge that his supervisor was doing so.

Establishing and maintaining these types of conventions is crucial when breaking the fourth wall. You must decide: who is allowed to address the audience? Under what conditions? Does anyone else on camera react to this strange behavior?

No set of conventions is better than another; but consistency is critical. It ruins the video's credibility if conventions are not obvious and consistently maintained. For example, it would not work to have everyone acknowledge the camera in one scene only to mysteriously lose this power in other scenes.

Interviews

For credibility and to introduce a new perspective, you can't beat hearing the short and skinny from someone who's been there. A colleague respected by your audience can discuss techniques and procedures. Customers can open a few eyes with comments on quality and service, and recognized experts can lend stature and credibility. Good use of interviews can be effective in addressing the "reality backlash" acknowledged earlier.

Interviews are best used for segments within other formats, or as continuity to hold together other elements: a customer relating an experience can be inter-cut with a dramatization of a specific situation and a discussion of why it was optimal or how it could be improved.

Combining several interviews can project a sense of balance. The news show *60 Minutes* is a good example of the documentary convention of intercutting interviews that express opposing viewpoints to simulate a moderated debate.

As the writer for a show incorporating interviews, you have two basic responsibilities that go beyond developing the show's tone, structure, and content: The initial script must provide an idea of how the interviews will work within the structure of that script and what content they will deliver; secondly, it's a good idea for you to write the interview questions, to help ensure that the tone and content of the answers will be consistent with your vision for the show.

Case Study #1, "Opportunity Into Excellence," is an example of how the initial script simply lists the points that will covered by the interview:

Interview with Philip Jason.   NARRATOR: Philip Jason is Director of Operations for EMC.

EXCERPTS FROM INTERVIEW WITH PHILLIP JASON, MAKING THE FOLLOWING POINTS:

- Career paths are kept challenging.
- Top performance is rewarded with one of the best compensation packages in our industry.
- EMC recruits only those who are ready to take initiative and constantly strive for improvement.

Another option is to write "anticipated responses" into the script, or examples of what you think interviewees will say. This is risky. The client or producer may decide that's exactly what they want, and if they are too inexperienced to know better, they may ask people to read your exact lines rather than to respond to questions in their own words.

This usually results in an embarrassingly wooden performance. It's obvious that the person is reading a script, so not only is your show ruined by bad acting, its credibility is ruined because it *is* acting—rather than a spontaneous expression of personal opinion or experience.

Amateurs are good on camera in two situations: responding in their own words to intelligent questions and doing what they normally do the way they normally do it. Asking them to read a script or incorporate specific phrases is asking for footage that will be an embarrassment to all concerned.

From the "points to be covered," in your script, develop questions that address those points. Interview questions for the preceding example included:

➢ Why is EMC a good place to pursue a career?

➢ How would you describe the careers at EMC?

➢ What makes a career at EMC different?

➢ In what ways are career paths kept challenging?

➤ How is hard work and achievement recognized?

➤ How would you describe the compensation package at EMC?

➤ How do pay and benefits at EMC compare with the rest of the industry?

➤ What is EMC looking for in the employees you recruit?

➤ How important is initiative in a candidate for employment?

As with the research questions, there is a redundancy in these interview questions. That's in case an answer to one question does not give you the concise statement or tone you need. Asking another similar question gives the interviewee another chance to approach the same information from a slightly different perspective. That's often more effective than asking for a rephrasing of an answer already given. The phrasing of the new question may be just the slight difference in perspective needed to set off the idea or the wording the interviewee couldn't quite get while answering the earlier question. Some interview questions may be skipped by the interviewer if there's nothing else needed on that point.

How Interviews Differ From Research

There are critical differences between the research questions you asked earlier and interviews to be included in your show. During research, your only concern was to gather information. It was a fishing trip. You let the client or content expert run with it, unconcerned with how the information was expressed, as long as it was there. Little control was needed.

During on-camera, or on-microphone, interviews, you already know what you want. Your concern is to capture on video someone concisely articulating what you already know—or at least suspect. A lot of control is needed.

You need to ask questions that are precisely phrased to keep the interviewee on a specific subject and speaking from a specific perspective.

There's a lot of difference between the answers you would receive if you ask a restaurant owner the following two questions:

➤ "Why did you choose to cook with electricity?"

➤ "What were the factors you considered when deciding whether to cook with gas or electricity?"

They both address the same information. But the first question will probably yield answers that are an obvious endorsement for cooking with electricity, while answers to the second question are more likely to yield an even-handed statement of the considerations that a restaurant owner faces when deciding whether to cook with gas or electricity.

If your client is positioning itself as a research facility for helping customers make up their own minds, answers to the first question would defeat that purpose because of its obvious promotional tone, whereas answers to the second questions would be closer to the desired tone of commitment to open-minded research.

The best interview questions are usually open-ended; they require a discussion rather than a yes, no or specific fact. They are specific enough to keep the interviewee on the subject and broad enough to let opinions or insight come through.

Closed questions also have their place. They can be used to qualify whether a group of questions is appropriate for an interviewee.

For example, "Have you ever used the product?" may be a good qualifying question to ask before soliciting any further opinions—which may be freely given based on assumptions rather than actual experience. Asking if someone is a member of a union, political party or religious group may decide for you which set of questions to ask.

Short answer questions, such as "How large is your dealership?" "Where are you from?" and "How long have you been with the company?" can further qualify an interviewee and also give you something to edit into the show so that your subjects can introduce themselves to your audience and provide a basis for their credibility.

Interview Question Templates

Certain phrases are consistently effective in setting up interview questions. They include:

1. What has been your greatest challenge while …
2. What has been your greatest reward from …
3. What is the most important opportunity that has been created by …
4. What is the primary benefit of …

5. What surprised you most …

6. What was the most unusual or surprising benefit …

7. To what extent were your expectations about _____ met?

8. To what extent do you feel …

9. What was the most effective technique that was used …

10. What has been the biggest impact …

11. How successful has _____ been in …

12. What needs does _____ meet that can not be met by other means of _____?

13. How does _____ differ from …

14. What's different about …

15. What are (were) your major concerns …

16. What makes your organization/product/service different from other organization/product/service?

17. What is your impression …

18. What advice can you give to people facing the decisions/experience you've been through?

19. How would you rate the quality of …

20. How does _____ contribute to _____?

21. How well does _____ provide/maintain/support/etc. _____?

22. What is the significance of _____?

23. How would you describe _____ to a friend?

24. How does this _____ change your opinion about _____?

25. What do you think would motivate _____ to do this?

26. What does this tell you about commitments or plans (YOUR ORGANIZATION) has made for its future?

Notice that many of these questions follow a strategy of asking for a single thing, such as "greatest challenge" or "greatest reward." This helps to focus the person being interviewed. When you ask a broader question, such as

"What were the challenges …," it can be overwhelming. The interviewee may feel obligated to think through *all* the challenges that were faced, assuming that quantity is more important the quality. The opposite is actually the case. One pithy example usually delivers more useful information than a list that provides little detail or insight.

And if that *pithy* comment is not forthcoming, your extemporized follow-up question is of course, "Any other significant challenges/rewards/etc." In this way you direct the interviewee to dig down into their insights, fully exploring each lesson learned in order of importance, rather than skating over a list of hastily recalled generalizations.

Several of the questions focus on surprises and differences. The strategy here reflects the earlier-stated observation that audiences are typically informal, informed and in a hurry. Being *informed* means that many audiences have the same background and expectations as the interviewee. If this is the case, the audience doesn't have much interest in how the subject of your show is just like what they already know or expect. They want to know what's new. They want to focus on the surprises and how to prepare for them. So that's where your questions need to lead the interview

Another helpful guideline is to understand that people are more interesting when talking about personal experiences rather than abstract concepts. Focus your questions on specific examples rather than broad generalities. Anyone can have an opinion, but the credibility to back it up comes from experience.

When you interview, it's often a good idea to explain that your questions probably won't be heard by the audience, so you need answers that are complete sentences. It's then a judgment call whether to make interviewees keep trying until they do work an answer into a complete sentence. Single phrases can often be interwoven with voice-over to create an effective segment. Complete sentences aren't always necessary and when you force amateurs into numerous retakes and unfamiliar speech patterns, they may lose what composure they started with, taking with it their credibility on camera.

Simulated Interviews

The problem with interviews is the lack of control. You may never get that perfect statement that will make a key point. An option combining the control of a tight script with the spontaneity and conversational tone of an interview is to hire actors to portray real people responding to questions.

You've seen it on TV commercials. You know it's an actor saying those clever things about the product, but it's easier to become involved with a actor speaking from your perspective or taking a third-party point-of-view than with an actor who takes the company's perspective.

A show on fertility counseling opened with three different couples talking straight to the audience about the problems and needs that prompted them to seek help. It was sensitive, personal information that most people would never be comfortable telling to strangers. So actors delivered the lines.

As the show progressed, the couples were seen together in a counseling session, each asking questions appropriate to their characters—giving everyone in the intended audience a sympathetic on-camera character with whom to identify. It was obvious that they were actors, but the audience could accept it. It provided the control needed to make an already long show as concise as possible and it created an alternative that was more involving than listening to the counselor give a lecture to the camera.

The secret is to be honest. Use simulated interviews for what they will contribute to the show's style, tone or pacing, not as an attempt to deceive the audience.

Documentary

The term documentary says more about a show's tone and intention than its format. Documentaries can be a combination of several formats: voice-over, on-camera spokespersons, interviews or dramatizations.

The strength of documentary is that it deals with what really exists or has already happened. It has a factual and unbiased tone. A documentary on satisfied customers can lend credibility through second party endorsement. A documentary on success stories from using a new sales or management technique has the feel of honest advice from a more experienced colleague. A documentary on your company's facilities or operations could be used as informational programming by schools or television.

The downside of documentaries is that many people think they're dull. Generations of droning narrators, spokespersons posing in lab coats and self-righteous attitudes about giving people what's good for them, have all had their effect.

The obvious response to this perception is to avoid these clichés and maintain a tone and pace that does not assume your audience is brain-damaged—but this works only if your audience will watch in the first place. So, although the documentary is an effective format, you may want to call it something else.

Video Magazine

The video magazine has a more popular image than a straight documentary, from which it evolved. The main differences are that the video magazine deals with several topics and it is usually done as a series.

The use of on-camera spokespersons enhances the appeal of a video-magazine, giving it more warmth and personality; selecting the right spokespersons is critical to establishing the show's tone. When they are done well, internal video magazines are effective in broadcasting information, recognizing initiative and contributions, and promoting a team consciousness.

A secret to creating effective video magazines is to respect your audience's intelligence; inform rather than manipulate. To be taken seriously, video magazines must deliver substance, rather than function as a cheerleader or a conduit for obvious propaganda.

Newscast

Like the video magazine, this is a good format for tying together several unrelated stories or formats. On the downside, newscasts inherently violate the operative concept of showing it with pictures rather than explaining it in words—since the most commonly used shot is the talking head.

It's tough to find visuals for all of those words. An easy out is to do video-magazine-type inserts, with the newscaster speaking from the environment being reported on. But location shoots get expensive—after already spending budget on a news-set. An alternative is to put all of your budget into going on location. Why spend money creating an artificial environment for your newscaster to appear in when real environments are usually more interesting and always enhance the story? This possibility makes the video magazine format look even better.

On the lighter side, the pomposity of most TV news shows makes them an easy target for parody. Humorous reporting on your competition's products and marketing strategies can effectively deliver hard information, while implying to your audience that your products and support are so much better it's funny.

Day in the Life

Although sometimes fictionalized, a day-in-the-life show also has a documentary feel. Its tone can vary from hard-edged drama, to humorous send-up, to a respectful hero treatment. It's particularly effective when one of your objectives is to motivate and reward the audience, because there's tremendous home-movie appeal in seeing the familiar, and there's tremendous validation in seeing someone just like yourself immortalized on the screen.

For a variation, a fictionalized day can provide continuity for interviews with real people speaking about their typical day. Intercutting between two or three typical days can help to contrast and compare. Or the day of a real person can be dramatized as we hear that person talk about it in interview excerpts and voice-over.

Genres and Parodies

Genres and parodies have the advantage that they come with their own conventions and expectations. If you add an imaginative twist to those expectations, the show gains impact. By simply imitating the conventions, you're only adding one cliché on top of another.

Detective Shows

These seem to be most popular with informational video makers. Although too many weak attempts have been made, an anti-hero whose value system is shown to be superior to the morals of the more influential among us is appealing to most people and another good telling of this tale is always welcome.

On a more literal level, this genre makes it easy to intrigue the audience with finding out the truth. Logic and reason become steps to solving a puzzle, rather than dry facts to be memorized.

Game Shows

This is a natural format for training. Contestants are rewarded for answering questions and demonstrating skills.

There's something warmly comforting about a game show: We feel superior because we don't take it too seriously, but we still enjoy guessing the answers.

Hit Movies, Plays or Musicals

Just the mention of a well-loved film or play can put an audience in a special mood. The audience is already familiar with the language and conventions, so little time is necessary to set the scene. Since they already know the characters, they are grounded in a comfortable familiarity and are more willing to accept new information and ideas from these old friends.

For your show to hold up over time, it must be based on a true classic. This week's biggest box office smash may be a fading memory by the time your video is seen, and unless key scenes or lines of dialogue have become part of our group consciousness, references to them may seem contrived and confusing.

It's much safer to go back several years to shows such as the Wizard of Oz, South Pacific, Star Wars, or the like. These are true myths. Like the Greek classics, they live in our media and in our memories more through being a constant source of reference than through our audience's actually reading or seeing them.

Once you've selected your classic, study its tone, emotions, and message. Don't dwell on trivia. Oblique references may add depth and intelligence to a parody, but for an informational video, it's best to play off of the most familiar associations. Obscure references are more likely to baffle than intrigue an audience.

Courtroom Drama

Since it involves comparison of facts and defending one's position, a courtroom drama is a good vehicle for introducing ideas or techniques that may not yet be fully accepted. For example, a salesperson can go on trial for not being aggressive enough when closing a sale, only to prove to the jury that being more responsive to the customer's needs is really the more effective means of building a loyal customer base.

Through flashbacks, dramatizations can show us how the incident actually happened, the events leading up to it, or show the investigation as an expert witness points out the most crucial details.

Obvious uses for courtroom drama are the many legal questions faced by any organization: discrimination, harassment, product liability and so on. A single case study can provide a backdrop for a general discussion of the major points. The courtroom scene itself could be a series of flashbacks that bring up the points on which current procedures are based. Intercutting among several trials can contrast different interpretations of a law and how they hold up in court.

Comedy

Comedy can be the most effective as well as the most difficult format to use. Humor helps your audience open up to new perspectives and insights. It rewards them for paying attention by giving them a laugh every time they understand a point.

Humor is sometimes criticized because it can distract from the content, but this is only the case when humor is misused. John Cleese is a successful British comedian who starred in Monty Python's Flying Circus and his own television show. He also founded the Video Arts company, which became successful producing training videos for business. Here's what he said in an interview:

> "There's a right way and a wrong way of using comedy. The wrong way—the old way they used to do it in Britain—was to have a straight script written and then hire someone to come in and put in some jokes. This was hopeless. If the jokes didn't work, it was embarrassing. And if they did work, the audience remembered the jokes and forgot the lessons."

> "The right way to use comedy is to make sure that all the humor arises out of the teaching points themselves. So that every time that audience laughs, they're taking a point. And if they remember the joke, they've remembered the training point."

The operative concept here is:

Humor must be based on your training or selling points

There are several levels on which to do this. For example, the basic premise of the story can be humorous, such as a mad-cap adventure: If your organization has a policy of making deliveries within a certain time limit, show an extreme situation, such as delivering an oil pump in darkest Africa.

If the training or selling point is that you hand-off delivery to only the most dependable local carriers, you could illustrate this by showing a precarious trip in a dugout canoe or by the carrier hacking through dangerous jungle. Your client's use of modern communications could be illustrated by showing a wireless network powered by a hand-cranked generator.

And none of this requires an expensive location shoot. Since it's comedy in the first place, you can be loose and whimsical. A cardboard cutout canoe and a few palm fronds can set the stage. Stuffed animals can suggest the "danger." Crank up the sound effects for more humorous potential

A more realistic premise could exaggerate problems closer to home: flat tires, airline strikes, confusing addresses, vicious guard dogs. Each predicament demonstrates that contingency procedures and resourcefulness save the day. The final shot becomes the delivery person, cool and composed, right on time, expressing an attitude of "no problem, just doing my job."

Parodies of a genre have potential as a humorous premise. A tough-guy detective could chase down the culprits who are stealing time, holding productivity ransom, or murdering competitiveness.

A training series for a restaurant chain parodied "Close Encounters of the Third Kind." An alien from another galaxy came in to order a meal, driving home the point that many customers may not be familiar with the menu, so it's the host's responsibility to conscientiously describe menu items and to not make assumptions.

Another way for humor to develop naturally from a training or selling point is to create humorous situations. There are two of them: normal people in extraordinary circumstances and extraordinary people in normal circumstances. An archeologist digging in the jungle is not humorous. But it could be funny if some important files have become so lost in an antiquated filing system that an archeologist is brought in to find them.

In the other type of humorous situation, an office worker on vacation uses the search logic employed by his company's new filing system to find the priceless artifact that had been eluding a team of top archeologists.

The following excerpt, from "Blazing Quotas," is another example of characters in unlikely situations. It's a western produced for a financial institution. Black Bart and his boys are terrorizing the townspeople with oppressively high fixed rate mortgages, until the town unites to form its own loan company.

Part of the humor develops from seeing two-fisted cowboys gathered in the saloon to grapple with complicated financial issues from the next century. The training point is that the features they decide on are the most effective against a tough competitor who will stoop to anything.

INT.   SALOON—NIGHT

The townspeople have gathered and are already well into a discussion of Black Bart's evil ways.

> JOHNNY JOE ARMSTEAD
> Black Bart needs some honest competition is what he needs.

> ANNA LEEA
> Yea, a place where honest citizens can get fair home loans.

> HANK
> With rates that don't go up ... while Bart keeps ya stuck in escrow.

> ZEKE
> Or while he stalls the paperwork.

> JOHNNY JOE ARMSTEAD
> Hey, ya know what—we could form our own loan company.

The crowd begins showing some enthusiasm.

> ANNA LEEA
> That offers affordable home loans!

The crowd cheers.

> JOHNNY JOE ARMSTEAD
> And gives good, honest service.

The crowd cheers.

> ANNA LEEA
> We could even offer adjustable-rate mortgages.

The crowd is very suspicious of this foreign idea.

> JOHNNY JOE ARMSTEAD
> You mean, like with a rate tied to T-bills?

The crowd hates the idea.

> ANNA LEEA
> Well then, how about the National Mortgage
> Contract Rate?

The crowd warms up slightly to the idea in general.

> JOHNNY JOE ARMSTEAD
> I know! We'll tie our adjustable rate to the 11th
> District Cost of Funds Index!

The crowd likes it—big time.

Another opportunity for humor to develop from training or selling points lies in creating humorous characters. Humorous insight can often be gained by showing the world from the perspective of a colorful character: the old prospector, the "rad" surfer, the oblivious professor, the good old boy, time travelers, foreign visitors, animals or even inanimate objects.

In developing a creative approach, humor can be based on any of these four levels: premise, story, situation, and character. Each one creates another opportunity for your humor to develop naturally from a training or selling point.

Humorous Guidelines

To create these opportunities effectively, there are certain guidelines. First of all, the premise must be believable. Intentionally blowing up a car is not humorous. Attempting to make a minor adjustment that sets off an escalating chain of dilemmas that result in a car blowing up might be humorous.

Comedic style is either broad or subtle. Attempting to do both isn't likely to work. Will Ferrell does good slapstick. Jerry Seinfeld is subtle.

A Jerry Seinfeld-type character throwing in a little slapstick would be confusing, not humorous.

"Voice," discussed in an earlier chapter, becomes even more important when you're writing comedy. Humor is an attitude, a point of view. It's based on a specific view of the world. Is your show taking the view of a curmudgeon or a wide-eyed innocent? Do you feel it's technical malfunction or operator error that's usually to blame? Are men mere putty in the hands of women, or are women the victims in a man's world?

Either side of those, or any other arguments could be humorous, but there's little humor to be found in the middle—unless the humor is specifically based on the difficulty of making up your mind in such a confusing world. There may be irony in agonizing over whether to take the stitch in time that will purportedly save nine, or to save the waste that is alleged to be caused by haste.

You must develop your voice and create a specific language for your script. The more specific your language becomes and the closer it's association with a specific group or character, the more humorous potential you create. Woody Allen once stated that he used "whitefish" in his stand-up act because it made people laugh, while "trout" did not.

When you understand your voice and language, you express ideas concisely, with wit and intelligence:

➤ If you can't set a good example, you can at least be a horrible warning.

➤ Always remember that you are unique. Just like everyone else.

➤ If you can't do anything about it, don't.

➤ There's an old proverb that says just about whatever you want it to.

Not only is there humor in these phrases, they also express ideas and opinions quickly and powerfully.

Humorous Techniques

In developing humor for anything from your premise or story-line, to gags and one-liners, there are several basic techniques to consider:

Connecting two or more ideas with irony

Example: "Every generation laughs at the old fashions, while religiously following the new."

The irony in a management training show can be that the manager thinks he's doing a great job because he's always frantically busy fixing every detail; when in actuality, he is sabotaging his entire department by his inability to delegate.

Twisting expectations

Example: "A person carefully stepping over a banana peel on the sidewalk falls into an open manhole."

For negotiation training, a twisted expectation could show that an IRS agent coming in to perform an audit is so polite and courteous that the person being audited revels the little secrets she had vowed no one would ever be able to force out of her using intimidation.

In a show introducing an electronic component to the sales staff, the premise was that the director of marketing built a robot to do housework. This robot then decided on its own that it wanted a career outside the home—working with a cousin on the automated assembly line that manufacturers the new component. The humor developed from a robot behaving unexpectedly. This excerpt begins as Yvette, the robot, attempts to prove a mastery of product information by reciting a list of product features.

> YVETTE
> … Mechanical angle: 275 degrees nominal.
> Torque: 5 ounces per inch maximum …

Dennis spots a brochure on the workbench and holds it up accusingly.

> DENNIS
> Your cousin sent this, didn't he?

> YVETTE
> He emailed it to me. (BEAT) It's a product
> brochure.

Dennis models the brochure for the audience.

> DENNIS
> I've seen them before.

> YVETTE
> Humans who buy cermet trimmers find this
> particular product brochure very persuasive.

Dennis looks at the brochure with renewed appreciation.

> DENNIS
> It **is** one of our better efforts.

> YVETTE
> And humans who sell trimmers find them
> dynamite selling tools.

> DENNIS
> Dynamite?

> YVETTE
> It's a human term.

> DENNIS
> I know.

> YVETTE
> It means good. Like the Bourns 3323 trimmer is
> dynamite. See?

Yvette picks up a trimmer from the workbench and tosses it to
Dennis.

> YVETTE
> (continuing)
> And also where the action is.

> DENNIS
> What action?

YVETTE
A whole new market. Bourns is selling 3323s to
distributors now ...

Exaggerate and distort

Example: "Coffee too thick to stir but too wet to plow."

In a show introducing a company's new line of toys to toy buyers, the toy market was portrayed as the perilous science fiction world populated by many of that year's best-selling toys. The company itself was portrayed as its own line of space-faring robots with extraordinary powers, who were easily defeating their enemies, represented by the competition's line of space toys:

> "An ancient and revered intelligence has evolved into a new, more potent marketing force: so responsive, so versatile that the lumbering competition is being left in its vapor trail. So come on, step aboard the Starcruiser Revell."

Pushing logic to the extreme

Example: "If shirts come in extra small and extra large, why not an extra medium size."

In a show on quality improvement, the audience is asked if they would apply often accepted workplace standards of "close enough is good enough" to their personal lives: "Would you accept 99 cents on the dollar when cashing your paycheck? Would you pay full price for a car with a scratch in the paint? How often is it acceptable for a pediatric nurse to drop a newborn infant?"

Commenting on the facts

Example: "... and how bad is it?" A show on air pollution could show a future in which scuba gear must be donned to go out on the street.

In a show introducing a new monthly statement format to bank personnel, a customer was so pleased with the improvement that he brings in flowers for a teller.

When you are considering humor in your show's premise, story line, one-liners, individual gags, and scenes, run down this list of techniques to spark your imagination by sending it off in a promising direction.

Humorous Precautions

A useful precaution when writing humor is: Don't offend. Humor inherently reveals the frailties and foibles of the characters portrayed. Handled well, it creates characters who are vulnerably human. Done poorly, humor becomes a vicious attack on a specific group. And there is no group you can attack without jeopardizing the effectiveness of your show.

Management can't be attacked; aside from the fact they're paying you, it's an underlying goal of virtually all informational shows to *encourage* teamwork, not undermine it. Customers and clients aren't a suitable target; the other underlying goal of most shows is to increase service and responsiveness to these groups. Even the competition isn't always a safe target; members of your audience may use and respect their product, may have been working for them recently or have friends who work there. This leaves only the audience themselves—the last group you would ever want to offend.

The only suitable villain is usually an abstract: indifference, an inability to delegate, carelessness, lack of product knowledge. These evils can be personified in a character, but it's then usually a good idea for that character to be redeemed by exorcising that demon and embracing your message by the end of the show.

A more effective variation is to create a fictitious competitor who is so extreme that they can't be mistaken for any real person or organization—Black Bart and his boys, in the earlier excerpt, being an example. Bart remains bad to the bone right to the bitter end, because he's such an obvious caricature that no one is likely to see him as representing a real person or group.

Other precautions boil down to good taste and common sense. Racial humor, sexist remarks and demeaning stereotypes are never a good idea. Sexual innuendo may be appropriate for some audiences in some situations, but basing an entire show on an obviously sexual theme is probably a bad idea.

Humor is serious work. The experience you create for the audience may seem silly and chaotic, but for that experience to be effective in achieving your show's objectives, the process of creating the chaotic silliness must be highly focused and buttoned down.

The secret is to think. Don't just show something; show it in a way that's imaginative. Basically, give your audience what they want but in a way they're not expecting it. Being humorous can be the most fun you'll ever have writing, but it will also probably be the *hardest* work you'll ever do.

Specialized Formats

At times, the situation calls for a specialized format. Three examples are candids modules, music videos, and a technique I've heard called "Can the Wizard."

Candids Modules

Often called—somewhat dismissively—a "Happy Faces" module, this format is part family album and part music video. For sheer fun, motivation, and camaraderie, you can't beat it for closing an event, promoting next year's event or re-living fond memories.

Candids modules consist of candid stills or video shot during an event, then edited to appropriate music. Though loose in tone and feel, the best ones follow a structural logic: chronological, alternating between active and tender moments, a running gag, alternating between groups and individuals, or alternating between work and play.

If you are also producing/directing a candids module, think carefully before using much motion video. We remember events as a series of stills: those telling moments that live in our memories as the essence of what was special. A well-paced sequence of stills is usually more effective in helping an audience remember those special moments, as their memory fills in the emotional detail

A downside of candids modules is that the family-album appeal works only with the people involved or their friends and family. Don't inflict these on non-participants

Music Videos

Like any video, it still must tell a story. Even with the best of music, if the people on camera simply dance around and act cute, the show just sits there—pointless and boring. A music video must take the viewer somewhere, be structured with a logical sequence of scenes that obviously develop a theme, convey a message, and reach a conclusion.

Can the Wizard

There are no rules, only guidelines; and sometimes it's best to throw out the guidelines.

I heard this story from the manager of a large in-house video facility. An internal client they had never worked with insisted on ignoring all of their strenuous suggestions for planning and pre-production procedures. He insisted on simply talking to the camera.

On the appointed day, he showed up late and his only visual support was a flip chart with hand-written notes that had suffered the smearing effects of water damage.

The resulting video was the production-value disaster that the video manager anticipated, but the client insisted it be made available to anyone requesting it—as he disappeared back out into the organization.

Within a few months, this became the most requested video in the organization's entire library. It turned out that the mysterious client was a well-known researcher in an area that was currently hot. Advancements were being made so fast that he had no time to properly organize his findings, much less publish them, and anyone aware of his reputation was more than willing to overlook the video's flaws to get the hottest info direct from the source. It also helped that the client was a bit of a character who projected great amounts of enthusiasm.

This situation is so unusual that it may never happen to most of us, but the story illustrates that every show is different and must be evaluated on its on strengths and objectives. If you force octagonal pegs into square holes you will get only splinters. If you ever have the fortune to work with a genuine Mr. Wizard, don't dilute the magic; just get that person on video any way the wizard wants to do it.

Elements of Structure

"We may take Fancy for a companion, but must follow Reason as a guide."
—Samuel Johnson (1709–1784)

In addition to format, there are several other elements of structure requiring decisions. Making these decisions is not a linear, fill-in-the-blanks procedure. Depending on the type of show you're scripting and how your mind works, you may be simultaneously making decisions on several different elements of structure while working out format, or even before that point in the process.

For many shows, a good idea for an opening, a premise or any of the elements may be the springboard that motivates all other decisions on format and structure.

The order in which you make your format and structural decisions is not important. The important thing is to consider them all, take your best ideas from wherever you can get them, and keep working on them until all of the elements of structure in your script flow seamlessly together.

The creative process is organic. The human mind is incredible in its capacity to simultaneously manipulate interconnecting, shifting variables. But to analyze those variables we must impose some sort of order. The following is as good as any:

Premise	**Theme**
Ending	**Image system**
Central idea	**Continuity**

Premise: The Idea That Starts the Story

The opening and ending of a video are its most critical parts. They must function as bookends, in that they both address the same idea with the same weight and tone: the opening states your premise and the closing confirms that your premise has been proven.

Your premise is an assumption that motivates the structure and action of the rest of the show. It's the idea that the rest of the show must prove credible. It poses a "what if?" question.

The premise for a management training show could pose the question "What if we compared the manager to the skipper of a racing yacht?" The structure of the show is then based on introducing the different management techniques and illustrating how they are applied during a race, then showing how those same techniques are also effective in an office environment.

The premise of a product information show may be, "What if a sales-person explained how a solid grasp of product knowledge helped him to close a big sale?" Rather than presenting product knowledge in the abstract, the show illustrates how it helps close sales.

Grabbing attention is the first measure of a good premise. It must immediately involve the audience, making them hungry for what comes next. But obvious gimmicks may create resentment when your audience realizes how cheaply they've been fooled.

A good premise also has substance. It clearly motivates the rest of the show's structure, leading logically up to the fundamental message you want your audience to accept—knowing that this may require them to change their minds about a few things.

The best way to change someone's mind is to first agree with their ideas. Confrontation usually causes defenses to be raised rather than minds to be opened. But if your first statement, or premise, reassures your audience that they are correct in their thinking, you can build on that with a logical argument showing them how they may become even more correct by accepting your message.

In addition to grabbing attention, a good premise provides an apple-pie statement with which your audience can easily agree: "Races are won by seconds." "Knowing more means selling more." This then becomes the foundation from which you can launch a rationale that drives home your central idea.

The premise in Case Study #1, the employee orientation, is that the secret behind EMC's success can be found in the story of how the company was founded and that it is exemplified by the founder himself.

This premise grabs attention by hurling the audience directly into a moment of high drama: a business owner going bankrupt and a more resourceful man stepping in to save the company. It's easy for the audience to accept, because it's a retelling of the American dream: hard work and resourcefulness paying off.

The rest of the show naturally flows from this premise by showing how the values and business strategies that rescued Elgin Medical Labs from bankruptcy have worked to make EMC a success.

The premise in Case Study #2, the sales training show, is that a new salesperson is turning to a successful and more experienced employee for advice. For a dramatization such as this, the premise usually needs to be a decision made by a character that begins the chain of events that moves the story to its conclusion. It is decisions that show character and prompt the action that follows—not abstract facts.

Facts are not premises. For example, "Experienced employees have something to share with new employees" does not motivate any action. Though that fact may be true, it doesn't cause anything to happen, or anyone to learn anything. Before we can have a story, someone must decide to act. In Case Study #2, the premise can be stated as, "What if a new employee decided to ask a more experienced salesperson for advice?" That simple decision becomes the premise for the whole dramatization.

It's a believable premise, because the character is motivated by wanting to earn higher commissions, so the show has credibility. If the premise of the show was that a new-hire in accounting was asking about sales techniques, the show would not be credible.

This "seeking a mentor" premise has additional advantages in that the audience is also newly hired salespeople who will be hungry to know how someone else has found success in their situation; they will probably also be curious to find out how others get along with their co-workers.

Credibility is enhanced by making these characters something other than goody-two-shoers trying to get in good with the boss. They're motivated by making more money and furthering their careers.

This premise in Case Study #2 motivates the rest of the show's structure because Carol must now give Jerry some advice. Credibility is further enhanced because she is responding to a sincere request for help—rather than just telling a junior employee what's good for him.

Ending

A well-structured presentation goes full circle. The premise sets up what you're trying to accomplish and introduces the theme and central idea. The ending ties together all of the points that answer the "what if?" question posed by the premise.

A good ending includes some sort of a summary and a restatement of the central idea, so there can be no question in the audience's mind about the point being made.

Case Study #1 ends with a summary of three core values, reminding new employees that company growth and changes in the industry are creating new opportunities, and if they heed the values on which the company was founded, they can advance "as far and as fast" as their ability will take them.

Case Study #2 is designed as one module in a series of training shows. Its ending must provide a feeling of closure for one topic, while creating a natural transition into the next topic. To solve the transition problem, a time element is used as a dramatic device. An implication of the premise is that Carol, the more experienced salesperson, is staying after work to give tips to the new guy. Carol may be kind and generous but it's too much of a stretch for her to give up an entire evening. So the show has a credible device to motivate a logical ending at any point: Carol says "Just look at the time … gotta go."

In terms of instructional design, the ending creates closure by wrapping up the segment, which is about having "an attitude of customer service." The topic is summarized as the conversation comes naturally to an end. The fact that the new guy is beginning to catch on is illustrated by the line:

> JERRY
> Then by the time you made the sale, you even
> knew her name.

Carol's line confirms Jerry's observation and adds another training point: a tip for discreetly finding out a customer's name; it also reviews the main points of the section:

> CAROL
> Of course. I got it from her credit card. It's up
> to you to take the first steps. Smile. Take an
> interest. Take responsibility for satisfying every
> customer.

Jerry's line restates what this segment has all been about:

> JERRY
> So it's all attitude?

Carol's line then confirms the importance of this segment's topic, sets up for her "it's late" line and implies that there's more to come:

> CAROL
> Not all attitude, but you'll never be a success
> without it.

With the instruction concluded, the time element device is used to bring this segment to an end.

> JERRY
> So what else?

> Carol checks her watch.

> CAROL
> So it's getting late; why don't you just work on
> that attitude of customer service, and we'll talk
> more tomorrow.

A few more lines of banter get some points across on dressing for success and the show is over.

The premise establishes the new guy asking for advice, the ending resolves that a mentor relationship has developed, and in the process, the first clump of knowledge has been imparted.

Central Idea

Let's be realistic about the power of video. A single show isn't likely to change anyone's life. We've done a good job if our audience retains one or two main points. It's much better to leave your audience with one memorable insight than with a dozen forgettable details.

If you bombard your audience with too many ideas, they blur together. Later, when someone favorably impressed by your show must provide a justification for the conclusions they now hold, no specific reason comes to mind—only that the video left them with a warm and fuzzy feeling.

One step you used to get organized was to decide on the central idea. Now, while you are writing the creative treatment, you have a chance to reassess your initial decision, making sure it still holds up and will work well with the other elements of structure.

Your central idea should be a single statement, but it can still be pretty broad, such as "We have the most dependable service." This one idea becomes a spine for the show; although there is concise focus on a central idea, that single trunk can support many branches of information.

There can be segments on the quality of the people working for your organization, the depth of training, the advanced equipment and the immediate shipment of replacement parts. Though each of these segments introduces new and different information, they all tie back to that central idea of "We have the most dependable service."

Without a central idea, your audience is simply bombarded with unrelated facts; they're left on their own to sort it all out. They may reach a conclusion that has less of an impact than the central idea you have in mind, or they may reach an incorrect conclusion, or—most likely—they'll simply be confused.

In Case Study #1, a number of values had to be conveyed, a number of executives had to speak, and the audience needed to gain a feeling for how the company began and how that heritage has shaped its growth.

The central idea developed while getting organized was:

"Take initiative to find problems and solve them."

This still seems like a good spine that will support all of the show's objectives. It supports the premise that the secret of the company's success can be discovered in how it was founded—applying this central idea is exactly what the founder did when starting the company. The three core values can all be introduced as guiding principles to follow when you "take initiative to find problems and solve them."

The three values also provide an obvious structure within which three top executives speak on topics of equal weight. And most important, this central idea is good advice to any new employee who wants to get ahead in a company growing by fits and starts in an industry experiencing rapid growth.

In Case Study #2, we are considering the central idea,

Develop an attitude of customer service

It concisely states the overall change we would like to see in audience behavior. It provides motivation for including in the show information on several different sales techniques and options for handling different situations. It supports the premise that a new guy is asking a successful salesperson for advice, and it is the type of advice that could credibly be given.

Theme Line

Three-word battle cries are what motivate groups to action. Extended treatises, examining every implication, are of interest only to intellectuals—and even intellectuals need that decisive battle cry to arouse them to their task.

A show's theme line provides that battle cry. It's the phrase that best represents the central idea. Most themes also serve as the show's title. A theme may be based on a literal analogy or background, such as:

- ➢ Sports
- ➢ Science fiction
- ➢ Historical events
- ➢ Detective story
- ➢ Space exploration
- ➢ American West
- ➢ Patriotism

Whether or not it has a literal basis, a good theme is expressed in a short phrase that both makes a statement about the show's subject matter and introduces a concept supporting the central idea. Examples include:

- ➢ A Shape For All Seasons
- ➢ Building A Winner
- ➢ Heritage of Performance
- ➢ Partners for Profit
- ➢ Proud to be the Best
- ➢ Quest For Sales
- ➢ Simply the Best
- ➢ Synergy In Selling
- ➢ The Quality Advantage
- ➢ Tradition of Success

Strong imagery and high impact are essential to a good theme. It also must make a certain amount of sense without having to be explained, while at the same time be broad enough so that the presentation can bring new and deeper meaning to it. Characteristics of a good theme are that it:

- ➢ Has a meaning on multiple levels.
- ➢ Is short and powerful.
- ➢ Has a surface/literal meaning that's intuitively obvious.
- ➢ Hints at a deeper meaning.
- ➢ Supports the show's central idea, premise, ending, and continuity device.

Good themes are hard to come by. Many long hours of research and thinking may go into a single three-word phrase.

In Case Study #1, the central idea, "take initiative to find problems and solve them," logically supports the values and heritage, but does not effectively position EMC as to whether it's top quality, low budget or somewhere in between. The theme needs to take this idea one step further, helping employees decide how good is good enough and which priority is tops when several priorities seem to be in conflict.

During research, the client stated its positioning to be no-compromise top quality. The free association list supports this in that the words quality and excellence are included in several places. The theme must reflect this top quality positioning.

The central idea is based on the adage "turn problems into opportunities,"—an idea that is familiar to most people and ties into the American dream. By taking that adage one step further and adding a fresh twist to help it transcend the cliché, a strong theme is created:

Opportunity Into Excellence

In Case Study #2, a theme is needed that is appropriate to the entire series of video modules. "Secrets to Selling," "Selling Smarter," and "Professional Selling" were all considered, but they don't promise a strong and obvious benefit.

For an audience that is both young and new to the company, we can't assume strong company loyalty. The theme must promise a benefit that will bring personal reward and will be of long-term value even though the audience may not stay with the company. The theme must also be an ultimate goal that motivates the audience to learn a wide range of skills. The theme that covers all these bases is:

Success In Selling

The word success has strong appeal. And this theme will support further amplification beyond simply closing sales, because success means a better income and earning respect in a profession. This theme can be taken even further to imply that learning to be a success in selling means learning the interpersonal skills necessary for success in any career.

On first hearing, this theme has strong connotations. Strong alliteration gives it good punch—apart from any specific meaning. It's also broad enough to support additional levels of meaning as the show unfolds.

A danger in going for strong, catchy themes is that of falling into sloganeering. The difference between slogans and themes is meaning. A slogan is often empty rhetoric; a theme must have meaning and substance. If you can't provide a strong rationale for a theme when you are asked, "What does it mean?" keep working.

Beware of puns, clichés and empty phrases that simply sound good. Being cute and clever is amusing, but it won't hold the weight that a theme must carry.

Image System

The impact of video comes largely from its visuals. Seeing is believing. Seeing is also a level of communication that does not have to be reduced to a verbal explanation. The *look* of your presentation may leave a stronger impression than all of the words that are spoken.

Think about your favorite movies. Each one has a certain look to it: comedies often have an exaggerated, cartoony look; action-adventures may have a gritty, dark look; Woody Allen films portray a New York known only to the imaginations of wealthy liberal intellectuals. These visual realities convey the central ideas of these shows. Though the art director is primarily responsible for creating this look, it's based on an "image system" created by the writer.

An image system has two main elements: background ambiance and specific symbols. If your central idea ties in to your organization's heritage of craftsmanship, you may call for locations and backgrounds that recall the shops of master craftsmen from an earlier era. A craftsman's tool can be established as a symbol of craftsmanship. It can then appear prominently on a desk or table in a later scene or become a design element in the graphics.

Look for the telling details that visually embody your central idea. In Case Study #1, "Opportunity Into Excellence," the general background ambience for the show must convey quality and excellence. Every object must be immaculately maintained, clean, and gleaming. The people must be neat and well-groomed, moving with swift confidence, always in control.

During the tour of an EMC hospital, the writer was impressed by how precisely and intelligently the medical equipment was arranged. So in the visual for the code blue alert, there's a specific suggestion for a cutaway:

> Cutaway of a hand reaching for a scalpel or similar medical instrument emphasizes how intelligently organized they are and within an instant's reach.

This is the type of telling detail that will help bring the appropriate look to life. It's a level of visual detail not normally expected from a writer. Some may even argue that it infringes on the domain of the director or art director. But visual descriptions in the script are intended only as suggestions and guidelines that may be changed during production. Calling out specific details is a conscientious attempt to stimulate the imagination of others on the production team. Including such attention to visual detail will help to separate your work from the work of hacks.

In addition to the telling details that create the overall background ambiance, an image system includes specific icons and symbols. A tasteful arrangement of fresh flowers could become a good icon, visual element, continuity device for Case Study #1. It conveys an extra touch of quality and concern. Flowers help bridge the gap between high-tech medical technology and the warmth of human concern.

IBM created a similar icon by using a single rose in early advertising for their personal computers. It softened the computer's high-tech image, making them more acceptable to the computer phobic.

A more practical benefit to flower arrangements is that they make excellent visual elements to place in the foreground to frame up shots. They're also a good cutaway shot, or the beginning for a rack focus shot.

Another possible source of symbols for this show is it's opening scene. Period scenes usually create high visual impact. An object from that earlier era can become an icon—a piece of medical equipment that first appears in use in the opening scene, then as part of an exhibit or as an item of room decor in a lobby, then as the subject of a photo or painting decorating an office. That one icon then represents the heritage that is being handed down from the company's founder to every stage in its growth.

The most important aspect of this show's visual system is its treatment of people. Without being so trite as to say, "our people make the difference," we demonstrate this fact by concentrating most of the visuals on EMC employees in heroic and flattering situations. They are the center of attention. It's your basic monkey-see-monkey-do approach to orientation. Rather than lecturing on how to behave, this show gives many specific examples of the proper behavior to emulate.

In Case Study #2, "Success In Selling," the image system must be warmer and more relaxing. Rather than situations of life or death, it deals with enhancing customer satisfaction.

The background ambiance must be clean and must tastefully display an abundance of product—a visual enticement to come browse for that perfect something. This is an opportunity to reinforce training on how a department should be stocked and maintained, without saying a word or adding to the show's length.

As with the first case study, people are crucial to the look of this show. The new guy's transformation into a professional salesperson will be symbolized by an improvement in his wardrobe, behavior, and grooming as the series progresses. Spitting out his gum in the ending of the case study script is a visual metaphor for discarding his immaturity and cynicism.

Carol, the experienced salesperson, must symbolize what we want the audience to become. Her demeanor and the way she is treated by the camera must create a character that the audience will want to emulate: confident and respected, very responsive to her customers while still being very true to herself.

In an earlier draft, Carol brought one of the latest, high-end electronic gizmos into work. This worked within the script as a symbol for the success she's enjoying, as well as a prop to motivate a conversation with Jerry about the financial success that's possible. It was cut in the interest of time, but it illustrates the way that props and symbols carry an impact that words alone can't approach.

A large part of your show's impact will come from its look—whether you intend it to or not. It's part of your responsibility to consider a show's image system. You must have in your mind a detailed vision of what your show will be like on the screen, so even if you do not go into detail describing visuals in the script, everything you write will be influenced by the show you are envisioning. If your show's look is not intelligently designed to strengthen the show's impact, what is created by default may weaken and even mock everything you put into the words that are heard.

Continuity/Flow

Continuity is the logic that drives your show from one segment to the next. It can be as obvious as a subtitle saying "Two hours later," or as subtle as following the natural flow of a dinner conversation. The best continuity devices also tie into the theme, central idea and image system. Typical ways to arrange segments of a show include:

➢ Chronological/historical.

➢ Follow the steps of a process.

➢ General to specific.

➢ Specific to general.

➢ Geographic/spatial/structure of a system.

➢ Topical/categorical.

➢ Day in the life.

➢ Order of importance.

➢ Problem, cause, solution.

Corporate image shows often start with a chronological history of the company. Not only is this lazy writing and a clichéd approach, it undermines the effectiveness of the show. Think how much more involving it would be to first give the audience a reason to care about that history.

> **Example:** In a product introduction video, we took a patriotic stance, building up to a presentation of Thomas Edison as an embodiment of the American spirit of courage and vision. We showed his invention, the "voice writer," and only then did we introduce three brothers in Nashville, demonstrating how their own courage and vision brought that technology to the people who needed it most.
>
> The full momentum of waving flags and everything that's right about America had our audience up and ready to feel good. By showing that selling office equipment is part of that America, we put some magic back into their lives, showing them how their work-a-day efforts really are part of a heritage they can be proud of.

Compare that level of emotional experience to what an audience takes home from a self-obsessed chronology about your company starting from humble beginnings a century ago.

In addition to the overall logic of a show's flow, some shows use specific transition devices to go from segment to segment. When a newscaster on location says, "back to you …" the audience knows exactly what's happening and they expect a new face to pop onto the screen. That's a transition device.

Many video effects make effective transition devices. A simple dissolve or wipe are well accepted transitions to a later time or a different place.

A clock-face wipe more literally implies a passage of time. A page turn effect was used in a travelogue show, that as a structure, had a couple showing off a photo album of their vacation pictures. For more ideas, take a look at the video switcher that will be used for the on-line edit of your show.

A word of warning: although it's good to understand the effects available and to have a specific effect in mind as you mentally run through your show, *do not burden your script by specifying video effects,* unless the effectiveness of that segment hinges on an unusual use of effects that could not be implied by the spoken words or action.

A script littered with video effects is the sign of an amateur bent on proving a grasp of the obvious. Clients, content experts and account executives who don't understand the terminology are confused and distracted by them. And the production team members, who do understand the terminology, are often insulted by the writer infringing on their area of authority; it seems to imply that they are unable to make such basic decisions for themselves.

Video effects are not the only transition devices and certainly not the most imaginative. In an employee relations show informing employees about a change in management, a racing sailboat was used to show how a skipper and crew illustrate sound management principles. Every time the show went back to a scene on the boat, the audience knew that a new management strategy was about to be introduced. When the show went back to scenes of the office, they knew to expect an explanation of how that strategy is now being applied within their organization.

In a video designed to convince businesses to lease office space in a new building, part of the building's positioning was that it embodied the heritage of Pasadena, a city with a distinctive architectural style. Each segment began with a full-frame shot of an architectural detail from one of the city's prominent buildings. That shot then dissolved to a similar detail on the new office building, providing both a visual transition and also making it obvious that this new building incorporates the city's architectural flavor.

Camera moves, such as a zoom and tilt, or a rack-focus shot can introduce new segments. Cutting back to a map, graphic or flow chart provides an obvious transition. In Case Study #1, "Opportunity Into

Excellence," discussion of three *core values* provide the show's structure. A visual transition is created by cutting to interviews with top executives, each one discussing one of those values.

Literal transition devices such as these are often not necessary. You need only a transition statement, such as:

"Over the years …"

"Today …"

"It began as an idea …"

"At every step of the process …"

"After talking with …"

"Consider the advantages of …"

"Further advantages …"

"Another superior achiever …"

"Even among the best, there is a smaller group who have distinguished themselves even further."

Simplicity is often the best transition. Simply state the topic of the next segment:

"Recycling is another strategy for managing solid waste."

"Containerization was introduced to the port …"

"In the tool section, merchandise displays …"

"Green spaces separate neighborhoods …"

Case Study #2 follows the natural flow of a conversation. Flashbacks are included in the show, but they usually occur within a segment rather than as transition devices to open new segments. Phrases in the dialogue that move the show into new segments include:

➤ "… how about just a few good tips?"

➤ "Sounds good in theory, but you know how busy we get."

➤ "So, what else?"

Transitions and continuity devices can be very dramatic or barely there, whatever is appropriate to the overall structure. The only absolute is that your show needs some sort of obvious logic to drive it from one segment to the next.

After deciding on continuity and flow, you may want to revise your outline. It was suggested that your initial outline be simply a list of content points that are not necessarily in the order they would occur in your show.

If your flow departs from this initial outline significantly, you may want to revise it to follow the intended flow of your show, to help you stay organized while you are writing the treatment and script.

Applying the Elements of Structure

In addition to applying the specific elements of structure, there are two guidelines that will help improve your structure:

Show it, don't tell it

Abstracts on the track, specifics on the screen

This second operative concept is based on the fact that you are working in a visual medium and the fundamental truth that abstracts are difficult to photograph. In short, say everything you can in pictures, then put the rest into words.

Case Study #1, "Opportunity Into Excellence," is about values and heritage. Heritage can be represented visually: the opening scene does this by telling the story of how founder Jim Spanner turned a bankrupt medical lab into a thriving corporation. Values are abstracts, they must be presented in words. The show is structured so that the top executives can speak the words explaining the abstracts, while the visuals show examples of "concern," "excellence," and "economic strength."

When the specifics are on the screen, the voice-over never has to literally say "An example of concern for patients is the way we handle a code blue alert." If a code blue is unfolding right before the eyes of the audience while the voice-over is talking about concern for the patient, it's pretty obvious that the visual is illustrating the abstract being discussed. Our audiences have been well trained by films and television to accept this convention.

To verbally explain it to them is redundant, a waste of time and a violation of the "write for your equals commandment:"

Thou shalt respect the intelligence of thine audience

Case Study #2, "Success In Selling," includes many abstract theories of how and why to improve customer service. The structure chosen for this show provides a very natural motivation for these abstracts to be explained by Carol in voice-over, while the flashbacks show specific examples of their application.

Establish Format Conventions Early

Conventions are all of the techniques and devices your show uses: interviews, examples, talking directly to the audience, being able to hear the thoughts of the characters. No convention is always right or wrong. But to be used effectively, conventions must be established early to give your audience an idea of what to expect throughout the show.

An on-camera spokesperson is a commonly accepted convention. But if this spokesperson is not seen until the final segment of your show, it's jarring to your audience. They wonder where this person came from or where they have been up to this point in the show.

In Case Study #2, "Success In Selling," it feels very natural for the visual to be a flashback that presents an example of what Carol is explaining—because this technique was established early in the show. If the rhythm of the show was established without the use of this technique, and all of a sudden a flashback was thrown in toward the end of the show, it would seem contrived and unjustified.

As a guideline, any devices or techniques you intend to use need to be established within the first third of your show.

CHAPTER 7

THE POWER OF DRAMA

Dramatizations

"Every novel should have a beginning, a muddle, and an end."
—Peter De Vries

It is safe to generalize that most audiences care more about people than about things or ideas, which gives rise to the tell-a-people-story commandment:

> **Thou shalt illustrate how others have embraced thine message and prospered.**

A traditional linear story takes the audience from the beginning to the end of one person's tale. This is the typical use of dramatization. Other uses include vignettes illustrating points being made by interviews, a spokesperson or narrator. Video magazines can include dramatized segments. Even a straight voice-over narration can be strengthened by visuals that show people acting out a story.

Here's an example of how glimpses of several stories added power to a show selling uninterruptible power supplies for mainframe computers.

A flash of electric current etches out a stylized information grid, each node representing a business or government agency.

MUSIC: BOLD AND PROMISING.

SFX: SURGE OF ELECTRICITY AS IT ETCHES OUT A SCHEMATIC OF A STYLIZED INFORMATION GRID.

NARRATOR: The power and pulse of our information revolution:

One of the nodes zooms out from the grid to become an inset of a scene from the interior of a bank floating over the grid background.

BANK EMPLOYEE INTO PHONE: Your remittance account deposits total $10,583 (BEGINS FADING OUT) as of 1:00 this afternoon.

Inset zooms back into the grid to become one of its nodes.

SFX: SWOOSHING BACK INTO GRID.

Inset an airline reservation counter.

RESERVATIONS CLERK: That's two first-class seats from LAX to Houston (BEGINS FADING OUT) confirmed for Monday, May third.

Inset zooms back into the grid to become one of its nodes.

SFX: SWOOSHING BACK INTO GRID.

Inset police dispatcher.

POLICE DISPATCHER: ... victim is lying in the front yard. (BEGINS FADING OUT) EMT unit is in route to the crime scene.

Inset zooms back into the grid to become one of its nodes.

SFX: SWOOSHING BACK INTO GRID.
SFX: BURBLE OF VOICES: ship 28 cartons ... will be arriving ... confirmed on the 24th. at 2:00 pm ... cleared for takeoff on runway ... KEEP UNDER NARRATION.

NARRATOR: With the efficiency of networked computers comes new power ... new opportunities.... and ... a constant danger.

Sine wave appears across bottom of screen, indicating AC current.	SFX: TONE OF SINE WAVE.
Overlay straight horizontal line representing ANSI standard.	Even when wall current is well within ANSI (an'-see) standards ... even in a room perfect
Inset hand adjusting thermostat.	for human comfort ... a micro-second deviation ...
Spike travels down sine wave.	SFX: DISSONANCE CREEPS INTO SINE WAVE. NARRATOR: ... can bring disaster.
Warning lights flash on grid.	SFX: CRESCENDO OF WARNINGS AND ALARMS.

Though no individual's story was more than a brief glimpse, the sum of those stories effectively dramatized how business can be crippled and lives endangered by computer failure; turning a technical message into an involving drama.

The Power of Examples

In addition to being more involving, dramatizations are usually more effective instructional design, because they provide examples of how training or selling points are applied.

Seeing someone go through a procedure is usually the best way to learn it, as implied by the operative concept:

Show it; don't tell it.

Rather than having a spokesperson explain to the audience what they should do, consider dramatizing a real situation where there's pressure and real-life complexities and where something meaningful is at stake.

If additional commentary is necessary, simply cut to a discussion or explanation. A character can "break the fourth wall" to talk directly to the audience, a narrator can make comments, or a spokesperson can enter the scene, or you can literally cut to a class responding to discussion questions on the points just illustrated, then cut back to the action to introduce the next point.

In a training program for insurance claims representatives, the show follows a new employee as she works on her first insurance claim while a more experienced claims rep acts as her mentor. The audience has two interrelated stories to follow: following a likable young woman trying to figure out her new job and struggling along with her more experienced colleague as he tries to figure out how to share his knowledge and insight with her. It's an involving story and certainly an improvement over listening to a narrator explain how to fill out forms and follow procedures.

To add another level of interest and strengthen the instructional design, every time a clump of new information is introduced the dramatization is intercut with a class that discusses how the characters are handling their cases.

Aristotle's Elements of Drama

"The aim of art is not to represent the outward appearance of things, but their inward significance."
—Aristotle (384—322 B.C.)

While technophiles may consider any piece of production gear more ancient than last Tuesday to be verging on obsolescence, the components that make up a good story remain as constant as our basic human emotions. Aristotle pretty much nailed it when he included the six elements of drama in his *Poetics*.

Though often rehashed, this list of has yet to be proven inadequate by any theatrical presentation—from ancient Greece to modern Hollywood. This is Aristotle's list:

> ➤ Opsis—everything pertaining to appearance, including costumes, sets, and props.
>
> ➤ Melos—Composition of the music.

- ➢ Muthos—story or plot.
- ➢ Ethos—moral inclinations of the characters; qualities of the heart.
- ➢ Dianoia—intellect of the characters; qualities of the head.
- ➢ Lexis—Composition of the words, divided into two parts: diction and melody; and the fitting together of the words in rhythm and its overall sound.

The relative importance of these elements remain a traditional diversion during literary lunches and writers' workshops. Aristotle wrote, "The plot, then, is the first principle, and, as it were, the soul of a tragedy; character holds the second place." Academic discussion notwithstanding, for your story to have full impact, all six of the elements must be good.

Opsis, Melos: Sight and Sound

Opsis evolves from your image system, discussed in the previous chapter. The visual descriptions in a script are best kept broad and open to interpretation, but it's still necessary for you to see in your mind the look of the show you're trying to create. It's your vision, so the more complete that vision becomes in your mind, the more powerful the words will become that go down on the page.

The same is true with the music track. First hear the music, to fix in your mind the emotion the audience must feel. Then write the description of the music cues to convey to the production team the emotions to create. The more descriptive the better:

- ➢ "Hip and confident, with a street-tough beat."
- ➢ "Restrained anticipation, building in excitement."
- ➢ "Lively, active, full of purpose."
- ➢ "Ethereal theme with a touch of expectancy."
- ➢ "The tone pulls back to controlled activity with computeresque effects in the background."

The creativity that goes into your visual and music descriptions helps shape the final show just as surely as do the words that will be heard by the audience. Well written descriptions are the sign of a professional.

They set an example for the production crew of the level of detail and creativity you expect from them, while helping them understand the power or the subtlety you are attempting to get on the screen.

Muthos: Dramatic Structure

A good story has a few bumps in it. It's not very involving to watch a hero walk away with an easy victory. The villain or obstacle needs to get the upper hand twice. Typically, the villain—or problem—is in full flower as the story opens, then comes on even stronger to squash the hero's initial success.

Premise

Your premise, an important element of structure discussed in Chapter 6, is the basic assumption that motivates the rest of your show's structure and action. The dramatic structure arises out of the premise, which is usually set up by a decision made by the protagonist or hero. He decides to see the doctor about his leg pain; she wants to apply for management training; they decide to build a sundeck in the backyard.

Once this decision is made, an obstacle or villain gets in the way; and the roller-coaster begins.

Planning the Roller-Coaster

The basic three-act dramatic structure is really very simple: Boy meets girl. Boy loses girl. Boy wins girl back. It's also quite effective and has been holding audience interest since well before Aristotle wrote his list.

> ➤ **Act one**—the hero is prevented from fulfilling the decision made in the premise.
>
> ➤ **Act two**—the hero bravely intensifies effort and almost prevails; but then, the problems get bigger, the villain gets meaner or something else overwhelming knocks the hero back down.
>
> ➤ **Act three**—the hero has been changed into a better person because of all this and is now able to come back strong and prevail.

Analyze virtually any popular movie or television drama and you will find this basic three-act structure.

In Case Study #2, "Success In Selling," the first act ends with the lines:

> **JERRY**
> That's all a little philosophical, Carol; how about just a few good tips?

> **CAROL**
> Develop an attitude of Customer Service.

It's now obvious that the new guy is in for more than he bargained for. His initial decision was to pick up a few quick tips on making more money. Now a new hurdle has been thrown in his way. He'll have to work on his attitude before even hearing about those quick tips he wants.

The second act is usually the bulk of any story. In informational shows this is where most of the content is delivered. In Case Study #2 it includes all of the training up to the lines:

> **JERRY**
> So it's all attitude?

> **CAROL**
> Not all attitude, but you'll never be a success without it.

Jerry now understands that becoming a success in selling is more involved than he imagined. So he has to face another choice: remain the cynic he's always been and say, "not worth it," or face up to the challenge and do whatever it takes. He says:

> **JERRY**
> So, what else?

With that line, Jerry demonstrates that he's made a critical decision, which is examined in more detail later. For now, it's enough to understand that act three is when the story is ready for the big ending. In a movie, this could be the big battle that leads to final victory. In a romance it's likely to be when he finally sweeps her off her feet. In Case Study #2, "Success In Selling," it's when Carol and Jerry have established a good student/mentor relationship with which they are just sure to be happy ever after.

Since the Case Study #2 show is the first in a series of several modules, on one level it could be considered the first act for the whole series—with the premise that Jerry is ready to learn all that Carol will teach him. But it is also a complete 3-act story in itself.

Tension and Release

Good stories have good pacing. High-energy excitement resolves into a relaxed and soothing scene. Serious moments are balanced with comic relief. Escalating success—at least early in the story—needs to be broken with a failure. This was done in the excerpt from "Blazing Quotas" used earlier:

> JOHNNY JOE ARMSTEAD
> Hey, ya know what—we could form our own loan company.

The crowd begins showing some enthusiasm.

> ANNA LEEA
> That offers affordable home loans!

The crowd cheers.

> JOHNNY JOE ARMSTEAD
> And gives good, honest service.

The crowd cheers.

> ANNA LEEA
> We could even offer adjustable rate mortgages.

The crowd is very suspicious of this foreign idea.

> JOHNNY JOE ARMSTEAD
> You mean, like with a rate tied to T-bills?

The crowd hates the idea.

It's an in-joke. It parodied the decision that the bank's management actually had to face. But more importantly, in terms of dramatic structure, good ideas need to be broken with a clunker, to bring everyone back down to earth and to show them struggling with their conflict.

Happy Endings

End happy and demonstrate that it's happy; don't just bury it in the dialogue. A close-up on a customer with a big smile doesn't do it either. Develop a device that shows your character is happy. Maybe your hero is leaving work early to see the kid's little league ball game. Making a sales quota is reason to be happy. Or a happy couple could be hosting a backyard barbecue on a redwood deck that was established as the object of their desire in the opening scene.

Ethos, Dianoia: Interesting Characters

Think about a person you find interesting. How would you describe that person? It would probably be in terms of where they're from, specific experiences that have shaped them, specific things they are now doing and what they are currently trying to overcome or accomplish.

It's the same with the characters you create. Characters who are broad generalities are usually boring. They have no motivation … no conflict. They're cardboard cutouts. In short, they lack back stories.

Back Stories

Even for minor characters, it's always a good idea to write a back story. This is a thumbnail sketch of their lives before they appeared in your story. Where are they from? Who are their people? What kind of jobs have they had? What do they want out of life? What conflicts are they facing? Are they introverted or extroverted … analytical or intuitive?

Then, for every situation and every line you can ask yourself, "how would a person like that respond?" Push it a little bit. Make them a little extreme. It will make your show more involving and it's always easier to pull back some than to pump more energy into a story that's bland and dull.

Conflicts and Villains

Drama is characters dealing with conflict. With no conflict there is no drama, and a hero can be no stronger than the villain or conflict that must be overcome. This open secret of basic dramatic theory is somewhat harder to apply in informational media than in entertainment, because your choice of villains is sharply restricted.

There is virtually no group that can be portrayed as flat-out bad or stupid without jeopardizing the effectiveness of your show.

It's usually necessary to create an abstract villain: misunderstanding, a poor attitude, or an improper technique. In Case Study #2, Jerry's cynicism and indifference provide the conflict he must overcome.

Decisions

We judge people by what they do more than by what they say. The best means of developing a character is by showing how they make decisions: An aggressive character can be established by showing him push through a crowd. A very honest person would be sure to leave all company office supplies behind when leaving for the day.

Once a character is established, your audience is more easily involved in seeing how they react to situations and the reactions of other characters. Are they going to remain true to type, or have they gained an insight that will change the way they think or act?

Having a character experience change is fundamental to a good story. It's not much of a story if the characters don't move on to a higher level of knowledge. Even worse, if there's no change in your characters there is no behavior for your audience to model—keeping in mind the operative concept:

Change the Audience.

In great literature, characters experience profound change. In informational media, we're more concerned with changes like embracing a more effective management style, following safety procedures or enjoying a benefit our product provides. In any case, it's called a *revelation*. Like the rest of us mortals, your protagonists must "learn things for themselves." And in the best drama the audience sees when that happens. *See* is the operative concept here, since the protagonist virtually never acknowledges their revelation.

Exclaiming "I've seen the light" or "From now on I'm (whatever)" are painfully obvious and melodramatic. Instead, we often see a steely look of determination take over the hero's face. At this point it helps to have something symbolic to hurl into a fire that has been conveniently placed in the scene.

The revelation then must manifest itself in a decision. Typically this is the decision that begins the third act. The protagonist has finally become a better person who can rise to the final challenge. In a movie, this may start the final battle or propel the detective to snare the bad guy in a web of his own deceit. In an informational video, it may be when the manager unites the workgroup into a productive team, or the patient retains her dignity despite losing her hair.

In case study #2, "Success in Selling," Jerry set up his revelation by effectively challenging Carol with the line:

JERRY
So it's all attitude?

With this line, we understand that Jerry is still holding out for the "few tips" that will help him improve commissions. He asks a leading question, by stating what he wants to hear: "… it's all attitude." This is his last hope, as he tries to boil it down to a single issue that he may be able to master quickly.

His hopes are dashed by Carol's line, stating that attitude is only a necessary first step:

CAROL
Not **all** attitude, but you'll never be a success
without it.

Jerry is now on the spot. A good director would give him a few beats of close-up as he ponders his decision … maybe he takes a deep breath as the revelation sinks in that this is not going to be quick and easy, and may even be a turning point in his career, if not his life—if he just lets it.

The success of the story turns on whether he will make the same decision he probably would have made before his conversation with Carol, back when he was looking for "a few tips." The answer is in his line:

JERRY
So, what else?

His revelation has driven a decision to step up to the challenge, wherever it may take him. A few lines later there is even a dramatic touch of spitting out his gum, which symbolizes that he's casting off some of his cynicism and ready to enjoy a more fulfilling attitude. Rather than learning a few quick tips, he's now on his way to becoming a success in selling.

In order for the audience to appreciate the profound change that is being driven by your protagonist's revelation, they need a comparison. This is called foreshadowing. You've seen it in most movies, when a first-act scene shows the protagonist go down to a humiliating defeat, or prove unable to afford a simple necessity. You just know, or at least hope, that by the end of the movie the hero will rise far above ever experiencing that again.

In case study #2, "Success in Selling," Jerry's later revelation is foreshadowed when he asks Carol to "… give me a few tips on how I could do a little better with my commissions." He's clearly motivated only by the money, and not even very motivated by that, in that he is interested in doing only "… a little better."

This creates a more interesting story for the audience. We like to see characters grow and change. And that is possible only if you foreshadow early just how much improvement that the hero needs. Just as the only way to add stature to the protagonist is to build up the villain or challenge they are facing, the only way to make their revelation more profound is to foreshadow with a dramatization of how much room there is for improvement in their life.

Human Interest and Happy Endings

Your characters have lives outside of the workplace that can add interest. Your opening can show a character working late. That alone can be a good device to establish that the character's having some sort of problem and it can be made even more involving if you also reveal that it's causing him to miss his kid's band recital.

With that bit of exposition planted in your audience's mind, you have a perfect set up for a happy ending. Through embracing whatever it is your show's trying to sell, your character can happily walk out of the last scene with plenty of time to spend with the kids that evening.

This device works in many situations, if you keep in mind your characters' back stories and what they want out of life. An elderly patient can want a clean bill-of-health before taking an important vacation. A manager can discover that win-win negotiating techniques learned on the job help her reach compromises with her husband. A clerk can find new self-esteem in his personal life by leaning to take initiative.

Lexis: Writing Dialogue

Good dialogue is both natural and concise. Your object is not to write like people really talk—most people are pretty boring most of the time. Your object is to write as they *would* talk if they took 30 minutes to carefully consider every sentence.

Add color to your dialogue. Go to your character's back story and see what type of slang they'd use. Are they sailors, athletes, world-travelers, musicians? Can you slip in some regionalisms?

Almost every region of the country is represented by a book on the habits and speech of the locals. Collect a library of these and every time you need a speech-pattern for a new character, simply choose a book and develop a character from how it describes the locals.

Jump into the middle of conversations. There's usually no reason to include the "Hi, how are you?" Cut right to the relevant comment. Stay only long enough to make your point, then move on to the next scene.

Exposition

Informational scriptwriters have to get content across. Screenwriters have exposition. Exposition is the term used by the literati to describe all of the factual information the audience needs to understand the story.

In a murder mystery, it's all the clues adding up to "who done it?" In an action-adventure it's all the information about who's on which side, how well are they armed, what's a pretty girl like that doing here, and what's with this big grudge that seems to have everyone so worked up?

Exposition can be deadly dull. Audiences have a low tolerance for shows beginning with explanations about who's who and what's going on, or in which characters deliver lines such as, "As you know, General, our troops are outnumbered five to one. They've received no supplies for 3 days. We have no air support. And gallant Captain Chandler can't hold out much longer."

Audiences feel the same about your shows. They want action, not talking. Watch for the techniques used in movies to handle exposition. This can be a good education in how to incorporate content into your scripts. They first make the audience hungry to know why, then reveal only just enough exposition to move the story forward. They also follow the operative concept:

Show it; don't tell it.

Don't stop the action so the characters can slip in a little lecture. Keep it moving, so instead of a lecture, your characters are commenting on the action.

In Case Study #2, flashbacks are used to provide action. Rather than a lecture, Carol comments on what is being seen.

Involving All Characters

Many informational shows are cursed with a "Gee Mr. Science" style of insulting your audience. This is dialogue in which one character delivers all of the content, while the other character's lines all boil down to "Oh, I see," and "Gee, that's interesting." Not only is this stupid and unrealistic, it wastes screen time and bores your audience.

It's better to have all characters contribute to the conversation. Even if one character is the expert and another just learning, the learner can still make assumptions.

The following excerpt from a patient information show on angioplasty begins in the middle of a discussion between a patient and his doctor. Although the patient has no medical background, his lines can still be used to introduce the symptoms into the conversation ...

> PATIENT
> ... a lot like muscle cramping, y'know? Not real serious. Like a charlie horse down there in my lower leg.

> DOCTOR
> It might be some kind of blockage in one of your arteries.

> PATIENT
> But it really feels more like a muscle thing.

> DOCTOR
> It can feel like that sometimes; like, do you ever have pain in your feet or your lower legs when you climb stairs?

This style of dialogue sounds more natural and involving and it gets information across more effectively. Every line both responds to the previous line and also introduces new information.

Here's an example from Case Study #2, the sales training video.

> JERRY
> Sounds easy, but you just naturally have a way with people.

> CAROL
> You know what rapport means?

> JERRY
> A good friendly type of relationship?

> CAROL
> Right. And it doesn't just happen. You have to **build** rapport. Get involved with the customer, notice details, show an interest.

In terms of delivering a list of facts, there's no reason that Jerry couldn't be left out and Carol given a larger block of dialogue, similar to, "That's because I understand rapport, which is the ability to create a good friendly type of relationship. And it doesn't just happen ..."

But that's a lecture. And Jerry just standing there listening is not visually interesting. It's better on every level to hand the dialogue back and forth, with each character saying only a few words at a time.

Also notice the syntax of the dialogue. It's clearly conversational and wouldn't sound right if these lines of dialogue were transferred straight into the paragraph format of a book—any more than words lifted out of a textbook would sound like credible dialogue. In well-crafted dialogue, some words are left out. Certain things are assumed. Because these are lines being spoken by people with personalities that we are getting to know, some of the communication is taking place in subtext.

Subtext

Most of us mean more than we actually say. A parent storming into the house shouting at the kids to "clean up this mess" is communicating his current emotional state, his attitudes about child rearing, his position of dominance, and perhaps a reaction to the kids' earlier behavior. All of this information is being communicated as "subtext"—not so much what is said but how it is said.

Have you ever been watching a good movie and thought to yourself, "I know exactly what he's thinking and how he's trying to manipulate those other characters?" You were following the subtext.

"On the nose writing" is having characters say exactly what's on their minds. It sounds amateurish and melodramatic, and its prevalence in informational media has helped to earn it a reputation for being unimaginative and boring.

Referring back to the patient/doctor conversation, after the doctor gives a brief description of an angioplasty procedure, the patient responds, "So you'll have to use one of those catheters on me?"

The actual words bring up an important point, but the real emotional message is carried in subtext. This patient is frightened and apprehensive, and this message is delivered more convincingly and with more drama by a good interpretation of his line about the catheter than it could be if he simply stated his fears.

In Case Study #2, Jerry responds to Carol's line about trust and respect with:

> JERRY
> That's a little philosophical Carol; how about just
> a few good tips.

The subtext here is "I'm too hip for that, and I don't care anyway. Just show me the easy way." This is good dramatically because it demonstrates conflict between Carol and Jerry. A quote elsewhere in this book contends, "If you want an audience, start a fight." And that's what we have here. Characters with contrasting outlooks on life have tentatively agreed on a common goal: to help Jerry make more money. Now they have to work out on whose terms this is done.

By keeping this conflict in subtext, it is all the more interesting and takes virtually no additional screen time. Carol responds with:

> CAROL
> Okay, develop an attitude of customer service.

The subtext here is "Ok, I'm smart enough to play your game. If you want one-phrase answers, take this and see how far it gets you." This puts Jerry on the defensive, and rather than concede, by saying, "Ok, I see it's more complicated than I thought." He tries to break down Carol's strategic advice into a "quick tip" with the line:

> JERRY
> So I should like ... smile more.

This level of writing is more involving for the audience. On the literal level, they are hearing good advice on sales skills. In the subtext, they are having the fun of hearing two people engage in some low-level verbal sparring.

Part of what makes this conflict work is that it's credible. It's similar to what most of us have observed—or experienced—when people with distinctly differently personalities are thrust together. In this case, in contrast to Jerry's low-energy, Carol is a real go-getter. The ending shows that she's finished her closing duties and is headed for the door while Jerry's still taking his time. It's realistic dialogue. But the message is in the subtext and symbolism. By being on the ball, Carol gets to leave earlier. And when she answers Jerry's request to "Wait up," by saying "You hurry up," we are telling the audience that to keep up with the top performers, you're going to have to put out the effort. They're not going to cut back to make it easier for you.

When Jerry says, "I'm trying," it flows naturally as commentary on the literal action of leaving work. But more important, it also reconfirms—in subtext—the change in attitude he's just experienced. For the first time, he's really trying to become professional in his approach to selling.

He's rewarded for this effort. Carol's "That's a start," comments on the literal action while it also implies that making the effort is the first step and something for which the audience will be recognized and appreciated.

This dialogue may appear to be a few throw-away lines of banter, but it is actually a device for delivering carefully-crafted subtext summarizing what the show is all about.

Were this written in a more on-the-nose style, Carol would say something such as ...

> CAROL
> Well I'm ready to leave because I'm serious
> about my job, maintain a professional attitude
> and follow all the best practices that you were
> laughing about earlier.

This has Carol sounding like a prissy nag, and her lines come off as a self-righteous scolding. Which is not at all enjoyable for the audience because it is essentially they who are being scolded ... ahead of time, just in case they should "be a Jerry."

Jerry's on-the-nose reply would be something along the lines of ...

> JERRY
> Gosh Carol, you're right. I'm changing my
> attitude right now. So I can get my work done
> and leave on time, just like you.

It's hokey. It's not credible. And it sounds just like the dialogue in all too many informational videos. The training points, as well as the plot points, are exactly the same. But instead of enjoying a scene rich in subtext, with characters respecting each other's dignity by leaving just the right things unsaid, the audience is subjected to amateur theatrics that could easily leave them wondering whether the message is as far off as its means of delivery.

ON TO SCRIPTING

Pitching the Creative Treatment

"Credit goes to the man who convinces the world, not to the man to whom the idea first occurs."
—Sir Francis Darwin (1848–1925)

Once you've convinced yourself of the brilliance of your creative approach, it's time to convince the world. The essence of pitching the creative treatment is to gain consensus among all parties involved. You must convince the client and content experts that their needs are being met, and convince the production team that your ideas are practical within existing time and budget restraints.

Whether you're working on a student project or a corporate megaproduction, the principles are the same and the consensus is critical. Without treatment approval there's a big risk that someone may get a big, unpleasant surprise from your first draft script; and that someone is likely to be you, when you discover you've been working under invalid assumptions and you're forced to fall back several steps rather than one.

During initial research meetings it was the client's turn to talk. Your role was primarily to keep the answers coming by asking intelligent questions. When it's time to pitch the creative treatment, it's your turn to talk.

As in any good meeting, it's best to begin with a statement of your expectation of what you would like the meeting to accomplish and what the next step will be. In this case, your agenda is to present the creative treatment. Your expectation is to get approval on three things:

> Tone
> Structure
> Content

The next involvement you will have with the decision maker (or that person's representative) is when you return with a finished script based on the approved creative treatment.

Involve all Decision Makers

This is an approval point. Anyone who must approve the final show should also sign off on the treatment. It's simply good business. Explain that it will never be as easy and inexpensive to change anything as it is right now; which can be hard to say after pouring heart, soul and many hours into your creation.

If you're working through a recommender, be sure that person then presents the treatment to the decision makers and gets their sign off, or at least takes full responsibility for approving the treatment.

First Point of No Return

Carefully explain that this treatment is the first point of no return. The treatment approval meeting is the last point at which anything can be changed without affecting the budget or deadline.

By inviting and encouraging involvement now, you diminish the risk of being blind-sided by some new information at a later date. And if that situation does arise, you can politely explain that the process is being disrupted by saying, "this is the kind of input we were asking for during creative treatment approval."

What's Being Approved

Make clear that you're asking for approval on Ideas and concepts rather than specific words. Reassure everyone that when the finished script is presented, they will have ample opportunity to change any of the words. Then make sure they understand what they are approving.

> Briefly explain tone as the style and overall impression of the show.

> Briefly explain structure as the show's format, arrangement of segments and the creative approach that ties it all together.

> Briefly explain content as the main points to be covered and information to be included.

To be really buttoned down, you may include a content outline with the treatment. But I usually find that this is too much detail. Your purpose is to achieve general agreement, not to scrutinize nuances.

The analogy of the architect's initial rendering is often effective. Explain that you need approval on the overall impression the result will make, along with the basic layout and number of rooms. When you come back with the blueprint (script) there'll be plenty of opportunity to select the wallpaper and position the electrical outlets.

Although this is not the time to discuss specific wording, it may be a good opportunity to take suggestions on the best language to use to set the right tone. You should already have incorporated into the treatment many of the words on the language list created while organizing your research to write the treatment.

Now is the time to ask which words or phrases are appropriate and to ask for more suggestions on the jargon used by your audience. The more you can write with the words and language used by your audience, the more credible your show becomes. Don't expect clients to offer a lot of help here—or even to fully understand what you're asking for—but it doesn't hurt to ask. It can make the client feel more involved, and position you as being professional in your understanding of all the elements involved in scripting.

The big warning here is that the only thing worse than not knowing the jargon is using it incorrectly. Nothing blows credibility quicker than trying to write like an insider and failing at it. Be sure an audience member, or content expert, proof reads every word to ensure that any jargon, slang or language specific to the audience's trade or profession is used absolutely correctly.

Presentation

Presentation counts. The treatment approval meeting is the greatest test of your skills as a salesperson. Getting full approval of your treatment means that scripting will consist mostly of filling in the details.

This is no time to meekly hand out copies saying, "I hope you like it," and stammering out any reservations you may be feeling. Present it. And more than reading it out loud, put your full energy and enthusiasm into painting a word picture.

Enthusiasm sells. And the tone you set will be the first cue the client has about how they should feel about your creative treatment. If you show little confidence in your work, how can they have any confidence?

This does not mean high-pressure huckstering. Many writers are by nature less than flamboyant. This is not a problem, because you don't need to become aggressively extroverted to be persuasive. Overt aggressiveness is often the least effective approach to selling.

Everyone has their own style, and you are most persuasive when remaining true to your own style. Sincerity, confidence, and an ability to express your ideas are what is needed during a treatment approval meeting.

Practice reading aloud. Study public speaking. Take classes in debating, acting or standup comedy. You must learn to remain comfortable when a group focuses its attention on you. And this is not a skill that can be learned in private. You don't need to change your style or personality; you just need to improve your confidence and your ability to put energy into reading your own words.

Confidence is the key and you can't fake it. So a prerequisite for pitching your treatment is to work on it until you really do believe in it.

Edit. Edit again. Keep on editing until you are sure of what you have written. There will be changes. Make sure those changes come from new information you were not aware of or from personal preferences of a decision maker, rather than from you giving it any less than your absolute best.

Presentation Techniques

In addition to putting good energy and enthusiasm into your presentation, there are several specific techniques that may improve it.

The first is to simply set the stage. When you get to the creative approach section, explain that everyone has a hard time imagining what a show will be like from hearing a verbal description. Say, "Use your imagination." This simple request helps them feel they now have permission to relax. It helps them to picture in their minds what the show will look and sound like, opening up to the ideas rather than dwelling on the words.

Team reading is another technique to use if you are pitching as a group. Have different people read different sections of the treatment, saving your best reader for the creative approach. If the approach is written in distinctly different sections, such as voice-over interspersed with dramatizations, you can take this a step further by having different voices read the different sections.

Photos, Artwork and Music

You are asking your client to imagine a look and a sound. Give them some help. Bring in any visual support or recordings that may spark their imagination in the right direction:

> ➢ Music.
> ➢ Sound effects.
> ➢ Graphic art work in the style you are considering.
> ➢ Photos showing the sets, locations, props, or lighting style you intend to use.
> ➢ Existing or stock footage you are considering.
> ➢ Demo tape or head shots of actors with the look or voice you have in mind.

Show only very brief excerpts from videos if you use them at all. There's a danger that they will become the standard of reference and your show will be judged, not on how well it meets its objectives, but on how well it imitates other videos.

How Many Approaches?

Your clients need solutions. Don't waste their time by asking them to be your editor.

Some producers like to go into a treatment meeting with several approaches ready, and some clients like having the choice, but in most situations I feel it's the writer's responsibility to decide which is the one best approach and then put full effort into making it work.

Throwing ideas at a problem is usually a waste of everybody's efforts and often reflects a lack of respect for a writer's time and abilities. Creative approaches are not like tract houses that you inspect until you find one that you're willing to buy. Each creative treatment should be custom designed to be an exact fit. Alterations may be necessary, but just as an architect wouldn't complete several full sets of renderings in distinctly different styles for a single house, a scriptwriter doesn't need to complete several creative approaches.

There will be times when you're not even close, when you have to start over on a fresh creative approach. But generally your work will have more impact and your odds will improve when you put your full energy into something, instead of parceling your energies into several tentative ideas.

Disagreeing Without Being Disagreeable

There will be changes. Some will be obvious improvements. Some will be matters of judgment. Some won't be very good ideas. The best strategy for responding to criticism of your treatment is to accept all of the obvious improvements and matters of judgment. However, it is your professional responsibility to present your client with other options before allowing them to make what seems to you an obvious mistake.

Never say no. It grates on the ear and virtually never has the desired effect. Instead, explain why you did what you've done, offer a better alternative to what your client is asking for, or offer to work out the problem in your next draft.

This is when those sections on objectives and strategy become useful tools. Keep taking your client back to them as objective criteria for deciding which ideas are the best options. Counter attempts to make unnecessary additions by asking questions such as, "How does adding that help in achieving our stated objectives?" Question ill-considered changes by asking, "How does that change help to better achieve our stated objectives?" Or explain the rationale of an element being questioned in terms of how it's instrumental to your strategy and creative approach.

Your written objectives and strategies provide specific criteria by which every element of your script—or requested changes—can be judged. And having specific criteria is more persuasive than saying, "just trust me."

The creative process may be mysterious to your clients. They may not understand the thought process behind it, or see that specific guidelines exist. If you can explain that your ideas and elements are based on the basic principles of marketing, dramatic structure, and instructional design— rather than because they "just seem right"—you have a better chance of having your work approved and earning respect as a professional.

Asking "what's the problem?" is another powerful technique for cutting through the rhetoric to the heart of the issue. Approval meetings can get bogged down in pointless wheel spinning as people begin moving the words around rather than clarifying the ideas. If the discussion seems to be going in circles and focus has been lost, simply ask "what's the problem?" The most effective approach to getting your creative treatment approved is to focus on problem-solving rather than copy editing.

Unless your creative approach has been totally blown out of the water, it's usually not necessary to rewrite the treatment. It's an interim document, meant only as a tool for presenting your ideas and achieving consensus before moving on to scripting.

Developing the Blueprint

"When ideas fail, words come in very handy."
—Goethe (1749–1832)

With your initial sketch approved, it's time to put the blueprint together. While you were writing the creative treatment you should have made all of the major creative decisions on structure and approach, so you're now free to concentrate full creativity on bringing your treatment to life.

Scripting a high impact show is more like composing music than writing words to be read. Though of necessity, scripts are written in words, what you are really combining are sights and sounds. You are designing the plans for creating an emotional experience.

Just as written music is instructions to musicians, your script must be a set of plans that will clearly and quickly convey your vision to the production team that will be bringing that vision to the screen.

Page Formats

"A foolish consistency is the hobgoblin of little minds, adored by little statesmen and philosophers and divines."
—Ralph Waldo Emerson (1803–1882)

The mechanics of placing words on the page are often a central focus of advice and criteria on how to write scripts. I suspect this is because the objectivity of setting margins is easier to master and enforce than the subjectivity of the creative process. In short, neatness counts. If you do not follow an accepted script format, you risk having your work summarily rejected.

However, there is no single industry standard for the layout of words on the page. To be safe, ask your client or employer what format they prefer. Personal experience has been that any format that's legible, logical, and consistent will not be questioned by the more experienced in our industry.

The case studies follow a set of conventions that seem well accepted, and in my own work I'll generally select between those two formats without bothering clients with detailed questions on their page format preferences.

There are basically three page formats.

➢ Two-column—Case Study #1 being an example.

➢ Screenplay—Case Study #2 being an example.

➢ A combination of the two—an example of which is included after the discussion of this format.

Two-column Page Format

This is best for shows that are mostly voice-over. Since the visual description is directly across from the audio, it's easy to see exactly which goes with what, and in the recording session, the narrator has an unbroken column of copy to read.

Television news and commercials are usually written in some variation of this format.

A potential problem is that this format makes it easier for clients to read only the audio column and ignore the visuals. The following is a typical example of a script following two-column conventions:

VISUAL	AUDIO
Sign or subtitle identifies the Commercial Technology Applications Center.	MUSIC: SEGUE TO A THEME FOR CONFIDENT, BUSY ACTIVITY.
Moving shot or montage takes us past all of the activity at CTAC and into the kitchen.	NARRATOR: At the hub of this network is CTAC (see' tack), the Commercial Technology Applications Center.
Sign or subtitle identifies the Commercial Cooking Center.	SFX: SOUNDS OF A BUSY COMMERCIAL KITCHEN.
Caterer at work preparing for a food-function.	Within CTAC, the Commercial Cooking Center is a working kitchen, from which caterers service a variety of functions.
Small group observes food preparation.	It's also a proving ground, where the food service industry can research new equipment and new ideas—before making any commitment.

The following list describes the conventions.

Convention Descriptions

➢ Visual column—left 1/3 of the page.

➢ Audio column—right 2/3's of the page.

➢ Margins—½" on right, 1" on left side (to allow for binding), 1" top and bottom.

➢ Visual descriptions—Single spaced, normal capitalization; directly across from the audio that goes with it.

➢ Names—Upper case, followed by a colon and single space.

➢ Narration—Double spaced, normal capitalization. Some professional voice talent, particularly with news backgrounds, may prefer all caps, but most people find lower case with normal capitalization easier to read.

➢ Music and sound effect descriptions—Single spaced, all caps (to help differentiate it from narration).

Screenplay Page Format

This is best for dramatizations or shows with a lot of dialogue and live action. It breaks the show up into specific scenes. It's easy to skim through and count the different locations and sets. Pacing can be quickly judged by noticing the number of lines in each block of dialogue.

Most movies and TV entertainment programs are written in some variation of this format.

A potential problem is that this format breaks up narration—possibly into chunks as short as a single phrase—making it more difficult to follow its pacing and flow. It's also less intuitive in showing how the visual unfolds in exact synchronization with the audio. The following list describes the conventions. The line numbers to the left will help you refer to the descriptions that follow:

Screenplay Conventions

(1) INT. BRANCH CLAIMS OFFICE—DAY

(2) Maria has just returned to the branch claims office. GREG, a co-worker in drive-in auto claims, passes her walking through the office.

> GREG
> (4) I have those estimates on Bradshaw's car
> when you're ready.

> MARIA
> Thank you, Greg. I'll be by later.

(5) MOVING

(6) Maria hurries through the busy office, RINGING PHONES and other office commotion are heard in the background.

Arriving at her desk, Maria is surprised to see that it is piled high with field folders. Steve sits innocently working at his desk. Looking up, he greets Maria with a smile.

> MARIA
> So what's all this?

> STEVE
> Those are typical examples of what you might
> run into on bodily injury claims.

> MARIA
> I can't memorize all this.

> STEVE
> I know.

MARIA
(7) (SHE NOW UNDERSTANDS)
So maybe you should just kinda help me with
questions as they come up.

STEVE
I think that's what Elliot's been suggesting.

MARIA
Smart guy, that Elliot.

(8) FADE TO:

The following list describes the conventions.

Convention Descriptions

> ➤ Right margin of 1" with a 1.5" left margin, to allow for binding.

> ➤ Line 1—The scene heading tells whether the scene is EXTerior or INTerior, where it is and whether it is day or night, sometimes specifying a time of day such as sunrise or dusk.

> ➤ Line 2—Action description has 12 points of space before, or alternately the scene heading can have 12 points after. In either case it's effectively the same as double spacing. Character names are capitalized only the first time they appear in the script. Character descriptions contain only the details essential to the story (let the casting director decide on race, hair color and other non-essential details).

> ➤ Line 3—The character cue, which displays the speaking character's name, also has 12 points of space before, or alternately the action can have 12 points after (effectively the same as double spacing). Indent about 2.2" from the left margin. Use all upper case.

> ➤ Line 4—Dialogue is written in a solid, single-spaced block, with no space before. Use a right indent of 1" and a left indent of 1.5".

➢ Line 5—This is a heading. It should be used sparingly, as more than an action description and less than a scene heading. Some writers refer to a scene heading as a master scene heading (unbroken period of time in the same location), then use headings to set off specific segments of the scene. For example, the scene heading could indicate BILL'S HOUSE—DAY. The action could start in the living room. A heading of KITCHEN would indicate a cut to what is going on in the kitchen, in a contiguous period of time. A heading of SALLY'S BEDROOM then jumps to what's going on in Sally's bedroom. A heading uses all capital letters with 12 points of space before and after (double spaced).

➢ Line 6—SOUND EFFECT and MUSIC cues are written in all caps and included with the description of the action.

➢ Line 7—Parenthetical directions (also called stage directions) are single-spaced under the name, in parentheses with a left indent of 1.6" and a right indent of 2.1" (.6" narrower than the dialogue on both the right and left). Use these sparingly and only when an accurate interpretation of the lines isn't likely to be interpreted from the lines themselves.

➢ Line 8—Transitionals suggest a visual transition to the next scene. They are all upper case, flush right, followed by a colon and also should be used sparingly (they confuse clients, and offend directors and editors, who usually feel as if this is something they do not need to be told). The one exception is "FADE TO BLACK," which is usually expected at the end of the final scene and is not followed by a colon, or any other punctuation.

Several books on the market go into more detail on screenplay format and its conventions, the most widely accepted standard is Dave Trottier's *The Screenwriter's Bible*, included in the "Suggested Reading" list in the Appendix.

Combination Page Format

When shows combine significant amounts of both voice-over and live action, simply combine the two styles.

The advantage is that anyone can see at a glance what's voice-over and what's live-action. This helps in budgeting, estimating days shooting and length of recording sessions. It also reduces the chance of narration not being recorded during a recording session because it was mistaken for dialogue to be recorded some other time, and vice versa. An example of the combination format follows.

Combination Format Example

INT.   AN EXAMINATION ROOM   —DAY

Mr. Claudine and Dr. Reames continue their discussion.

> MR. CLAUDINE
> So how much pain will I have to put up with?

> DR. REAMES
> You'll feel a prick when they inject the local anesthetic. And with that area numb, you won't feel the insertion of the catheter.

> MR. CLAUDINE
> And that's it?

> DR. REAMES
> During the procedure—when they blow up the balloon—you might feel the same discomfort you get now when you exert yourself.

> MR. CLAUDINE
> So I'll be awake the whole time?

> DR. REAMES
> Right. This isn't surgery, so you don't need general anesthesia.

MR. CLAUDINE
So it's really no more painful than the angiogram
you need to do for the test?

Doctor and patient continue talking as we hear:

Angiography room.	NARRATOR: Angioplasty can be easily performed in the same facilities used for angiography. So if a blockage is found, it's usually easiest on the patient to immediately go ahead with the angioplasty.
Radiologist.	The same physician performs both procedures. This doctor is a medical specialist, called a radiologist.

Timing

One page of script generally equals about one minute of screen time. It's uncanny, but whether it's two-column, screenplay or a combination format; whether it's mostly dialogue, voice-over or action, this rule generally holds. It may vary by up to ten seconds a page for some pages in some shows, but on the average, one page is one minute.

CHAPTER 9

PICTURES AND WORDS

Thinking Visually

"Seeing is believing."
—variously attributed

Think how your mind works when you walk into an unfamiliar room. Simultaneously, and often unconsciously, you analyze the style and quality of the décor. You detect clues to the occupants' lifestyle and tastes. You size-up the people there. You notice anything having to do with your current areas of interest. You check out the mood of the person you are there to see—and it all happens within seconds.

It's not a linear process. You take it in all at once. It's a layered experience, delivering a lot of information. It's exciting, the same type of excitement that video can deliver—but only if it's thought out as a layered experience.

Visually, shots need to be thought out with three layers: foreground, subject plane and background. Subject plane is often all that's considered in many scripts. This leaves a valuable part of the screen unused. Even worse, it leaves two levels of the audience's attention uninvolved. It's more involving for our audience if they can glimpse things passing through the background or cropping up into the foreground to increase the density of information.

For Example, wall art can reinforce the image system. Background action can demonstrate the techniques that are being promoted.

Foregrounds can enhance the visual composition and incorporate props and icons that reinforce the show's theme.

> **Example:** A dramatization during a video on safety includes safety posters on the walls, people walking through the background putting on hardhats or other safety equipment as they walk out into the production area, and characters stopping to talk next to first aid cabinets or fire extinguishers. Safety equipment in the foreground frames up a shot, and a fleeting cut-away of one thing out of place foreshadows the emergency about to happen. That's a lot of reinforcement and scene-setting without a word being said, and only a second or two of extra screen time is needed.

This richly layered feel is what helps make high-budget commercials and movies so involving. Any visual detail or element of foreshadowing grabs audience attention, involves the audience more fully and demonstrates a level of quality and attention to detail that enhances the show's credibility and production value.

In movies, people rarely sit rigidly in place to talk. They pace in front of large windows filled with louvered blinds. They ride in elevators and rush through airports. These same techniques are even more appropriate for informational shows. If your client has factories, stores, shops or production areas, use them for backgrounds. Even if they tie into the show's main purpose only indirectly, they show what your organization is all about and reinforce your culture, make the show uniquely your own, and create more visually interesting shots than standard office sets.

Visual Humor

Background and foreground action are also opportunities to add humor. Upper management can pass, Alfred Hitchcock-like, through the background. This light touch can be more effective in communicating a blessing from management than a solemn shot of the CEO stating to the camera, "Executive management fully supports the directives presented in this video."

A spokesperson's appearance on camera can also be imaginative. Rather than walking into the frame, a spokesperson can unexpectedly pop up from the bottom of the frame, step out of a group, or appear from behind or inside of some object. A shot that tilts down from a tall building can end with the spokesperson leaning against a statue out front. A rack-focus shot beginning on a small object in the foreground or a large item in the background can resolve itself by bringing the spokesperson into focus.

A flip joke can add visual humor: A character makes a decisive statement, then a quick cut shows him in exactly the situation he's trying to avoid.

> Example: In a patient information video, the crusty curmudgeon with leg pain declares to his wife, "No way you're getting me in to see the doctor about this." A quick cut and we see him in the doctor's office ... smiling wife at his side.

It's a proven Hollywood technique. And in addition to injecting some humor, it bridges time quickly, while involving the audience's imagination in filling in the give and take that must have gone on between scenes.

The camera itself can be inside the trunk of a car, or inside a shipping crate. The scene starts in black, with muffled sound. Then, as the trunk or container is opened, the audience is jarred into recognition of this new visual perspective.

Extreme close-ups or extremely wide shots can make an audience wonder what it's seeing. By revealing the mystery, you have their interest—as they search the screen for another visual surprise.

Image Systems

Deciding on an image system was part of writing the creative approach. Now is the time to further develop that image system.

If craftsmanship is central to your message, you may have decided to open on a workshop from an earlier era. Now is the time to rethink that location. What type of workshop would be closest to the heritage of your client's organization? Would an early morning, evening, or night scene add anything? What props could be introduced and used as a recurring visual theme or symbol?

An image system can be thought of as a visual vocabulary; you develop it much as you developed a language list in the process of writing a creative treatment. Images have specific meanings just as words do, so consciously choosing to work with a specific set of images or words creates a distinct tone for your show.

Peaceful imagery helps bring a sense of calm to your audience and creates a perfect setup for introducing the thing, action or idea that will enhance their security. On the other hand, the angry buzz of an electric saw can introduce danger, foreshadow an accident or help build excitement.

If your show is about stalking sales leads in a jungle-like market, show your hero driving to sales meetings in a jeep rigged for heavy safari duty. A pith helmet can add to the effect. This symbolism needs no verbal comment, so it takes no extra time, but it adds impact and makes one of your message's fundamental concepts obvious to viewers.

Abstracts on the Track, Specifics on the Screen

This is one of the basic operative concepts. It means communicating as much as possible visually, reserving the narration and dialogue on the sound track for things you can't take a picture of. To apply this operative concept, first think through every bit of information you must convey; then ask yourself, "how can we show a picture of this?"

If your product comes in blue and green, a picture conveys this information without insulting your audience's intelligence by having the voice-over explain what they can see.

However, while you audience is taking in information visually you can also deliver the points that you can't take a picture of. Your product shot showing the two available colors can be complemented by a line such as, "Available in the two colors that research shows consumers like best." or "… in the hottest designer colors that consumers now demand."

Basically, your message should be on the screen. Narration and dialogue should be used primarily to comment on the visual or the action, explaining why your audience is seeing these images and why they should care.

Very often, words aren't necessary at all. The following excerpt is the introduction to a show promoting a planned community:

Sailing catamarans or other small sailboats.	SFX: SAILING SOUNDS.
Tennis racket hitting ball.	SFX: CROSS FADE SAILING SOUNDS WITH TENNIS GAME SOUNDS.
Happy, active, big barbecue party in a backyard.	SFX: CROSS FADE TENNIS GAME WITH BUZZ OF HAPPY CONVERSATION AT A LIVELY BARBECUE PARTY.
	UP LOUD THEN DRAMATIC CUT TO …
	SFX: SOFT SOUNDS OF WATER LAPPING ON THE SHORE AND LEAVES RUSTLING.
Couple in a reflective mood sitting on the shore at twilight looking out over the lake.	VOICE-OVER: If you could start from scratch—making your dreams real—
Camera follows their gaze out over the water.	how would you begin?

The visual and sound effects in the opening scenes make all the points that need to be made. They also create attention-grabbing dynamics: the subtle sounds of sailing building up to a loud barbecue party, then a dramatic cut to the quiet of the lake shore alerts the audience that something important is about to happen. You don't need words in every scene. Wall-to-wall narration is fatiguing to your audience. Give 'em a break.

Body Language

Actors have bodies as well as mouths—so use them. Body language can be very powerful subtext. Crossed arms communicate that a character has thrown up resistance to further discussion or new ideas. Propping feet up on a desk shows that a character is relaxed. Facial expressions often say more than words.

In the patient information show on angioplasty cited earlier, the visual description in one scene calls for a close-up on the patient's clenched fist. This shows that he's tense and worried without his having to say so.

Camera angles can add another layer of understanding. A low camera angle, looking up at a character, conveys strength and power; a high angle, looking down on a character, conveys weakness or vulnerability.

Including camera directions in a script is usually considered the sign of an amateur, but if you have a specific idea for using the camera that will not be obvious to the director from your script's content and action, suggest it in the visual description; just be careful to do it sparingly.

Painting With Sound

"Anything that is too stupid to be spoken is sung."
—Voltaire (1694–1778)

While visuals are the element of a show that is most likely to be remembered, the sound often has the greater impact on shaping the emotions felt by your audience *during* the presentation.

Music can set any variation of virtually any mood. Sound effects can heighten tension or bring a sigh of relief. Convincing background effects bring life and power to a setting that's only minimally suggested by the visual.

Think through the sound track. Make it work on every level. Be sure that everything on the screen that is capable of making a noise is also heard. Few mistakes make a show seem as dead and unconvincing as showing equipment or crowds without including the appropriate sounds.

You may not be involved in production and have the opportunity to make sure that ambient sounds are recorded and mixed into the track, but you can remind the crew to remember this crucial detail with sound cues in the script.

In addition to background sounds, specific sounds can be used to improve pacing or add impact. Here's an example of how sound effects were used as punctuation in a product information show for investment bankers:

A thirty-something couple play a competitive game of racquetball.	NARRATOR: There's a new breed of investors: active ...
	SFX: RACQUETBALL BASHING INTO WALL.
	knowledgeable ...
	SFX: RACQUETBALL BASHING INTO WALL.
	strong competitors.
	SFX: RACQUETBALL BASHING INTO WALL.
	They demand top performance from their investment portfolios, just as they demand top value and full service from their brokerage firm.

The sound effects add impact to the racquetball analogy, which was established using only the visual and sound effects. A verbal setup wasn't necessary. The track was there only to explain how the analogy conveys the show's message.

Wordsmithing

"In every fat book there is a thin book trying to get out."
—anonymous

When the words become fewer, the ideas become clearer. On the flip side, the better you understand your message, the more concisely you will be able to convey it. Selecting and combining the words for your narration and dialogue is the last decision you make in the writing process, but it's a crucial one.

Open Strong—Go for the Jugular

When starting each segment, and certainly when starting the show, open strong. Get right to the most important point and let your audience know why they should care. Obey the "Get to the point" commandment:

Thou shalt make it quick and snappy

The first sentence in the sales show for a planned community cited earlier asked, "If you could start from scratch—making your dreams real—how would you begin?" With this single sentence we involve the audience, state the premise of the show, reinforce a tone and clearly demonstrate that this is a show about a way of life rather than a place to live.

No setup was necessary. It got right to the point. The audience was grabbed and pulled into immediate action without any time for second thoughts.

Grammatical Decisions

Scripting is writing for the ear (words to be heard) rather than for the eye (words to be read). Since ears are used to hearing conversation, good scripts are usually conversational.

A simple technique for creating a conversational tone is to use contractions. Using contractions doesn't take much effort, it's quite effective and this easy step to sounding conversational shouldn't be overlooked. So don't write, "do not" when you're trying to be conversational.

For a writer who's creating a conversational tone, contractions aren't the only thing that'll do the trick; we'll analyze other techniques to show how they're effective in creating a more conversational style. You can increase clarity and impact if you check every sentence to see whether it can be improved by being edited into:

> ➢ Active voice
> ➢ Present tense
> ➢ First- or second-person voice
> ➢ Gender-neutral wording

The rules of grammar are looser for conversation, but they still apply. This section is not intended to teach these rules, but to help you make the grammatical decisions that will improve the clarity and impact of your scripts.

Active Voice

The term *voice* has both an editorial and a grammatical meaning. The *voice* covered earlier involved editorial decisions on what attitudes and values would shape the overall tone of your show. In addition to this editorial voice, there is a grammatical decision to make about every sentence: Is the subject of that sentence producing or receiving the action expressed by the verb? Is it passive voice or active voice?

Active voice is more powerful and involving. In the following pairs of examples, the first sentence is in passive voice; the second sentence is in active voice, the subject of the sentence is performing the action:

> ➢ A study of the proposal was conducted by our committee.
>
> *Our committee studied the proposal.*
>
> ➢ An inquiry about the building has been made by an investor.
>
> *An investor asked about the building.*
>
> ➢ There were many dead leaves lying on the ground.
>
> *Dead leaves covered the ground.*

The sentences in active voice are all shorter. This alone would be a great reason to write in active voice. But even more important, active voice has more power. It's more immediate and more effectively involves the audience.

Active voice is not always better. In some cases, the thing *receiving* the action is of greater interest:

> ➢ An equity of information is being created.
>
> ➢ Problems are best corrected early.
>
> ➢ Construction was completed in 1949.

But in most situations you can improve clarity and impact by writing in active voice.

Present Tense

Another grammatical device for improving power and immediacy is to write in the present tense. In the following examples the second sentence in each pair is in present tense:

- We have entered the digital age.
  It's the digital *age.*

- Our freeways are choked with cars.
  Cars choke our freeways.

- Rebecca has been an inspiration to us all.
  Rebecca inspires all of us.

The past-tense sentences sound as if they are referring to past events, or at least to things we now accept and don't feel much power to change. It sounds as if poor Rebecca is no longer with us.

"You" and "I" Have Power

Writing in first person enhances authority and immediacy. Your speakers are talking about what they've done and what they know. Speaking in first person means taking responsibility for your opinions and ideas.

Writing in second person helps involve the audience. When they hear the word *you* they know that the speaker is committed to reaching them as individuals:

- ➤ Hold the tool this way.
- ➤ You'll appreciate its lightness and design.

This concise use of second person draws viewers into the show, helping them envision and feel the experience you are trying to create.

It may occasionally be necessary to use the third-person when presenting case studies or using a documentary format, but it is most typically the choice of bureaucrats, functionaries and other timid souls who are attempting to avoid responsibility, tone down their writing, or increase their word count. If those are your intentions, feel free.

Writing Gender-Neutral

It's not our fault but writers of either gender must now torture our English syntax to atone for centuries of grammatically accepted conventions that used masculine pronouns and nouns in constructions that actually include women. Until a gender-neutral third-person singular pronoun is developed, it will be a frustrating task to avoid the offending pronouns we're stuck with—similar to telling composers that the note A-flat must never be heard in their music.

Phrases such as "he or she" and "his or her" are awkward contrivances that become annoying when heard with any frequency. The plural pronoun "their" is now widely tolerated in situations such as:

"Any person may choose their own solution."

But as pronoun and antecedent draw closer, acceptability diminishes:

"A writer and their solution may both be criticized."

Unless you can build your career writing only about inanimate objects, you'll have to learn techniques for gender-neutral writing. Reference books such as, *The Handbook of Nonsexist Writing*,[41] though sometimes strident, offer many useful suggestions. Most techniques for avoiding the dread pronoun can be divided into three basic approaches. Examples of each follow:

Make it plural

- When a student goes to school, he learns to read and write.
  When students go to school, they learn to read and write.

- As a nurse gains experience, more opportunities open up to her.
  As nurses gain experience, more opportunities open up to them.

- Every voter has a responsibility to his country.
  All voters have a responsibility to their country.

---

4   Casey Miller and Kate Swift, *The Handbook of Nonsexist Writing*, 2nd. ed. (iUniverse, 2001).

Eliminate the pronoun

- A handicapped child may be able to dress himself.
  A handicapped child may be able to get dressed without help.

- When a customer has a problem, help him solve it.
  When a customer has a problem, help solve it.

- A citizen is more likely to find fault when she's been treated rudely by a government employee.
  A citizen is more likely to find fault when treated rudely by a government employee.

Use second person

- ➢ *Anyone can become involved in improving his community.*
  You can become involved in improving your community.
- ➢ *The applicant must then provide her medical history.*
  You must then provide your medical history.
- ➢ *A car-owner can save money by doing his own repairs.*
  You can save money by doing your own car repairs.

Write Tight

Words to be heard are different from words to be read. Your audience can't visually fix the words in their mind, or go back and check the first part of a paragraph. Each phrase must make sense by itself. And your audience can't skim the dull parts or scrutinize the hard stuff.

With that in mind, it's obvious that your phrases and sentences must be tight and concise—quick to say and easy to grasp. In short:

Thou shalt make it quick and snappy.

You control the pace, so it's your responsibility to make that pace lively and involving. Careful word selection helps.

The following examples show how syllables can be shed and impact enhanced by paring down some of the corpulent terms that clog our information stream:

utilization - use

cognizant - aware

necessitate - need, or require

substantiate - prove

at their disposal - available

for the purpose of - to

at this point in time - now

revenue enhancement - tax increase

reduce to the basic elements - simplify

Liberate Your Verbs

Smothering verbs within a verb phrase is another waste of syllables— a style common in bureaucratic writing. This increases verbosity and smothers meaning. The following examples may be familiar to you:

make a choice - choose

take under consideration - consider

make an inquiry regarding - ask

make provision for - provide

is negligent in - neglects

conduct the negotiation process - negotiate

give a presentation - present

offer a suggestion - suggest

come to the conclusion - conclude

extend encouragement - encourage

facilitate privatization - privatize

I can imagine no instance in which the above phrases offer any advantage over the single-word verbs. So remember these verb phrases, they are your enemy. Here are a few danger signs to help you spot them:

➢ bland substitute verbs: make, give, take, come.

➢ Verbs or verb phrases ending in: -ive, -sion, -ment, -ization.

Look for them in every sentence. Liberating your verbs adds power to your writing and helps you obey the get-off-your-high-horse commandment:

Thou shalt not be pompous and obscure.

Avoid Redundancies

Though they are used so frequently they flow naturally into our writing, many redundancies that are best eliminated. They include:

during the month of June - in June

plan ahead - plan

first began - started, or began

actual fact - fact

report back - report

already complete - complete

never before - never

true facts - facts

basic essentials - essentials

final conclusion - conclusion

matter of hours - hours

most predominant - predominant

Weed out this redundant verbiage. It smothers meaning and these phrases are trite, conveying to an audience that little thought has gone into the writing. Above all, write simply. *Intelligence and scholarship are proven with sound ideas clearly stated, not with pretentious rhetoric.*

Power Words

Fewer words are usually better. One of the best ways to reduce quantity is to increase quality. If a point isn't clear, don't automatically begin fashioning a clause to explain it. Look for more precise words that don't need explanation. When you use powerful words to say exactly what you mean, you do not need to pile on extra words to explain what you meant.

Stamp out unnecessary adverbs and adjectives. Meaning is carried by your subjects and verbs, not by the words with which you surround them. Does "adding extra interest" say more than "adding interest?" Is a "very important feature" more impressive than "an important feature?" Usually not. Modifiers such as *very, much,* and *extra* may be the most over-used words in the English language.

Adverbs and adjectives are valid parts of speech and sometimes necessary, but in most situations, if your subjects and verbs don't convey the meaning or power you need, find better ones. Propping them up with modifiers is more likely to smother meaning than empower it.

A sentence that uses a general term such as *person* can be made more specific by substituting terms such as *thug, father, shop-lifter,* or *top performer.* Rather than *walking* into a room, that thug or top performer can *sneak, prance, strut* or *meander.*

Precise words have power. They don't need modifiers to prop them up.

The following list of words has been attributed to a scientific study done at Yale University to determine the words with the greatest power to grab and hold attention:

New	How to	Save
Discover	Safety	Health
Free	You	Guarantee
Love	Ease	Money

This next list is a completely unscientific sampling of some words that I have found add power to a sentence:

Deliver	Potent	Growth
Punch	Performance	Action
Enthusiasm	Confidence	Power
Vision	Clout	Depth of resources

Language

During research, you were advised to develop a language list, which should have been a useful tool in helping to develop your voice and creating the tone for your creative treatment. Now is the time to put that language to work again. Here's an excerpt from a script using the upscale hotel language list referred to in an earlier chapter:

Room interiors.	A spacious theme unfolds ... of large rooms for quiet relaxation;
Guest working in room.	or a tempo well-suited to business.
Design details.	Here, you'll find a tasteful harmony,
Amenities package, turndown service, robe.	accented with the grace notes of a warm and personal touch.
Hall and lobby details.	MUSICAL BRIDGE TO A MORE VIGOROUS THEME.
	You'll feel a rhythm that invigorates: a baseline of polished marble;
People on banquet floor during a large business meeting or special event.	a flourish of brass. The power of people and ideas—in concert, making dreams become real.

This language makes the symphonic metaphor obvious, without the narrator having to call attention to it. The writing is in short phrases, each one making sense by itself and primarily commenting on the visual. Together with the visual, the language creates an emotional expectation of what can be experienced by staying at this hotel.

Creating Communications Weapons

To help make your shows more concise, think of what you're creating as communications weapons. They must be fast, precise, packing maximum power into the least amount of size. Ornamentation and personal indulgences must not be allowed. Effective shows accurately target a precisely defined audience; they hit hard and they hit dead-on. Adding unnecessary elements jeopardize your client's mission and risk heavy losses.

Imagine that every word you include in narration or dialogue costs $100. This can be an accurate figure when you consider the number of people who will be seeing your show multiplied by the time it takes them to hear a single word. The cost in person-hours can quickly approach and even exceed $100, not even considering the cost per word to produce, duplicate and distribute your show.

$$1 \text{ second X } 25,000 \text{ people X } \$15/\text{hour} = \$104$$

So not only is verbosity dull and offensive, it's also financially irresponsible. You can't afford to be any more generous with words than with $100 bills.

Pacing and Flow

The best scripts are usually conversational in tone. The best phrases are short, with high impact and strong imagery. Consider this example:

> "In addition to the convenience of having only one number to call for any type of needed information, POST adds the benefit of responding promptly. For any request that cannot be handled within four hours, the customer is guaranteed a progress report within that same period of time."

There's nothing terribly wrong with that. It would be acceptable brochure copy. But it lacks the conversational tone, immediacy, and impact of the following:

> "To one-call convenience, POST adds speed: for any request we can't handle immediately, we provide a solution, or a progress report within 4 hours—guaranteed."

There's a certain pacing and rhythm that makes spoken words sound good: the "melody" aspect of Aristotle's Lexis. Here is a scattering of more examples:

➢ The hard work; the sacrifice; we don't mind it. That's what it takes, when you're Proud To Be The Best.

➢ … controls and instrumentation meshing car and driver into a smooth flow of reflex action.

> As the day goes legato, a setting sun works its magic. From the Towers Lounge, with its complimentary cocktails; to pool-side hors d'oeuvres … enjoy a sumptuous prelude … a perfect progression to the Italian elegance of Cardini's.

> In our residential sections, as in any community, we have different neighborhoods—each with its own character: Condominiums for single people and young couples; smaller homes for young families; and right on the lake, in Clipper Bay, are the larger residences—a home you could enjoy for rest of your life.

> Within the store, you want to see abundance: a lot of product; a lot of choice. Bay ends are stacked high; a visual statement that massive amounts of merchandise are available here.

These examples are also primarily commenting on the visual. They aren't intended to be heard alone. You can almost feel the edit points and you want to see what you're hearing about.

Some of these sentences may not be grammatically complete and correct, but they are what our ears are used to hearing. We tend to speak in short phrases rather than complete sentences.

Lists of Three

A good pace is often set when you use three phrases or items combined in a list. For example:

> Enhancing the setting is a balance of scale: the majesty of the San Gabriels … the comforts of a small city … and on the property—the humane scale of a campus.

> Whatever the future may hold, we'll be there: with a commitment to excellence, in a position of leadership, Proud To Be The Best.

> Innovative programs … creative solutions … for helping us achieve our primary purpose: delivering quality healthcare.

> For professionalism; for knowledge, for personalized service, and nationwide strength …

> Our history is one of leadership, recognized by those with whom we compete, as well as by those we serve.

Specific Techniques

In addition to rhythms of three, there are several words and techniques that will improve your writing style.

Subject First

It's a visual medium and often those visuals need to cover a lot of material quickly. It often helps the pacing and better motivates the edits to begin sentences with the subject of the visual. This is particularly appropriate when using still images rather than motion video.

Architects of Freedom float in the Festival of Roses Parade.	In the Festival of Roses Parade our first entry since the 1950's won the parade's theme trophy.
Close-ups of elegant details combine with PR shots of the ball.	At the Ambassador's Ball, the leaders of Santa Ana raised money for the "Art in Public Places" program.
Marching bands and helium balloons.	At Toys On Parade: 100,000 spectators and 300,000 television viewers saw the Christmas Season begin with the West Coast premiere of giant helium balloons.
Montage of parade and "Summer In The City" scenes.	Last year *was* spectacular. It was fun. It left a legacy and provides a foundation for …

Parallel Statements

Sentence structure that contains parallel construction is handy for a number of applications such as contrasting, comparing, balancing and illustrating associations:

> ➤ As every customer has differing needs, every relationship with a customer is individualized.

➢ Decisions start with people, so Daum/Johnstown starts with the best.

➢ It's not the hours you put in; it's the results you get out.

➢ After 73 years of making Isuzus, we're not about to start making compromises.

➢ The vitality of youth; the wisdom of experience; blended into career paths giving you the best person at every level of operation.

➢ Good marketing means more than pushing *out* a good image. At Pioneer we also take *in* good ideas—during focus groups and through consumer questionnaires.

Parallel construction is also a good approach to lists:

➢ The bottom line is professionalism that shows: when the people and projects are of the highest caliber … when negotiations are complex … when the pressure is on.

➢ It's a commitment … that takes people with specialized training; technology focused on specific applications; and management skills emphasizing cooperation.

➢ Saving a life … Building a city … Shaping the future … Life seems fuller when it's your effort 'Making The Difference.'

One-Upping

One-upping creates a rhythm with which you setup with the first phrase, then pay off with the second:

➢ We've set the standards, then moved those standards ever higher.

➢ Even among the best, there is a smaller group that has distinguished itself even further.

➢ After a decade of leadership, we're extending the lead.

Here

More than a useful adverb, *here* makes a good, quick transition from introducing a place to illustrating its importance. Within that illustration, it can add a more definite punctuation and make more obvious a parallel structure.

➤ Nissan training is like nothing you've ever experienced. Here, service technicians rule.

➤ In medical research and training, we're Making The Difference as a premier healthcare facility. Here, we explore the medical frontiers … Here, you will find dedication … Here, you will find people, known not for what they've acquired, but for what they've accomplished.

➤ Here is where our values are tested against reality; where our commitment to customer service can be measured to three decimal places (referring to testing the accuracy of gas meters).

With

Here's another good transition word with which to create a setup/payoff structure, or to emphasize parallel structure.

➤ With leadership comes growth—a 50% growth in sales every year since 1980.

➤ With creativity and innovation; with proven selling know-how; we build foundations for promotions and product launches.

➤ With every check that's written; with every deposit accepted; the Bank makes a promise.

When

With this conjunction, you can also create a setup/payoff structure, or emphasize parallel structure.

➤ The bottom line is professionalism that shows: when the people and projects are of the highest caliber … when negotiations are complex … when the pressure … is on.

> ➢ When you need it now. When you need it done right ...
> ➢ When your training's over; when your goals are set; when our future is in your hands ...

More

When you need a setup/payoff structure, when you need to emphasize parallel structure; *more* can do the trick:

> ➢ More than the world's largest UPS manufacturer—EPE is your only one-stop source for all computer environment equipment.
> ➢ More than quality products, Pioneer delivers quality marketing support.
> ➢ More than economy of scale, this centralized system makes it easy to stay current with changes as they happen.
> ➢ More than hard work; more than careful planning; our vision includes the force that binds our people to a unifying goal.

Positioning Statements

Certain phrases clue your audience as to whether this information is appropriate to them and their needs.

To Position the Audience:

> ➢ ... a business environment designed for those bold enough to lead.
> ➢ You've worked hard building a subscriber base.
> ➢ The next time you don't want to wait in line, can't take a chance on being bumped, or want to enjoy some top quality personal service:

To Position the Product or Property:

> ➢ A statement of preeminent distinction.
> ➢ A high performance ticket to the way you want to live.
> ➢ The smash 'em, bash 'em excitement that boys love.
> ➢ Rugged dependability.

To Position the Company:

➤ The team to make it perform.

➤ Service you can bank on.

➤ Making everyone's life a little better.

➤ We've made our commitment to the future.

➤ Being dedicated to excellence, it's no surprise that we've attracted the best and the brightest from throughout our industry.

Editing Your Script

"Creativity is allowing yourself to make mistakes. Art is knowing which ones to keep."
—Scott Adams, cartoonist creator of Dilbert (1957–)

Edit. Edit again. Keep on editing. Nobody gets it right the first time, so don't waste your time trying. Apply your seat to your chair and get your ideas sketched out as quickly as possible. Don't block yourself with concerns about voice, structure or grammar. No one's going to see this draft anyway. Don't get it right; get it written. *Then Edit.*

Good writing is good editing, going over every idea and phrase until you have complete confidence that you can present and defend your script to anyone—most of all to yourself.

If ever you feel it necessary to excuse your work as a "rough draft," don't submit it. Keep editing until you have enough confidence in it to present a *finished draft*.

Specific techniques for editing are included in a following section on "Rewrites and Salvage Jobs." But the real secret to editing is to simply put in the time going over your work again and again.

Relax and trust your judgment. You've been entertained and informed by moving-image media all of your life. You can recognize quality. You know when a show is leaving you confused or bored. Apply those same standards to your own work.

The Operative Concepts and Video Commandments listed in Chapter 2, are useful guidelines for identifying and applying your own quality standards. Copy these lists and refer to them often while you edit.

Run your show in your head, making sure that everything you have written will help create what you are envisioning as precisely as possibly. Be ruthless. If any content point is not necessary to meeting your objectives, throw it out. If any imagery or language is not consistent with your theme, throw it out. If any scene or segment does not work within your structure and continuity, throw it out.

You will create thousands of ideas, phrases, transitions and visuals that are very good by themselves, but do not work within the context of the show that you are creating. Be rigorous. You must throw them out or keep crafting them until they do work on all levels. It's hard. It's painful. It's what separates writers from hacks.

Every aspect of your script must be excellent by itself, while contributing to the overall impact of your show. Keep working on it until it's seamless.

Pitching Your Script

"You call this a script? Give me a couple of 5,000-dollar-a-week writers and I'll write it myself."
—Movie producer Joe Pasternak

When you've finished editing, you're ready to pitch. Follow the advice in the earlier section on "Pitching the Creative Treatment." Let everyone know your expectations, what they are approving and that the next step will be the producer taking your script to storyboard or straight into production. And it's always a good idea to remind everyone, "It's cheaper to change things on paper than it is after it's recorded, so scrutinize carefully. It will never be easier or less expensive to change anything than it is right now."

No Rough Drafts

Don't present "rough drafts." It leads to easy answers and sloppy thinking. When the term *rough draft* is seen or heard most people experience a drop in intensity. They've just been told that this is all practice. They'll have another chance at it. They can relax and not take this one too seriously.

Minimize this danger by calling it a finished script or at least a finished draft. Sure there'll be changes, but making changes to a finished script makes everyone—including you—think harder and make sure everything is done right the first time.

This strategy requires massive editing on your part before anyone else sees your work. This is good. It builds your confidence that every idea and every word has been rethought and honed to precision. When you present your finished script, you're selling something that you really believe in. It keeps you focused. It makes things real. It saves your time.

On-the-Spot Rewrites

Writers need time to think. Quick fixes during a meeting are nice when they happen, but don't depend on them happening consistently. Focus on understanding the problems, then fixing them in rewrite. Don't be thrown off by clients who want to copy edit.

If you're told to add this phrase here or include another sentence there, be sure you understand the problem before you automatically react. Throwing words at a problem is often the least effective way of solving it and you won't be able to develop any better solutions until you understand the problem.

If you sense any impatience over your reluctance to "just do it," politely explain, "If I understand the problem better, I may be able to come up with a cleaner solution that doesn't require adding more words." Keep going back to problem-solving. You're a writer, not a stenographer.

Rewrites and Salvage Jobs

Shop rates for all work performed—$25/hr.
If you watch—$50/hr.
If you help—$75/hr.

—variously attributed

The big question with rewrites is: yours or theirs? Rewriting your own work is a natural step in the process. Salvaging someone else's script is often more time consuming that starting from scratch.

In either case, you must decide how extensive a rewrite is needed. There are 4 basic levels:

➢ Word Changes

➢ Rewriting for language

➢ Structural rewrites

➢ Creative rewrites

Word Changes

This lightest of rewrites is basically just changing a few words or numbers to get your facts straight and your style more consistent with the client's preferences.

Terms may have certain connotations and specific meanings of which you were not aware. *Consumer* and *customer* are synonymous to some organizations but not to others. I've had a client take offense at the term *employee*, insisting that everyone in their employ is a *coworker*. *Divisions* may include *departments*, or the other way around, depending on client preference. These are relatively painless changes to make, but they may loom large in the mind of your client.

In several situations, clients have expressed great concern about a script being "way off," or needing "major changes." When I met with them, I discovered that the sales figures were off by 10 percent, or that I'd used a term such as "matrix management," when that was the label they used for a management approach that had failed in the past, and they were now "encouraging involvement."

For a writer these word changes are easy-to-make, but for the client they were major mistakes. So when anyone says your script needs "major changes," don't overreact. Ask "What's the problem?" You may find that a "major solution" involves nothing more than changing a few words.

On the other hand, when a client reassures you that "all the information's there, you just need to move a few things," you may have a major restructuring job on your hands.

In short, don't expect clients to understand your job or accurately assess the level of damage control necessary. Ours is not to ask "How bad?" Ours is to ask, "What's the problem?"

Rewriting for Language

Rewriting for language is more difficult than simply changing words. It includes rewriting for grammar, tone, and style. But since it's essentially a sentence-for-sentence rewrite, it's easier than changing structure or creative approach.

To shed verbiage and enhance impact, make all of the grammatical changes suggested earlier under "Wordsmithing." Here are a few examples:

> To the loggers, the forests were an endless resource that seemed to go on forever. They could not even imagine that they might one day be wiped out.

This paragraph can be made more lyrical and the confusing double use of "they" in the second sentence can be eliminated; yielding:

> The loggers had no idea that what seemed to go on forever might some day be gone forever.

Another example:

> Golf fans can enjoy watching the action or participate themselves in the Mayor's Cup Golf Tournament.

This sentence can be made even more active and energetic:

> Golf fans can take the challenge or watch the action at the Mayor's Cup Golf Tournament.

Another example:

> Many areas in this major city still don't seem like part of a city, or have a strong identity of any sort, for that matter. They are still like the area was before it became so rapidly urbanized.

This paragraph can be simplified:

> Many areas are still essentially blank slates—having less in common with a major city than with a short and rural history.

A more fundamental problem would be an inappropriate voice that talks down to the audience or is too didactic. In this case, review the segment on "Active Voice," envision a more appropriate relationship with your audience and attempt a sentence-for-sentence rewrite in the new voice.

Some scripts can't be salvaged this easily and fall into the category of structural rewrites.

Structural Rewrites

A script needs a structural rewrite when it's confusing, unfocused, and burdened with problems such as:

➤ Redundant sections.

➤ No motivating logic to the continuity.

➤ No clear central idea.

If any or all of these are the case, you'll want to take the script apart, while attempting to leave the individual segments intact and maintain the creative approach.

Outlining the show again may be helpful. File cards with a single section on each may help in shuffling these sections around. The outlining feature, provided by many word processing programs, is also an effective means of restructuring a show.

Restructuring is similar to assembling a jigsaw puzzle, in which some of the pieces need to be whittled a little to make them all create the proper picture.

You must first understand what that finished picture will be. So a crucial step in a structural rewrite is reviewing—or perhaps stating for the first time—the show's purpose, objectives, and structural elements.

With those decisions rethought and firmly in mind, review each section in terms of which objective it achieves, how it must be logically arranged within your approach to continuity and how it supports your format and creative approach. You may be able to delete or combine sections, thereby eliminating redundancies.

In an employee orientation show it may seem logical to mention information technology (IT) in both the section on administration and the section on internal communication. But seeing computer-related visuals twice in the same program may seem redundant to your audience. An important aspect of a structural rewrite is eliminating these redundancies. So you could cover IT in one section then cover only the communication processes it makes possible in the other.

This would most likely strike your audience as a logical progression through sections that each have a distinctly different look. Although both sections address IT-related issues, the first focuses on the resources and administration needed to make the technology work—supported by pictures of the technology. The other section focuses on the improved internal communication made possible—the benefits of technology—supported by pictures of people engaged in fulfilling work.

Once the sections are purged of redundancies and unneeded information, and reassembled according to the logic of your continuity, a language rewrite will help it all fit smoothly together.

Creative Rewrites

There are times when the script isn't even close. This happened on a project for an electric utility company.

Through a series of miscommunications, I understood that the purpose of their show was to sell the commercial cooking industry on the benefits of cooking with electricity.

The premise developed was that some ideas that worked well in the past work even better today; we developed the analogy of commuting by train.

Only after completing a finished draft was it revealed that the show's primary purpose was to position the utility's Commercial Application Center as a neutral testing facility and information resource. An obvious sales piece would contradict this message, so the script's premise and entire creative approach were shot right out of the water.

The only legitimate thing to do was start over again, scrapping the train idea. What evolved was a straight-forward documentary that opened with quick takes of restaurant owners talking about problems they had faced that were typical throughout their industry. This led naturally to showing how the research facilities helped them solve those problems.

The obvious subtext was that going electric was part of the solutions that were developed, but by making that a supporting idea rather than the central idea, the show lost its sales-pitch tone and became a public relations show—effectively positioning the utility as a research facility supporting independent research.

Although the same information was conveyed, the creative approach had to be completely revamped, which meant that everything other than the research had to be redone.

This often happens when a client supplies what they call a "finished script." "All the information's there, it just needs a little rewrite." Be careful, the qualifying statement that "it just needs to be jazzed up a little," or "put it into that format you guys use," can be interpreted to really mean that a creative rewrite is necessary.

Rather than saving you a step, this client may have added another one: you now have to decode the information from the initial "script" into the basic facts, research the audience, identify behavioral objectives, and take it from the top again.

Analyze the situation carefully before agreeing that a client-supplied "script" will make your job any easier or quicker.

LIFE IN THE FOOD CHAIN

The Corporate Environment

"The mark of the true M.B.A. is that he is often wrong but seldom in doubt."
—Robert Buzzell, Harvard Professor of Marketing, (1933–2004)

Although cultures at different companies vary they all share the basic values of our American corporate culture, and like all cultures, this one has its elite.

In early cultures the warrior class was the elite. They were the strongest, the fastest, and often the smartest. They took the risks and felt the pressure. In return they received the biggest share of the tribe's wealth and prestige.

Today, corporate executives are our warrior class. Check the ads in Forbes and Fortune and you'll find a culture that pays homage to no-compromise determination coupled with the expectation of ample reward. The underlying tone of most corporate media is determined by the values of our corporate executive/warrior class:

➤ Highly competitive.

➤ High value placed on initiative, assertiveness, and risk-taking.

➤ Facing an accelerating rate of change.

➤ All decisions ultimately determined by the bottom line.

To design effective corporate shows, we must understand this corporate culture. Of course, a certain degree of skepticism is always healthy—part of our role is to play the devil's advocate. But on the whole, if it doesn't make sense to us, we won't be able to convince our audience.

Guaranteed Non-Failures

As many now-forgotten computer companies have discovered, no purchasing agent ever got fired for buying IBM. And a guaranteed non-failure is just as attractive to those who make video decisions.

Innovation and economy have their appeal, but you can never overestimate the allure of safety. Most informational shows are basically tools. They don't need to break new ground. They just have to meet requirements.

This is why being buttoned down works. Clients need to feel comfortable that all the basics are covered and that there's plenty of reserve before any chances are taken. Which is not to advocate taking the most conservative approach—no one likes unimaginative drivel, either. Most clients want to challenge the peaks a little, but they want to do so with a guide they're sure will get them back safely.

The secret is to learn what your client considers creatively adventurous. While one client may think anything beyond wall-to-wall narration is dangerously progressive, another may be comfortable approving the corporate equivalent of "Star Wars."

Then, assess your own abilities. What approach will create an interesting challenge without jeopardizing your confidence? With these two decisions in mind, lead your client through a creative process that nudges their limit of creative adventurousness without allowing them to perceive danger.

If you feel that your organization needs to take a more creative approach to its productions, the quickest way of bringing this about may be to slow down and ease them into it one step at a time, consistently making every production a little bit more imaginative. Actively solicit comments on this increased creativity, then make the decision makers aware of any positive comments from other decision makers and the intended audience.

Virtually every example in this book has been paid for by a client, although not all of these clients would feel that *all* of these ideas were worth buying. Your message must be tailored to the needs of your audience, but your level of creativity must be tailored to the comfort level of your client. You really have two audiences for every show: the people who will watch it and your client, who must feel safe with your ideas before the intended audience will ever see them on the screen.

No Dull Subjects, Only Dull Writers

Informational scriptwriting can be a creative and rewarding job. In the first place, we aren't subject to the agonizing scrutiny applied to television commercials or entertainment media, and since many of our shows are never seen by the general public, we're often given more creative leeway.

For example, a show for bank personnel revolved around a Wild West poker game, with the individual players representing the bank and its different competitors. Dodge City could freeze over in August before customers would ever be allowed to see their bank portrayed as a pistol-totin' card sharp in a Stetson. But since this show was intended for employees, we got creative, our audience had fun and our point about the intense competition in the financial industry came through loud and clear.

Scriptwriters also work with an incredibly broad palette. Unlike writers in print media, we can simultaneously mix any number of elements: photography, graphics, music, sound effects, dialogue, color, lighting, narration, visual effects, pacing, camera angle … the list continues and grows more subtle. The point is that by applying imagination to mixing these elements even the most mundane topics present a creative challenge.

Exploitation

There is no shortage of people in this world willing to exploit you, just as there is no shortage of people willing to be victimized. They tend to find each other.

Many organizations put unrealistic demands on their people, either intentionally or from ignorance. They do not allow adequate time or resources for doing good work. They don't provide needed direction. They withhold recognition or praise, while relying heavily on intimidation and cynicism.

Many creative people working in such places allow their lives to be shaped, frustrated or squandered by people who know little about our craft, care even less, and consider a commitment to doing quality work a perverse form of egocentricity. Their motivation is power and control. They recognize and reward perceived political allies, while remaining oblivious to the quality of what goes on the screen.

They've often won their authority by manipulation and self-promotion, and by asserting that they "understand creatives and know how to keep them in line." They get away with it because there's a constant stream of talented individuals willing to hand over responsibility for their future in exchange for some perceived benefit. They may assume this will save them from being bothered by company politics or that they won't need to hustle for work.

It's a risky bargain. Don't assume that if you are excellent at what you do, you will be justly rewarded and spared the complexities of life in the food chain; to do so makes it all the easier for you to be exploited and deprived of what you feel that you deserve. Good work speaks for itself only when someone who appreciates it is willing to listen.

Some exploiters are worse than others and since your choice of employment options may not always be bountiful, you may need to work with some of these people. So the question becomes, how? We can't change them. Don't bother.

Don't expect exploiters to know when they've asked for too much. They will keep asking and taking with no regard to the toll on your health or personal life. Exploiters see you as a commodity to be used up rather than a resource to be developed.

It is not a good idea to play their game—they're much better at it. A wiser choice is to remain true to your own values. Be vocal in opposing any compromise to the quality of your work. This gives you the moral high ground. Rather than bickering over narrow self-interests, you are defending the integrity of your profession. And to best serve your profession, you must have a balanced life, time to do your work, and respect for your efforts. You may lose many of these battles, but every one is an opportunity to state your position. Determined consistency wins more respect and longer-term results than frenzied outbursts.

Even more important, take responsibility for your career and look for people who will respect and develop your talents. Take credit for your ideas and contributions. Self-promotion is a time-honored American tradition—and the *only* thing many people have going for them. Push for on-screen credit. Be there when your shows premiere. Write news releases to be sent to internal newsletters, appropriate Web sites, and industry trade journals. Maintain a profile at organization functions. Maintain a professional-looking Web site to showcase your accomplishments. Find the conscientious people within your organization and let them know they have an ally in you.

It's easy to be pushed into an endless cycle of putting every second into beating the next deadline. Don't do it. Throw the responsibility back where the authority lies. State, "You're jeopardizing the quality of our work by not allowing enough time." Don't automatically assume responsibility when someone else's mistakes in judgment lead to last-minute panic. And when you do take on such a project, make sure you are recognized for it. Negotiate the compensation up front: comp time, adjusting another deadline or hiring another person. If you quietly and valiantly clean up someone else's mess, you may quickly become taken for granted.

Know what you're looking for in terms of financial compensation, standards of quality, and control of your hours. If you get it, stay; if not, move. Don't waste time on who's right and who's wrong. It's pointless to become engaged in a battle of morals. Don't expect apologies or appreciation, and above all, never expect anyone to admit they've been wrong.

People who continue working in exploitive situations tend to be a bit bovine in their outlook: They just go through the motions, frequently grumbling about what "they are making us do now." They begrudge any effort expected of them and they may subconsciously prefer working in a situation where there's always someone else to blame and always an excuse for failure.

On the other end of the spectrum are situations in which people are appreciated and encouraged to do their best. Those in charge look out for their people and express appreciation for top performance. People working in these organizations tend to take an active interest in their work, take initiative, and show pride of accomplishment.

These organizations also tend to be the best in their field. To work there you need a high level of self-motivation and a commitment to giving everything you've got to every project. For mistakes and failure there's no one else to blame.

Where you work is who you are. Choose appropriately.

Ethics

"Bulls make money and bears make money, but pigs seldom prosper."
—Wall Street maxim

Currently, the world doesn't expect much from informational scriptwriters. We're the people who string the words together, with all the "important" decisions about the pictures being made by a non-specific someone else. So you may be able to get by if you write spoken brochures.

Some writers are paid to write skimpy scripts with visual descriptions that say little more than "appropriate visuals," or "visuals follow the action." These people have learned to dodge responsibility by saying, "Well, what do you *want* me to write, then?"

They do what they're told, contributing nothing. Then they complain that "They don't know what they're doing," "They keep changing their minds," and "They always give me such dull scripts to write."

They're taking dictation. Pity them, but don't emulate them.

Just Do It

You've finished a script you can be proud of and given it your best pitch. Your client wants a few days to go over it. When it finally comes back to you, it's covered with qualifying phrases and additional words you are supposed to add.

It would be easy to follow direction—a simple clerical exercise. It could also turn a well-crafted script into a tangled mass of bureaucratic jargon. The producer tells you, "just do it."

No one can fault you for doing what you're told, but consider the consequences of compromising the quality of your work. In the short term, this will not be a sample you are proud to show. In the longer term, you are reinforcing among everyone involved that this is the way to do things, and changing this attitude will only be more difficult next time.

Another consideration is that the resulting show may be an embarrassment—with your name on it. Detractors may use it as an example when making the point that "we've tried making videos and they don't work for us." Not only will you jeopardize your own future with this organization, you'll poison the well for others.

Never expect the client or decision maker to take responsibility for forcing you to create a worthless show. Nobody likes to admit a mistake. Keep in mind the five steps of a project that were facetiously described in Chapter 2. The fourth step was "Search for the Guilty." When embarrassing questions are asked, it's often easier to simply designate a scapegoat and punish that person than to honestly deal with complex issues. Your client may look around to see who the most expendable person is with some level of authority, and you are a likely victim. It's happened to me; it can happen to you.

Playing the scenario the other way offers no easy answers either. Your alternative to just doing it is to talk with the decision makers again. Ask for a chance to solve the problems that concern them in a way that better uses the medium, go through the script line-by-line with them, asking "What's the problem?" Then do whatever level of rewrite is necessary to solve those problems.

This is a lot more work for you, but don't expect this level of conscientiousness to be appreciated. You're also asking the decision makers to spend more time, so you may be seen as a trouble-maker. Choose your words carefully when you suggest this approach, you need everyone to understand that you are proposing this because of your commitment to quality rather than because you insist on doing everything your way.

You may lose a few battles. You may lose most of them, but by consistently advocating professionalism and quality, those who understand the situation will know that the problems are happening in spite of your efforts rather than because of them. And you have fulfilled your professional responsibility to point out the possible consequences of what you are being asked to do.

Alternatives to Saying No

Ultimatums and confrontations seldom work. The word *no* grates on any ear. Suggesting options is a better approach. In the "Just do it" scenario, it was not necessary to tell the client "No, these changes will wreck the script and I won't do it." Instead, you offered an option by saying, "I understand that there are problems and think I can offer a better solution."

The secret is to make a distinction between the person and the problem. Forget about who's right and who's wrong, and focus on problem solving. It's not necessary to teach the client a lesson, or to lecture on how the rhythm and flow of your creation is being destroyed. Focus instead on their positive contributions. They've identified some problems, so thank them for their effort and ask for the opportunity to solve those problems.

Rather than punishing them by forcing them back a step to do everything your way, keep moving forward. Try to understand their expectations and approach to problem-solving, then devise a plan that will accommodate both their way of thinking and a result with which you are comfortable. Keep in mind the operative concept:

Focus on results rather than process.

It's easier to get cooperation when you're all working for the same results, rather than you forcing others to learn a new way of doing things. This approach takes time, but far less time than going to war over whose way is better, or who's the expert. Cooperation is usually the only way to create a quality show. When they finally see positive results on the screen, most reasonable people are more likely to do things the right way next time.

Another alternative to saying no is to offer rationales. A well-crafted script is more complex than most clients—and many producers—realize. They may not understand the systematic approach you've taken. This book presents a vocabulary you can use to reveal the many levels of thought that have gone into your work.

If you are asked to make an ill-considered change, explain the problem it creates. For example, you might say, "the show's premise will not support that and if we change the premise it will weaken the presentation of the three points you've told us are the most important. So we can do that, but not without weakening the show's overall effectiveness."

This level of professionalism elevates the conversation past the level of "my ideas are better than your ideas." Your clients and colleagues can now appreciate that your script is more than a series of random inspirations and that any single change may create consequences that ripple throughout the script.

Become familiar with at least the basic concepts and terminology of dramatic structure, instructional design, and marketing. To effectively defend your scripts, you must be able to verbalize what you are trying to accomplish without having to resort to, "Just trust me or you'll be sorry."

Do They Need What They Want?

There will be times when you're asked to write a script for a show that you realize is either misdirected or a flat-out waste of budget. This most often happens during periods when you're desperate for work. So what do you do: Do what they want, or encourage them to fall back and reassess their needs?

To just do it may get you through to the next check, but what happens if those who signed that check realize they didn't get full value. Accepting blame is not a common trait among mortals. They are more likely to choose one of the following explanations:

➢ You or the production team didn't do it right.

➢ Video doesn't work for us.

➢ The results we get with video are too inconsistent to depend on.

➢ All of the above.

With any answer, you lose.

Taking the other course—reassessing their needs—may cost you the job you want, but there's also a chance that it could reveal that they need more than they initially realized and that it's work you can do. You could actually come out ahead, but even if you lose the job, you come out ahead long-term. You gain credibility and position yourself as a responsible team player, a safety check on decisions made by others. You've shown that you're more than a hack mindlessly doing what you're told. You're a professional who can think and can be trusted with more authority the next time around.

Get the Bad News Out Early

It's never easy to ask for more time or money. But if these issues arise, the sooner you address them the less painful it is.

If your deadline is tomorrow and this afternoon you're told to change everything but the right margin, don't expect anyone to realize that you'll need more time. Explain this fact to them *now*. If you fail to do so and also fail to meet your deadline tomorrow, you're the one who will be blamed.

Timing is everything. If you play the option game now and say "Sure I can make these changes, but I'll need more time," you'll position yourself as a good manager. If you wait until someone calls to ask, "Where's that script you were supposed to have had here an hour ago?" and you respond with, "I've been working on it three days straight, I've had only four hours of sleep this whole week and it's your fault for all these changes," you'll probably be perceived as inexperienced, a poor manager of your own time, and incapable of understanding the scope of the work involved.

As things get tense and revisions come fast, don't expect clients to keep track of whose decision at what time caused you to spend twice as much time as budgeted. Their concern is to get the show they need, if that is going to take more than you had bargained for, your only hope of being compensated—or even recognized—for your heroics is to arrange it up front.

As soon as you realize that any decision or action by the client will require more effort than you're willing to give away, ask for written confirmation of the decision and its cost. You can make your request in a very positive manner. Explain the consequence at the same time you accept the additional work. For example, you might say, "Sure I can add a segment on the product that just came out of R&D. It's an addition to what we had agreed to do, so we'll need to schedule and budget another few hours of scripting and it will probably increase time in production, but I'm sure we can handle it for you."

If the client agrees, get written authorization. Depending on your organization, this may take the form of a change order, conference report or a memo. It doesn't need to be elaborate—just something on paper to remind your client that in the heat of the battle they agreed to pay for the consequences of their decisions.

It's simply good business and extra comfort factor. Any reasonable client will appreciate knowing up front the consequences of their decisions as they are made.

The other approach—doing whatever it takes and sorting it out later—virtually guarantees hard feelings all around. The client may honestly not have realized they would be charged overages. When you ask for them after the fact, it sounds as if you let the situation get out of hand and are now looking for someone to pay for your mistakes.

Good news is a nice surprise. But bad news only gets worse. Get it out of the way right away.

Legal Considerations

"I don't know as I want a lawyer to tell me what I cannot do. I hire him to tell me how to do what I want to do."
—J.P. Morgan (1837–1913)

The needs of our industry fall on both sides of the copyright laws: we need protection for what we create and we need to be able to incorporate the copyrighted work of others into our shows.

Copyright

In 1978, a completely new copyright statute came into effect, providing greater protection for the creators of intellectual property and making it easier to get that protection—so easy in fact that it's automatic.

According to information published by the Copyright Office (http://www.copyright.gov/video/script.html):

> "Registering an original work with the Copyright Office is not required to maintain copyright protection under the present law. Once an original work is written down, recorded, or tangibly fixed in an acceptable form, it is, in effect, copyrighted, and no action by the Copyright Office is necessary."

There are however some advantages to registration: It establishes a public record of your copyright claim, it's a necessary step in filing an infringement suit and it allows you to collect attorney's fees in addition to actual damages and profits if you have to take a case to court.

Registration is fairly simple. Send in a completed application form, a filing fee (check or money order), and one copy or your script if it has not yet been produced and distributed, two copies if it has.

It is best to send all three items to the Copyright Office at the same time and in the same package. Send this package to:

> The Register of Copyrights
> Copyright Office
> Library of Congress
> Washington, D.C. 20559–6000

Information on the fee currently being charged, and the page from which application forms can be downloaded, can be found on the Web site maintained by the Copyright Office: http://www.copyright.gov/.

Although the copyright notice was required prior to March 1, 1989, it is now optional. If you choose to display it on your script or finished video, it should be clearly visible and contain the following elements:

➢ The "c" in a circle symbol ©, or the word "copyright," or the abbreviation "copr."

➢ Year of first publication.

➢ Name of the owner of copyright.

In practice, most informational shows have little value to anyone other than the clients for whom they are created, so unless you have created a script that has a potential for additional applications, it may be of little value to register it.

On the other side of the coin, you must be careful not to violate the copyrights of others. This becomes an issue when your specify music or existing footage or images.

It's never a good idea to specify a popular piece of music in a script unless your client is willing to pay for synchronization rights to use it (synchronization means using it on the sound track so that it becomes a component of the production, rather than simply playing back the music by itself). It can be anything from annoying to absolutely impossible to obtain these rights. So the best music cues are simply descriptions of the style of music you envision or the emotions it must evoke.

Original music can then be composed to order, or library music can be used. Library music is specifically arranged and recorded to be used on film and video sound tracks. Rights to use it are easily and relatively inexpensively arranged, usually through the facility producing your show.

Well-known and commonly used visuals are similar to music, in that in most cases somebody owns them and will want to be paid for their use. For more common footage, like old newsreels and Hawaiian sunsets, this may be well within your budget, but even a few seconds of a recent movie or prime-time TV show can be prohibitively expensive. So if your idea for a creative approach involves existing images, it's best to research their cost and availability before putting any more work into that idea.

Despite how easy it is to take visual or audio assets off the Internet, it is critical to understand:

Just because it's on the Internet, doesn't mean it's free

And even if an asset is made available for free use, there are often stipulations. For example, clip art may be made available for free use only in non-commercial applications. So be sure to read and understand all legal restrictions on anything you download for use in a video.

Yes, it can be a long and tedious process, But a lot less painful than being taken to court for violating the copyrights of a deep-pockets corporation eager to make you an example that will strike terror in the hearts of others who may also consider stealing intellectual property.

Work for Hire

This is the exception to owning what your create. "Work for Hire" means that the employer and not the employee owns all copyrights to everything created by the employee within the scope of that person's employment.

If you draw a regular paycheck, it's pretty straightforward: your employer owns all rights to everything you create within the scope of your job.

But an independent contractor is not normally considered to be "working for hire." If you are a freelance writer working on a project basis, your client owns only the rights you specifically agree to sell. All other rights still belong to you. This is usually a technicality, since most informational scripts are too specialized to have much resale potential.

Some organizations ask independent writers to sign work-for-hire agreements, usually as part of a contract or agreement. So if you sign an agreement containing any language that states you are performing a "Work for Hire," be aware that you are signing away all rights to whatever you create within the scope of that agreement.

Fair Use

This is the legal doctrine that allows you to use limited amounts of copyrighted material without authorization from the copyright owner. The bad news is that this doctrine offers no specifics on how much use is "fair use." The guidelines it does offer state:

> "Determining whether the use made of a work in any particular case is a fair use ... shall include (1) the purpose and character of the use, including whether such use is of a commercial nature or is for nonprofit educational purposes; (2) the nature of the copyrighted work; (3) the amount and substantiality of the portion used in relation to the copyrighted work as a whole; and (4) the effect of the use upon the potential market for or value of the copyrighted work."

All considerations about fair use are variable. An in-house video used at only one school for teaching children how to cross the street safely will probably be held to a lower standard than a store display promoting a new product from one of the Fortune 500.

Shows seen only by employees are held to a lower standard than shows intended for the public. Shows done for a local charity can take greater liberties than shows done for a large corporation. As your profile increases and your pockets deepen, your level of caution must rise.

Where the Jobs Are

"The closest to perfection a person ever comes is when he fills out a job application form."
—Stanley J. Randall

Informational video writing is a good job for generalists. There is a wide range of skills needed and potential clients include all of the organizations in the many areas of business, government, healthcare and religion. A certain amount of specialization is possible. Entire careers can unfold within the confines of healthcare, training, the aerospace industry, or any combination of subject area and type of scripting with which a writer can balance income with interest and ability.

Many writers market more than one complementary skill. Writer-producers are probably the most common. In smaller operations, a single individual may handle the entire writing and production process.

Government agencies are particularly prone to creating job descriptions suited only to total renaissance persons—then expecting them to work for entry-level salaries. As unrealistic an expectation as this may be, a government job can be an opportunity to gain experience with the types of ideas that do and don't successfully make the transition from script to screen.

Writing jobs fall into two basic categories of employers: in-house departments and independent production companies. Production companies are the smaller of the two job markets and the more competitive. They are generally looking for more experienced writers and often prefer writer-producers.

Production companies are usually lean on staff. Few have more than ten permanent staff members and most consist of only one or two partners, often writers themselves, who hire creative and production help as needed. Within this environment there's little opportunity to learn as you earn or work your way up.

In-house jobs are the more common entry-level positions and usually offer the more stable career opportunities. Job descriptions vary widely, from full-time scriptwriting to writers who handle everything from brochures to speeches and Web sites.

The Job Search

Just as the best of ideas must still be sold, even the most talented writers must actively market themselves. Entry-level jobs may be found on university placement bulletin boards, *career* pages of company Web sites, employment Web sites or Web sites such as http://www.craigslist.org. But most jobs and assignments are filled by word-of-mouth. So take classes, join organizations formed by people working in communication, training, marketing, public relations, Web site design or other areas in which you prefer to write. Get on the board or directors. Develop a network of colleagues who can help you find the opportunities you seek.

When looking for work, attitude is everything. Don't look for favors. Look for problems and position yourself as a problem solver. Let prospective employers know that you're ready to help them.

The Business of Writing

"If you could sell your experience for what it cost you, you would have a fortune."
—Herbert Prochnow

Staying Fresh

Audiences are often similar in their needs and problems, so a certain repetition can creep in. It's easy to get stale, even cynical. But there's no excuse for it.

Writing is the perfect profession for any curious person. You can legitimately assure yourself that learning virtually anything about anything may someday be of value to your writing. It's the perfect excuse for developing a wide range of interests.

Any sport, craft or physical activity can become an analogy for concepts not easily photographed. Every minute in front of a stage, screen or television can be a chance to better understand your craft.

Reading classic literature or the current business gurus may provide just the point of reference you need when you work through a problem with clients or colleagues. History, politics, and current events illustrate the wide spectrum of human behavior that you are now attempting to mirror and shape. What's happening on the front page and the business section is probably shaping what you'll soon be writing about.

Enjoying music and creating your own music can help you understand how to discover and focus emotions, and how different sounds evoke different realities. It also provides another point of reference when working with the many former and current musicians in this business.

Your responsibility as a writer is to be fully aware of your world and experience the dynamics of its constantly changing realities. Keep your horizons open. Long slavish hours at your desk, focused only on cranking out bland scripts that no one can fault will most often lead to a downward spiral of diminishing returns.

As a writer, you're supposed to be the team member whose ideas are wilder, whose imagination is wider and who can see the excitement in every-day lives. Don't worry about pushing things a bit. There will never be a shortage of obstructionists and bean-counters to reel you back in.

Most clients understand that it's relatively easy to tone down a script that's ventured too close to the edge, while there's little that can be done with the flat and cynical script—except to throw it out, find a writer with some fresh ideas and start all over again.

Scripts Are Never Finished, Only Abandoned

Anything as complex as a script can usually be made a little better if you lavish a lot more time on it. If you get obsessive about your scripts there's a danger that simple projects can become endless epics.

Being buttoned down means knowing the level of quality needed, hitting your mark, then moving on.

To achieve this enlightened state, resolve to make time to do things right the first time. If you fall into the habit of promising yourself to fix it later, you will begin a downward spiral, falling further behind with every new job and never working up to your full potential.

Set deadlines. Sweat and bleed right down to the wire. Then forget it. It's far better to concentrate on making the next one better than to be continually salvaging the last one.

Working Freelance

To do freelance work you must know your craft, know the market and be able to work without supervision. It's no way to begin a career or to get into the business. Most organizations willingly train permanent employees, but it's unfair to expect an organization to provide the training you need to write one script, then watch as you ride off into the sunset to use your experiences as a freelancer. But working as an independent contractor is a viable option once you've gained enough experience to be confident that you can fend for yourself in handling most situations.

Writing is often the first thing that an in-house department or an independent production company farms out. It allows them to select the writer with the most appropriate style and level of expertise for a project.

In practice, one or two writers usually end up taking most of one client's work, but there's still that perceived need to be able to call in a specialist while the regular freelancer is cut loose to run the pasture—without adding to the overhead.

Breaking into this cycle takes good timing and perseverance. "Giving somebody new a chance" sounds good in the movies, but it's not likely to happen if a writer they've been happy with is available. Look for an opening when the proven favorites are too busy, out of town or otherwise indisposed. Then the producer has a problem. Position yourself as the solution.

When you work freelance, several matters of a financial nature become important. You need to understand pricing, contracts, the danger of writing "on spec," and how to charge for client-initiated rewrites.

Price Sensitivity

There's not much price sensitivity in informational scriptwriting. If there is an amount budgeted for writing, the producer will most likely try to get the best scriptwriter available for that amount. If you attempt to get your foot in the door by undercutting that price, you will most likely position yourself as a writer who isn't worth that much, rather than get a chance at the job.

Standard practice is to price scriptwriting by the finished minute: at the rate of $200 per minute, a ten minute script would cost $2,000. There are other pricing formulas, such as percentage of budget, estimating the time required, or averaging earlier projects. All of them tend to average out over the long-haul; none of them can accurately predict the true cost of the next script you bid on.

Deciding on your standard rate is even more subjective. You must know both your own level of expertise in relation to your competition and what the market will bear. Charging too much can price you out of the market, while charging too little can give the impression that you're not very good.

Over the last several years quoted rates have ranged from $100 to $300 per finished minute—producers quoting on the low side, writers quoting on the high end. However, there is no "standard" price for a script, any more than there is a standard price for dinner out.

Dinner for some means a burger and fries. Others demand fine dining. And just as you could never sell fast food for the price of gourmet cuisine, you can't sell marginal scripts for top dollar.

Expectations concerning writing fees can also vary widely by size of market. In larger markets, such as New York and Los Angeles, people are more likely to consider a writer as a professional, who would expect to be paid at a rate similar to architects, engineers and other design professionals. While in smaller markets, you may run into the attitude that writing a script is something you are doing "on the side" and would charge only a few hundred dollars.

In any size market, don't assume you can start at the top. And don't assume that every organization will recognize and be willing to pay for top quality work. Needs and sophistication vary. There are low-budget shows for which only token amounts are budgeted for scripting, and there are people willing to write for that amount.

If you can do better, you will first have to prove it, then find the clients who can both recognize and afford that level of quality. Positioning yourself in the market takes a consistent and assertive marketing effort and a brutally honest level of self-assessment.

Every time you're refused an assignment find out why. If you "don't fit the requirements" of an organization, ask for advice on an organization where you might be a good fit. Keep talking with anyone whose opinion you respect. Solicit honest critiques of your work and your potential. Keep pushing until you find the niche where you can work up to your ability and be fairly compensated.

Contracts

Though contracts are often thought to be a good idea, my experience has been that few producers actually go to the trouble of signing a contract with a writer. When they do, it's usually a rehash of standard business practices and copyright regulations that would be binding even without the contract.

Large organizations may have a standard contract that must be signed by all vendors. These are usually so broad that they have little bearing on the realities of scriptwriting. In other cases, the legal department throws in so much boilerplate that no one understands it and it may even contradict itself.

I was once asked to sign a contract that went on for pages. And evidently, I was the first to actually read it. On one page, it specifically stated that in order to maintain my status as an independent contractor, I had to continue accepting work from other clients who do business in a similar area (a big issue with the Internal Revenue Service). Another page specifically *forbade* me from accepting work from other companies doing work in similar areas while I worked for this one company and for the following year.

On pointing out this discrepancy, I was sent to talk with the staff attorney. He basically said, "If you want the job, sign it. Everybody else does." I signed, with a glint of glee at the thought of this company taking me to court to enforce either side of this contradiction.

If you are required to sign a prepared contract, "work for hire" is the most important phrase to look for. As described earlier, agreeing to work for hire means that all rights to your work go to the party hiring you. You may not re-sell this work to anyone else and the other party may reuse all or any parts of your work in any way they see fit.

This is usually a moot point. Most informational shows are too specialized to be of any value in other situations. Usually, you're not losing anything of a financial nature by working for hire, but you may still be concerned about the precedent being set.

Every right you allow to go to the party hiring you has a potential value—however slight. If in the contract they specifically ask for all of the rights, you should receive something in return. If they claim that the additional rights have no value, they should then be willing to strike the work-for-hire clause. If you don't make a point of this now, and a job ever comes along in which the additional rights *do* have a value, you may hear "You've always worked for hire before, so we can't change that now."

Don't feel shy about marking out or adding anything to a contract. *Everything's open to negotiation until you sign.*

The best advice I've heard on the wisdom of tightly written contracts came from Greg Killingsworth, of Killingsworth Presentations. He said, "A contract's only as good as the people signing it. If someone is intent on exploiting you, a contract won't stop them. If someone is conscientious, you don't need a contract to protect you." I didn't sign a contract with Greg, but I did send him a letter of confirmation.

The body of that letter read something like this:

> Thank you for choosing me as your writer for the Zenith Development video.
>
> To confirm our conversations, I understand that the video is to be seven minutes or less in length. It will be based on information and material I receive during our meeting with your client.
>
> My deadline for the creative treatment is Wednesday, November 2. Deadline for the finished script will be 10 working days after client approval of the treatment.

I further understand that my writing fee will be $2,000. I will be billing this in halves: half in advance (invoice enclosed), with the balance due on client approval of the script. Both invoices will be due within 10 days of receipt.

Please let me know if any items in this letter do not match your understanding of the agreement we reached over the phone.

This is an interesting and exciting project for me and I'm very glad to be working with you again. Thank you again for providing this opportunity and please let me know if there is anything else I can do to help ensure the success of this project.

This letter is short and relatively informal, but it concisely states all of the dates and numbers on which agreement is necessary. Inviting the other party to "let me know if any items in this letter do not match your understanding of the agreement" reinforces the idea that negotiations are still open, but that if everything is acceptable, the paperwork is finished and we can all get to work.

This approach may seem overly casual to a corporate attorney, but it's more prudent than what is often expected. It's one more buttoned-down step toward ensuring that everyone has realistic expectations before the project starts.

Writing on Spec

Don't write on speculation unless you have something clearly to gain. Producers are often asked to submit creative treatments as part of a competitive bid. They can then recoup their expenses by marking up their costs for the productions they eventually provide—such as costs for the script. As a writer, you don't have anything to mark up. There's no reward for taking the risk; if you get the job, you receive your normal fee. If you don't get the job, you lose the time you could have spent looking for a job that doesn't have to be done on spec.

With that stated, the realities of the marketplace are that you have to pay some dues. There are some situations in which you *do* clearly have something to gain by writing a spec proposal. You may need more material in your portfolio, want to get your foot in the door or you may not have the job or income level you desire.

If you're serious about writing—write. It's better to write on spec than not to write at all. A good place to draw the line is between creative treatments and finished scripts. Asking that a creative treatment be included with a proposal is a valid request, but I would question the professionalism, integrity or both of anyone who asks to see a finished script before offering payment.

Charging For Rewrites

Some writers place a limit on number of rewrites they will do within the initial budget; they charge extra for anything beyond that. My feeling is that it's the writer's responsibility to ask the right questions, manage the situation, and otherwise do what it takes to deliver an acceptable product. So the writer keeps rewriting until the script is approved.

What keeps this from becoming a blank check is a concise treatment. The treatment functions as a specification sheet. If rewrites are necessary because the writer didn't interpret the approved treatment to the client's satisfaction, it's the writer's problem. However, if the client wants a rewrite to add or change something that is inconsistent with the approved treatment, an additional rewrite fee may be appropriate. This gives both parties incentive to get things right the first time.

Keep good records of the different drafts of a script and the changes made on each one. If things get out of control and the requested changes start putting you right back where you were with an earlier draft, you can legitimately renegotiate your fee based on this additional work created by the client's inability to provide clear direction.

Taking Initiative

"Even if you're on the right track, you'll get run over if you just sit there."
—Will Rogers (1879–1935)

Informational video and the means by which it is distributed are evolving. This gives the role of "writer" some latitude. Authority and respect go to those who take the initiative, who know what they want and make their own opportunities.

It's up to you to decide whether to be a respected professional or a stenographer posing as a writer, allowing others to make the decisions in your life.

The process presented in this book has been well accepted by most people who've tried it, but it's by no means standard practice in the industry. The industry has no single established set of procedures for researching and writing scripts. Don't expect everyone to be familiar with all of the terminology or to automatically stand up and salute these ideas. Again, it takes initiative to create a good working environment.

In many situations you may have to explain and sell this process. Try it. It's worth it. Nothing's fail-safe, but this comes closer than anything else I've been able to find in over two decades of searching for something better.

APPENDIX

- *Research Questions*
- *Case Study #1*
- *Case Study #2*
- *Suggested Reading*
- *Periodicals*
- *Organizations*
- *Glossary*

Research Questions

Who's the Audience?

- Age range?
- Educational range?
- Gender balance (and does it matter)?
- Racial balance (and does it matter)?
- Decision makers or recommenders?
- What are they doing now: Dealer? Employee? Customer? Sales rep? Student? Government official? Hospital patient? New hire?
- What would they rather be doing (career or life goals)?
- What are they like:
    - Traditional or trendy?
    - Family oriented or career oriented?
    - Independent self starters or need close supervision?
    - Loyal to company or shopping around?
    - Take pride in working hard or looking for the easy way out?
    - What is their self-image?
    - Leisure time activities or interests?
- Previous knowledge of the subject?
- Do they understand the jargon?
- Who would they tend to trust most delivering this type of information?
- Are they price sensitive?
- How motivated are they to learn this information?
- What are their main concerns?
- What is the employee/customer turnover rate?
- What are their options (main competition/option to client)?
- Does the audience know each other?
- How do they feel about each other: Friends? Competitors? Business associates? Part of an elite group?

What's the Problem?

> ➤ Is there a problem that this show should solve?
> ➤ Should the audience's perception of the client change?
> ➤ Are there any bad habits we are trying to overcome?
> ➤ Are there any typical misconceptions that must be corrected?
> ➤ Are there any problems the audience has had with the client in the past?
> ➤ Any negative preconceptions or prejudices we need to dispel or be aware of?
> ➤ Any positive preconceptions on which to build?

How Must The Audience Think Or Act Differently To Solve The Problem?

> ➤ What is the primary impression you would like your audience to leave with?
> ➤ What do you want the audience to do differently after seeing this show?
>   - ▪ Is the desired result measurable?
>   - ▪ Will it be, and how will it be done?
> ➤ Is there pre-testing or some sort of formative research on current audience attitudes, impressions or skill levels?
> ➤ Is there a call to action (ask for the sale)?

The Message

> ➤ What are the main benefits to our audience?
> ➤ What are the specific features/skills to include?
> ➤ Are any features, benefits or services proprietary?
> ➤ What are the most common problems in learning or using this skill?

> ➢ What are the most common mistakes?
> ➢ What are the areas of greatest frustration when learning or using this skill?
> ➢ What are the main teaching points to include?
> ➢ Is there a specific positioning statement …

  - ▪ For the company?
  - ▪ For the product, service or technique?
  - ▪ For the on-going program/promotion?

Background Information

> ➢ How have these objectives been accomplished in the past?

  - ▪ What worked about it?
  - ▪ What didn't work about it?
  - ▪ Why change now?

> ➢ How do you feel about using actors to portray your people?
> ➢ How do you feel about incorporating interviews into the program?
> ➢ Are there other videos, Web sites or other media that have been effective in meeting these same objectives?
> ➢ What is the projected life of the show?
> ➢ Is this presentation part of a larger effort, and if so what is it?
> ➢ Are there any positioning statements (organization motto), logos, graphics, jingles or ad campaign themes that should be included or complemented by this presentation?
> ➢ Are there any broader goals or programs that this show should support?
> ➢ What books/influences have been shaping thinking on this subject within the organization?

How Will the Program be Used?

➢ Size of audience?
➢ Captive audience or passing by?
➢ Self-standing; within a seminar; part of a sales presentation?
➢ Type of room; auditorium; trade show booth?
➢ Any live positioning statement before presentation?
➢ Any Q & A or wrap-up after presentation?
➢ What will the audience be doing immediately before and after the presentation or meeting?
➢ Any printed collateral material?

Who Will be Administering the Program?

➢ What is their experience with this type of program?
➢ How polished are their presentation skills?
➢ Will there be a facilitator's/user's guide?
➢ What is their level of involvement in designing this program?
➢ What will they already know about this program; has there been any effort to promote it?
➢ If the video is intended to be self-standing; what type of introduction and directions will the packaging include?
➢ What type of follow-up is planned?

Production Details

➢ What's the budget?
➢ When's it due:

  ▪ Treatment?
  ▪ Script?
  ▪ Finished show?

- ➤ Production format?
- ➤ Distribution format?
- ➤ Limits on running time?
- ➤ Any restrictions on photography: location, studio, animation, special effects, stock, etc.?
- ➤ Professional talent, employees or a mixture used on camera?
- ➤ Any existing footage, photography or artwork that can be used?
- ➤ What else will the client be able to provide, in terms of locations, people, props, assistance and materials?
- ➤ Name, email and phone number of contact person?

Case Study #1

CREATIVE TREATMENT

for an Employee Orientation Video

Prepared for:

Elgin Medical Corporation

BACKGROUND

With growth come challenges. EMC's rapid growth means that the current one-on-one approach to orienting new employees is no longer effective. Supervisors simply don't have the time, have often not had an adequate orientation themselves, and many are not adequately prepared to express and pass on EMC's heritage and values.

To remedy this situation, the personnel department will begin conducting a formal orientation for all new employees, including a personal welcome from a counselor, a video, an employee handbook, and packet of other printed information. New employees will receive this orientation individually or in small groups.

The primary audience for this orientation will range in age from recent college graduates to mid-30's. Most will have a BS degree or higher in a healthcare-related major, the balance having degrees in business, computer sciences, and social sciences.

To be effective this orientation must be honest, particularly concerning EMC's growth. It has not always been smooth. Normal growing pains have been intensified by dramatic and sudden changes in the healthcare industry. During previous periods of regrouping, layoffs have been necessary. So rather than security, we promise opportunity to those who can take initiative in readily adapting to change.

Objectives

Our overall goal is to make new employees as productive as possible as soon as possible—through providing a clear picture of what they should expect and what will be expected of them.

More specifically, after experiencing this presentation our audience will be able to:

> ➢ Describe the basis and direction of EMC's heritage and growth.

> ➢ Identify the three values on which they are expected to base their decisions and actions.

> ➢ Identify EMC's positioning as a provider of quality healthcare.

> ➢ Determine that taking initiative is expected and rewarded behavior.

> ➢ Describe the role of EMC's top executives in guiding the organization according to values they are proud to affirm and live by.

> ➢ Seek out opportunities for improving their work, their career, and their company.

STRATEGIES

Our basic approach is to let top management speak directly to new employees, with their words, with their ideas and with their actions.

More specifically, we will.

> ➤ Use Jim Spanner's founding of Elgin Medical Labs as an example of the initiative and entrepreneurial spirit that is now expected of all EMC employees.

> ➤ Place main emphasis on the core values and goals that make EMC successful.

> ➤ Let top executives speak for themselves in excerpts from interviews during which they discuss the values and heritage that have shaped EMC.

> ➤ Show EMC employees in action, demonstrating the commitment to quality and excellence that is now expected from every member of the audience.

> ➤ Identify typical opportunities for improving operational efficiencies and patient care that Elgin employees have developed, and that now stand as examples to be followed by our audience.

CREATIVE APPROACH

Opportunity Into Excellence

The plaintive wail of a Jazz saxophone takes us back to the fifties. A man in a white lab coat stares out a nighttime window; his now bankrupt medical lab behind him.

A new refrain brings a fresh energy. Success is in the air, as our narrator tells the story of Jim Spanner buying that lab and turning it into a multi-million dollar corporation; a venture built on the philosophy that EMC follows to this day: Turn problems into opportunity; and Opportunity into Excellence.

A patient in surgery … the condition … critical. The scene becomes an analogy for the current state of the healthcare industry. As we see the banks of expensive equipment and the team of specialists, our narrator provides an explanation for medical costs that have become unbearable: those in charge are experts at treating patients, but inexperienced in business management.

As doctors filled the operating room, we now see professional business managers gathered to secure the future of EMC. Our narrator confirms that professional business management makes the difference at EMC.

Founder and president Jim Spanner is introduced, as he states EMC's business philosophy and its three core values: Care and concern for people, commitment to quality and excellence, and continued growth and economic strength.

A code blue alert hurls us back into the reality of running a hospital, while serving as an example of the care and concern shown to patients. The message is that quality will never be compromised, costs are reduced only through reducing mistakes and duplication, using expensive medical equipment more efficiently, and creating an environment allowing everyone to work at their highest level of productivity.

Philip Jason is introduced as the Director of Operations, as he explains the first core value: Concern for people.

A montage of EMC employees illustrates "commitment to quality and excellence," as CEO Kenneth Johnson is introduced to explain the implications of this second core value.

We flashback to the early days of Elgin Medical Labs to begin a quick review of the milestones in EMC's history: becoming a pioneer in investor-owned hospitals, opening subsidiary companies EMC data processing and MedCord.

Jim Spanner is introduced again to talk about the business strategies that have made this growth possible.

A chart of EMC's growth helps illustrate that growth has not always been smooth, but that those who can turn change into opportunity have consistently found success in their careers at EMC.

At an EMC hospital, we see a patient wearing the uniform of one of the companies participating in a preferred provider program. As his visit gives a visual summary of the preventive healthcare services now encouraged, our narrator explains how EMC is entering into partnerships with businesses to help reduce medical costs.

As the patient is discharged, we see the hospital's executive director on his way to visit several departments. Our narrator explains that every hospital and every subsidiary is autonomous, and that this philosophy of delegating responsibility extends to every employee.

Everyone at EMC is expected to take initiative in making decisions based on the three core values. The values are reviewed, with visual examples of their application.

Our narrator then welcomes the new employees to EMC, reminding them that they are now working for a dynamic company, that change will come fast—and not always smoothly—but that with each change comes the opportunity to advance as far and as fast as ability will allow.

VIDEO SCRIPT

Title: **Opportunity Into Excellence**
Prepared for: **Elgin Medical Corporation**

It's night, in a vintage 1950's medical lab. In the background a man in a white lab-coat stares out a window.	MUSIC: EARLY-FIFTIES TIN PAN ALLEY TUNE. NARRATOR: In 1958, the Doctors' Diagnostics Company was facing bankruptcy.
Close-up on the man.	It's owner saw nothing but problems.
Early portrait or at-work shot of Jim Spanner, President and Founder of EMC.	Jim Spanner, an employee of only two years, saw opportunity.
The signature of Jim Spanner going on the dotted line.	He bought the company.
Early logo.	Changed the name ...
Close-up on hands busy with 50s-style lab equipment.	And within a year Elgin Medical Labs was profitable.
A line-graph showing EMC's growth animates onto the screen, then becomes the border for a split screen showing a montage of action shots from throughout the history of EMC.	MUSIC BECOMES ACTIVE, CONFIDENT AND CURRENT. Over the years that small medical lab has grown into a $ 500 million health-care company ...
EMC logo joins the graph as the only stationary elements while the montage continues.	Elgin Medical Corporation: EMC ... Our path to success has not always been smooth, but its course has never varied from Jim Spanner's original philosophy of turning problems into opportunity ...
Screen dissolves into title graphic: "Opportunity into Excellence."	... and Opportunity into Excellence.

An operation's in progress, the screen fills with the readout of an EKG or similar instrument, registering a critical situation.	MUSIC: SEGUE TO A THEME EVOKING THE TENSION OF A MEDICAL EMERGENCY. Recently, there've been plenty of problems in the health care industry.
Camera pulls back to reveal more expensive equipment and a large surgical team.	Health care has simply become too expensive. And there's a reason for it.
Visual begins stressing the surgical team, particularly the doctors.	Traditionally, hospitals have been managed by people who were experts at treating patients, but knew little about managing a business.
A group of EMC executives gather around a conference table, in a composition matching the previous shots of the surgical team.	EMC has changed this by bringing sound business management to the delivery of health care. Our Founder, Jim Spanner, explains how:
Scene dissolves into a graphic. The title of which is "EMC Core Values." The three values are added under the title as they are stated. —Care and concern for people. —Unswerving commitment to Quality and Excellence. —Continued growth and economic strength.	SOUND BITES FROM INTERVIEW WITH JIM SPANNER MAKE THE FOLLOWING POINTS: • Building for the future. • Preventing problems before they happen. • Basing all decisions on three core values …
Close-up on ceiling speaker.	SFX: CODE BLUE ALERT.

A quick montage shows the staff of an Intensive Care Unit responding to the Code Blue.

Patients are an obvious focus for our care and concern. No decision will ever be made to reduce the quality of care received by an EMC patient.

Instead, we find ways to deliver quality health care more efficiently:

Employee enters data into a computer.

reducing mistakes and duplication ...

A mobile CT scanner is seen pulling up to a hospital.

using expensive medical equipment more effectively ...

A door or wall sign identifies an office of Employee Assistance Services. A brief scenario shows a couple in counseling.

and creating an environment that shows our care and concern for those who work here.

An Executive Director and corporate management are on a walking tour of a hospital. Include senior management if possible.

By turning the business of health care over to business professionals ...

Surgeons during an operation.

physicians are free to do what they do best.

Montage of EMC employees at work.

And this philosophy carries over into the respect we show for our employees.

Interview with Philip Jason.

Philip Jason is Director of Operations for EMC. EXCERPTS FROM INTERVIEW WITH PHILLIP JASON, MAKING THE FOLLOWING POINTS:

• Career paths are kept challenging.

- Top performance is rewarded with one of the best compensation packages in our industry.
- EMC recruits only those who are ready to take initiative and constantly strive for improvement.

Earlier graphic of core values showing the first two, with "Commitment to Quality and Excellence" highlighted.	NARRATOR: In short, EMC hires employees who have already dedicated themselves to our second core value: Commitment to Quality and Excellence. People with the same attitudes as expressed by EMC CEO Kenneth Johnson …
Interview with Kenneth Johnson.	EXCERPTS FROM INTERVIEW WITH KENNETH JOHNSON, MAKING THE FOLLOWING POINTS: • Putting forth your absolute best makes life more fulfilling. • We'll do what ever it takes to provide the best care for our patients. • We expect every employee to contribute new ideas on how our service can be improved.
Earlier graphic showing core values, highlighting third value: "Continued Growth and Economic Strength."	NARRATOR: Our first two core values are possible only through a dedication to our third and final core value: Continued growth and economic strength.
Lab seen in opening with two lab-techs in mid-50s hairstyles productively busy.	Our growth began when the newly renamed Elgin Medical Labs faced its first major crisis: Memorial Hospital was having severe financial problems.

Period photos of Memorial Hospital.	The lab couldn't afford to lose this major customer. So investors were found and Memorial Hospital was purchased.
Early logo of EMC.	This bold step made EMC an early pioneer in investor-owner hospitals.
Map of the region, as small EMC logos pop on to indicate the growth of EMC.	Over the decades, we've added more hospitals and medical support service companies,
Logos for EMC Data Processing and MedCord.	including EMC Data Processing, our computer services company, and MedCord, our medical records company.
Fleet of trucks used for moving CT scan and other equipment among hospitals.	With growth comes economies of scale—a principle that founder Jim Spanner has applied since EMC's beginnings.

SOUND BITES FROM INTERVIEW WITH JIM SPANNER MAKE THE FOLLOWING POINTS:

- Centralized labs serve several hospitals.

- Cost to patients can be kept lower.

- Larger labs can afford to hire better qualified and better compensated technicians.

- Through sharing centralized services, smaller hospitals have access to resources they could not otherwise afford.

Quick picture story showing a patient wearing a uniform of a company participating in a health-care program being treated and discharged.	EMC is also an innovative leader in cooperating with businesses to develop other cost-saving strategies, including Preferred Provider Systems, a health maintenance organization, and other group-health options.
As the patient leaves the hospital, the picture story follows the paper trail, showing that MedCord is automatically updating the patient's records and that billing paperwork has been streamlined by membership in a Preferred Provider System.	Economies of scale bring consistency and savings to high-volume tasks, but for making decisions, EMC needs diversity and quick response.
Montage showing an Executive Director walking through his hospital, stopping to talk with various employees.	So every EMC hospital is autonomous. Executive Directors have complete authority to run **their** hospitals **their** way. This autonomy is applied throughout EMC.
Director stops to check in on a representative from MedCord (identified by a logo on a name badge or piece of equipment) installing a system upgrade.	Every subsidiary operates as an independent business …

The name of a department is seen on a door, as the Director enters. The employee being visited takes this opportunity to show off an improvement that has been made in one of their systems.

every department has operational independence and every employee is encouraged to show initiative in applying our three core values:

A sub-title shows the name of each core value as it's mentioned, as the visual illustrates an example.

Care and Concern for people—including our patients, our doctors, all EMC employees and the people in the communities we serve ...

Commitment to quality and excellence—in the health care we provide and in every aspect of our operations ...

Growth and economic strength—based on sound business practices and effective management.

Candid scene if possible, of a medical team congratulating each other after a difficult and successful medical procedure.

So welcome to EMC. You're now part of a strong and growing team.

Cutting back to the opening shot in the 50s lab begins a quick cut montage taking us forward in time to the present day.

Change comes fast, and not always smoothly ...

But with each change comes opportunity, and by turning that opportunity into excellence you can advance as far and as fast as your ability will take you.

MUSIC: UP FULL TO END.

Case Study #2

VIDEO SCRIPT

Title: **Success in Selling**
Prepared for: **Bokman's Department Stores**

INT. A DEPARTMENT STORE—NIGHT

At the end of a busy day, JERRY, chewing gum and apathetically dressed, is straightening up around the cash register as CAROL, an obvious professional, is saying good night to a customer, MRS. ANDERSON.

> CAROL
> And thank you for coming in Mrs. Anderson ... I hope that birthday party goes well for you.

> MRS. ANDERSON
> Thank you Carol, I'll see you later.

> CAROL
> Good night.

Carol joins Jerry in closing up their department for the night.

> CAROL
> A good night, huh?

> JERRY
> You did all right ... and earlier you were saying you'd be able to, ah ... give me a few tips on how I could do a little better with my commissions?

Checking her watch, Carol sees that she does have a few minutes.

> CAROL
> Okay. Let's start with the basics then. Selling is communicating. It's all of those interpersonal skills you need for any kind of success.

> JERRY
> You mean like ... gaining people's confidence?

CAROL

That comes with it. When you start selling like a professional, people just naturally start treating you with more trust and respect.

JERRY

That's a little philosophical Carol; how about just a few good tips.

CAROL

Okay, develop an attitude of customer service.

JERRY

So I should like … smile more.

CAROL

A good start. Your face is your attitude.

JERRY

Well what about the attitude some of these customers bring in here—they're not exactly rays of sunshine.

CAROL

All the more reason to smile. Smiling is contagious.

DISSOLVE TO …

Sequence showing Carol approach MR. WATKINS, a customer with some spare time. Carol comments in voice-over.

CAROL
(Voice-over)

If **you** set a tone of friendly respect, you're more likely to get a smile and respect in return. It's like welcoming a friend into your home …

Sound fades up on Carol's conversation with Mr. Watkins.

> CAROL

Of course you're welcome to browse. Make yourself at home. My name's Carol, I'll be glad to help you with any questions.

DISSOLVE BACK TO ...

the current conversation.

> JERRY

Sounds good in theory, but you know how busy we get around here.

> CAROL

Most customers understand that ...

DISSOLVE TO ...

A busy day in the store. Carol is helping MR. FRIEDMAN, a customer in a hurry. Mrs. Anderson, the customer from the opening, walks in.

> CAROL
> (Voice-over)

but still, no one likes to be ignored.

Carol glances up to make eye contact with Mrs. Anderson.

> CAROL

I'll be with you in just a minute.

> CAROL
> (Voice-over)

All it takes is making eye contact, a smile and a few words on when you will be able to help them.

DISSOLVE BACK TO ...

the current conversation.

> JERRY
> Sounds easy, but you just naturally have a way with people.

> CAROL
> You know what rapport means?

> JERRY
> A good friendly type of relationship?

> CAROL
> Right. And it doesn't just happen. You have to **build** rapport. Get involved with the customer, notice details, show an interest.

DISSOLVE TO ...

the most recent example, Carol is now ready to help Mrs. Anderson, who she had asked to wait earlier.

> CAROL
> I'm sorry to keep you waiting.

> MRS. ANDERSON
> That's all right.

Carol notices that Mrs. Anderson has several packages.

> CAROL
> Looks like a busy day.

> MRS. ANDERSON
> I'm giving a birthday party for my 10-year-old tomorrow.

> CAROL
> Let me combine all of those packages into a bigger bag for you. I can hold it at the cash register while you shop.

                    MRS. ANDERSON
          Thank you.

As Carol accepts the packages.

                    CAROL
          What can I help you with today?

DISSOLVE BACK TO ...

the current conversation.

                    JERRY
          Then by the time you made the sale you even
          knew her name.

                    CAROL
          Of course, I got it from her credit card. It's up
          to you to take the first steps. Smile. Take an
          interest. Take responsibility for satisfying every
          customer.

                    JERRY
          So it's all attitude?

                    CAROL
          Not **all** attitude, but you'll never be a success
          without it.

                    JERRY
          So, what else?

Carol checks her watch.

                    CAROL
          So it's getting late, why don't you just work on
          that attitude of customer service and we'll talk
          more tomorrow.

                    JERRY
          Okay, let's call it a night.

They start going through the final correct procedures for closing down their department.

> CAROL
> And one more thing—the gum?

Suddenly becoming conscious of the gum he's chewing, Jerry places it in the garbage.

> JERRY
> Oh, yeah.

Carol gathers up her purse and begins heading for the store's exit.

> CAROL
> And if you want to be respected as a
> professional … dress like one.

After taking a quick assessment of his current style of dress, Jerry looks up to see he's being left behind.

> JERRY
> Hey, can't you wait up?

> CAROL
> Can't you hurry up?

> JERRY
> I'm trying.

> CAROL
> That's a start.

Jerry hurries to catch up with Carol, and as they walk toward the store's exit, the store lights dim to their after-hours level.

FADE TO BLACK.

Suggested Reading

Bernard, Sheila Curran, *Documentary Storytelling for Video and Filmmakers*, Boston: Focal Press, 2004.

Campbell, Joseph and Moyers, Bill, *The Power of Myth*, New York: Doubleday, 1988.

Campbell, Joseph, *Myths To Live By*, New York: Bantam, 1972.

Cartwright, Steve R., *Designing and Producing Media-based Training*, Boston: Focal Press, 1999.

Cartwright, Steve R., *Pre-Production Planning for Video, Film and Multimedia*, Boston: Focal Press, 1996.

Dichter, Ernest, *Getting Motivated*, New York: Pergamon Press, 1979.

Dichter, Ernest, *The Strategy of Desire*, Garden City, N.Y.: Doubleday & Company, Inc, 1960.

Donaldson, Michael C., *Clearance and Copyright*, 2nd revised ed., Silman-James Press, 2003.

Drucker, Peter F., *Innovation and Entrepreneurship*, New York: Harper & Row, 1985.

Drucker, Peter F., *The Frontiers of Management*, New York: Truman Talley, 1986.

Field, Syd, *Screenplay*, Revised Expanded ed., New York: Dell, 1984.

Frank, Milo O, *How to get Your Point Across in 30 Seconds or Less*, New York: Simon and Schuster, 1990.

Gronbeck, Bruce C. et al., *Principles and Types of Speech*, 11th. ed., Glenview, IL: Scott, Foresman & Co., 1986.

Jung, Carl G., *Man And His Symbols*, New York: Doubleday, 1969.

Landen, Hal, *Secrets of Producing and Selling Successful Videos*, Bristol, RI: Oak Tree Press, 2007.

Maslow, Abraham H., *The Farthest Reaches of Human Nature*, Magnolia, MA: Peter Smith, 1983.

Miller, Casey, and Kate Swift, *The Handbook of Nonsexist Writing,* 2nd. ed., iUniverse, 2001.

Ogilvy, David, *Ogilvy on Advertising,* 1st Vintage Books Ed edition, 1985.

Reader's Digest Editors, *Family Word Finder,* Pleasantville, New York: Reader's Digest Association, 1986.

Rosenthal, Alan, *Writing, Directing, and Producing Documentary Films and Videos,* 3rd. ed., Southern Illinois University Press, 2002.

Strunk, William Jr., and E. B. White, *The Elements of Style,* 4th ed, Needham Heights, MA: Allyn & Bacon, 1999.

Trottier, David, *The Screenwriter's Bible: A Complete Guide to Writing, formatting, and Selling Your Script,* 4th. ed, Los Angeles: Silman-James Press, 2005.

Zettl, Herbert, *Television Production Handbook,* 6th ed., Belmont, CA: Wadsworth, 1996.

Periodicals

Creative Screenwriting; 6404 Hollywood Blvd. Suite 415, Los Angeles, CA 90028; (323) 957–1405; http://creativescreenwriting.com.

Filmmaker, The Magazine of Independent Film, IFP, 104 West 29th Street, 12th Floor, New York, NY 10001; (212) 563–0211; www.filmmakermagazine.com.

Training Magazine, Nielsen Business Media, Inc., 770 Broadway, New York, NY 10003; (646) 654–4500; www.trainingmag.com.

Videography, NewBay Media, LLC, 810 Seventh Avenue, 27th Floor, New York, NY 10019; (212) 378–0400; http://www.videography.com.

Videomaker, York Publishing, Inc., P.O. Box 4591, Chico, CA 95927; (800) 284–3226, http://www.videomaker.com.

Organizations

American Society for Training and Development (ASTD); 1640 King Street, Box 1443 . Alexandria, VA; Phone: 703.683.8100; http://www.astd.org.

International Association of Business Communicators; One Hallidie Plaza, Suite 600, San Francisco, CA 94102 USA; Phone: 415.544.4700; http://www.iabc.com.

Society for Technical Communication; 901 North Stuart Street, Suite 904; Arlington, Virginia 22203; Phone: (703) 522–4114; www.stc.org.

International Society for Performance Improvement (ISPI); 1400 Spring Street, Suite 260, Silver Spring, MD 20910–2753; Phone: (301) 587–8570; http://ispi.org.

Glossary

Actors—as another nod to equality, many women in the acting profession prefer to be called actors rather than actresses, so the term actors may now refer to professional talent of either gender.

Analogy—making a literal comparison between one thing or situation and another; often comparing something difficult to grasp or visualize with something more familiar; e.g. As birds soar above the highest peaks, our imaginations can soar to new heights of creativity. see "metaphor."

Approach—see "Creative Approach."

Art Director—see "Designer."

Back story—a short history of a character's life before they appear in a story; including experiences that have shaped their character and motivations, such as: Where are they from? Who are their people? What are the conflicts in their lives? What do they want out of life? Are they introverted or extroverted ... analytical or intuitive?

Breaking the fourth wall—situation in which a participant in on-camera action turns to address the audience directly. The name comes from the fact that a typical studio set has three physical walls as background for the action and one imaginary wall separating the action from the camera. Talking to, or even recognizing the existence of the camera, "breaks" this imaginary fourth wall.

Buttoned down—being professional by being prepared. Following a specific process that anticipates and allows for different contingencies to better minimize frantic panic in the participants.

Central idea—also known as controlling idea, this is the fundamental concept linking all other ideas in a show. It's the single most important message the audience needs to take home with them.

Clock-face wipe—Special-effect video transition in which one image wipes away the next with a motion similar to the hands of a clock; often used to indicate passage of time.

Close-up (or Close Shot)—shot composed to fill the screen with a person's head and shoulders, or that fills the screen with an object.

Continuity—the logic and creative devices that motivate progressing from one segment of a show to the next.

Conventions—format and continuity devices that make up the reality of a show, establishing a pattern that the audience will accept. Typical conventions include: on-camera spokesperson, breaking the fourth wall and incorporating interview excerpts.

Copy edit—"copy" is the journalistic term meaning the words that make up a story or article, so "copy editing" is making word substitutions and grammatical corrections without substantially changing content or meaning.

Creative—In its objective sense, creative means all of the non-technical decisions that must be made about a show. The jobs of writer, director and designer are considered "creative" positions; people filling those roles are collectively referred to as "creatives," whether or not they *display* any creativity in the subjective sense of the word.

Creative approach—1. section of the creative treatment providing an active voice, present tense narrative of how the show will unfold on the screen. 2. overall way in which a show addresses its goals and objectives, providing the creative framework on which all of the elements of structure build.

Creative treatment—the "reality check" document that is written and approved before work is started on scripting; usually containing four sections: Background, objectives, strategies and creative approach. It's both specifications sheet and creative writing sample, giving the client a clear idea of what to expect from both the script and the finished show.

Cut—instantaneous change from one shot to the next. Most shots within a scene or segment are joined by cuts, rather than dissolves or other transitions.

Cutaway—a visual related to but outside the frame of the preceding shot. For a rural exterior scene, a bird sitting on a branch would be a typical cutaway. Cutaways are useful for adding visual details, and also give the editor a shot to go to for bridging time and salvaging dialogue shots or interviews that can't be used end to end. Cutaways are not normally included in the visual/action description, unless they are integral to the story unfolding in the visual or a suggestion for reinforcing the image system.

Designer—also Art Director. The individual responsible for a show's "look," designing the graphics, sets and special effects; usually the person who will create a storyboard from the script.

Dissolve—transition from one visual to the next in which the first fades away while the next simultaneously fades up to replace it, creating a momentary overlap. Traditionally used to indicate a new scene or a time lapse.

Exposition—information that an audience needs to understand in order to follow a story. Usually applied to entertainment or dramatizations.

Extreme Close-up—tighter shot than a close-up, composed so that part of a person's head, or an object, is cut off by the edge of the screen.

Flashback—v: to jump back in time and show something that happened earlier. n: a scene that takes place earlier than adjacent scenes.

Foreshadowing—A visual or spoken line that sets up a later scene. Seeing a worker shrug off using a hard hat could foreshadow that worker's receiving a head injury later in the show.

Format—the overall creative approach or type of show, e.g. voice-over narration, day-in-the-life, dramatization.

Framing a shot—providing a border. A tree to one side of a shot provides a natural "frame" for other visual elements in the same shot.

Image system—The logic and criteria that motivate what is seen on the screen to create a specific visual tone and message for a show. The show's "look." Image systems have two main elements: background ambiance and specific symbols.

Icon—A specific object, illustration, or person established as standard visual shorthand to symbolize a group, idea, value or category. A tennis racket could be an icon representing recreation; differs from a symbol in that symbols can be any one of a group of items used interchangeably as symbols of the same thing: any piece of sporting equipment could be a generalized symbol of recreation.

Interview questions—not to be confused with "Research questions:" Questions asked while an interview is being recorded with the intention of incorporating it into the final show.

Language—the vocabulary of phrases and specific words that help create the character and color of the show.

Location—place where a scene is shot; usually implies an existing environment, rather than a set created in a studio.

Metaphor—to attribute a thing or situation with a quality it does not actually possess, without literally stating one thing or situation is similar to another, e.g. Our imaginations can fly to new heights of creativity. see Analogy.

Montage—Series of related images or sounds cut together—often rapidly—to convey a single point or idea.

Multi-image—"an audio-visual presentation using a synchronized soundtrack and multiple projection devices that display images over one or more screen areas." (as defined by AMI, Association for Multi-Image International, Inc.) In practice, multi-image "projection devices" are usually slide projectors.

On-the-nose writing—style of writing in which the characters simply state the facts, leaving nothing to the audience's imagination; devoid of subtext; usually creating a show that sounds amateurish and melodramatic.

Page turn wipe—Special-effect video transition creating the illusion that a video image is on a page that peels off of the screen to reveal another image underneath; similar to turning pages of a book.

Positioning—n. the niche in which a person, place or thing has chosen to maintain an identity, e.g. the positioning of a Buick is between Cadillac and Chevrolet. v. the act of establishing or maintaining this identity, e.g. ads showing a Buick in up-scale situations are positioning it to high-income customers.

Premise—idea that opens the presentation; the assumption that motivates the structure and action of the rest of the show; the idea that the rest of the show must prove credible.

Producer—usually the person who controls the budget and decides who plays what roles. The person in charge. Liaison between the client and production team. For smaller budget shows, the producer may become involved in making most of the creative decisions and play a hands-on role in the production.

Production Values—details that enhance the quality of a show: well-crafted sets, beautiful locations, tasteful art direction, meticulous lighting, good direction and camera work.

Rack focus shot—shot that begins with something in the foreground in sharp focus and the background out of focus, often to the point of being indistinguishable—or vice versa. Changing focus throws the clear image out of focus, while bringing the other image or action—usually the point of relevance in the shot—into focus. Being quite dramatic, it can be easily overused.

Real people—people who are not professional actors; amateurs.

Research questions—not to be confused with "Interview questions:" Questions asked of clients or content experts as part of initial research; not intended for recording to be included into the final show.

Scene—A single event or exchange among characters with a unity of time or place. Implies a dramatization, shows that are primarily voice-over narration are usually thought of as containing "segments" rather than scenes.

Segue—To quickly cut from one audio source, or piece of music to another, keeping both at the same volume throughout; as opposed to a cross-fade.

Set—environment created within a studio as background and environment for filming or video taping.

SFX—standard abbreviation for sound effects.

Stock footage (or Stock Shots)—Footage or still visuals previously created for an earlier purpose. Usually from an organization's own library or bought commercially from a "stock house" or "stock agency."

Storyboard—comic strip-like row of pictures in sequence illustrating the different key shots that will make up the finished show.

Subtext—meaning conveyed by an actor in addition to what is literally being said; the "hidden meaning" or undercurrent in a scene.

Symbol—object representing a person, value, idea or theme; such as an antique tool representing craftsmanship; differs from an icon in that many different antique tools could symbolize craftsmanship within the same show, where an icon would be a specific tool or illustration designated as a visual shorthand for craftsmanship.

Theme—a short phrase that both makes a statement about the show's subject matter and introduces a concept supporting the central idea; often the show's title. Can also refer to the creative approach for a show, e.g., western-themed, sailing-themed, detective-themed.

Three T's—a basic fundamental of instructional design: Tell 'em what you're going to tell 'em; tell 'em; then tell 'em what you just told 'em.

Track (sound track)—all-inclusive term referring to all audio elements in a show.

Treatment—see "creative treatment."

Voice—literary term referring to the personality and motivating value system of a book, film or video; the attitude and tone taken by the writer in creating it.

White paper—A report, often of a technical nature, that provides a fairly detailed study of a specific issue. Usually produced by a company for internal use and to provide business customers with detailed information on products and services.

ABOUT THE AUTHOR

John Morley's been there. From working on staff in university video studios to freelancing for Fortune 500 companies. Along the way, over 300 of his video scripts have been produced, he has taught scriptwriting in corporate seminars and at the university level, and developed scriptwriting software used by thousands of writers.

After earning his BA in Broadcasting from the University of Florida, Morley worked as a writer/producer in school-based production facilities at Santa Fe Community College in Gainesville Florida, University of Florida and University of South Carolina.

A move to Atlanta to work with Jack Morton Productions brought projects from Home Box Office, Milliken Textiles, Georgia Pacific, and a transition into writing full-time. Since moving to Los Angeles in 1984, Morley has been working with clients including CitiBank, Mattel, Pioneer Electronics, and most of the Asian car companies, including Toyota, Lexus and Nissan.

In Los Angeles, Morley studied with the top screenwriting gurus, Robert McKee, Michael Hauge and John Truby. He developed a seminar on informational scriptwriting that was offered through Trudy's Writer's Studio and at numerous industry events, and he taught informational scriptwriting at California State University, Northridge.

His script-formatting software, Script Werx, is used around the world by writers working for corporations, government agencies, non-profits and television shows, including Saturday Night Live.

INDEX

978-0-595-44938-5
0-595-44938-7

CPSIA information can be obtained at www.ICGtesting.com
Printed in the USA
BVOW05s0900081214

377802BV00014B/55/P